BRANGWYN

IN PERSPECTIVE

Frank Brangwyn, c 1920

BRANGWYN

IN PERSPECTIVE

The Life and Work of
Sir Frank Brangwyn
RA RWS PRBA HRSA
1867-1956

Diana de Vere Cole

THE ONE ROOF PRESS
2006

Published by the
ONE ROOF PRESS
2006

ISBN 978-0-9535824-3-3

Cover artwork by the author. The image on the front is from Brangwyn's design for the device of the Avenue Press. On the back cover is a self-portrait woodcut, c 1935

CONTENTS

To the memory of Peter Holliday

ACKNOWLEDGEMENTS

Literary projects may be put into two classes. Some are like steamers that go in a regulated course to their destination, while others tack here and there like sailing ships *Walter Shaw Sparrow* [1]

Because of Brangwyn's capacity to work in many different styles and media concurrently, it has proved difficult to follow a linear course through his life story, bound as it was by his art. The titles of the chapters are therefore navigational aids rather than essays in themselves and are, like Brangwyn's beloved sailing ships, subject to some unavoidable tacking. Inevitably this short résumé cannot cover all of Brangwyn's adventures and achievements but its aim is to chart his progress through his artistic journey.

With his customary modesty and self-deprecating good humour, Brangwyn questioned the need for anyone to write about him. Nevertheless he accepted the books published in his lifetime and sanctioned them by distributing signed copies. Since the books are now out of print I have included many of the facts and anecdotes, as published. In the past it was not customary to provide scrupulous substantiation, so it has not been possible to verify all information, but where it is corroborated elsewhere it has been included. This biography is primarily informed by the knowledge I gained through my own family's long association with Brangwyn. My father worked with Brangwyn and after his death, at his house-keeper's request, bought The Jointure, his house and studios in the Sussex village of Ditchling. Both my parents were artists and, for a further forty years his former studios were in continuous use, by them and, later, for my own work as a painter, etcher and muralist. The studios are now used as a contemporary art gallery.

Rodney Brangwyn's biography, *Brangwyn*, published by William Kimber in 1978, has proved the bedrock of information for scholars and admirers of Brangwyn. My greatest thanks go to Rodney for letting me use his book so freely and benefit from the enormous amount of research supporting it. I would also like to thank the other members of the Brangwyn family. Michael and Margaret Brangwyn have been most encouraging and supportive and David and Margaret Brangwyn have been very helpful and generous. David Brangwyn holds the copyright to all the material not otherwise acknowledged in this book. Margaret has diligently researched new information regarding the Brangwyn family, particularly about Brangwyn's son, James Chesterfield Brangwyn.

Paul Liss has been unstinting in his support of Brangwyn's work and also of my efforts. My special thanks go to him and to Rachel Moss, a fellow Brangwyn dealer, for their work and their determination to return Brangwyn to the public recognition he once enjoyed and deserved. Libby Horner has become a leading authority on Brangwyn since she first visited me at The Jointure in 1997 to further her PhD studies. I commend her for her ensuing scholarship, for her forthcoming catalogue raisonée, her curatorship of the travelling Brangwyn retrospective in 2006 and her co-authorship, with Gillian Naylor, of the book of essays that accompanied it, also for her contribution to the book *Frank Brangwyn, A Mission to Decorate Life* published by Paul Liss in conjunction with the Fine Art Society for their celebratory Brangwyn exhibition in the spring of that year. I recommend these publications as companion works to this biographical study.

I am greatly indebted to Emma Worth for her expert editorial advice, to Andy Brown and Alan Hayward for photography. I salute Clare Willsdon for her serious study of Brangwyn as a muralist in her definitive book *British Murals 1840-1940, Image and Meaning*. My thanks go to Shirley Crowther at The Jointure Studios in Ditchling, Jennifer Mathur at the Ditchling Gallery, Ewan Clayton, Hilary Williams and Lucie Broadbent Smith at Ditchling Museum, Laurence van Kerkhoven at the Arents House, the Brangwyn Museum in Bruges, Judith Winnan at Fulmar TV for her documentary on Brangwyn's British Empire murals, to Sir Donald Sinden, Anne Morris, Andrew Hewson, Michael and Catriona Blaker, Shirley Clark and Tony Mott. I am also grateful to my family, Jemma and Jonathan Tetley, Cassian de Vere Cole, Virginia Broadbent, Joanna Varcoe and Susan Coster.

I am thankful for the help and friendship of Peter Holliday who encouraged me to write about Brangwyn. Our work for Ditchling Museum informed our study of the development of the Arts and Crafts Movement towards Modernism, with a special regard to the Ditchling artist-craftsmen. Regrettably, he didn't live to see this publication or his own elegant and scholarly biography of the eminent Ditchling calligrapher, Edward Johnston.

Peter introduced me to his friend and editor, Colin Maitland, whose advice, help and expertise has been crucial and invaluable in bringing this book to publication and above all I am grateful to him.

'A good westerly wind to Mrs Peacock's joy', 1944, ink, 20x22cm
'Buy War Bonds', poster
'Spain', general relief fund for the women and children of Spain, poster
Old Bridge at Rome, 1921, etching, 30x35cm
Brangwyn working on a stretched canvas
Brangwyn working at a lithographic stone
Installing the British Empire panels, 1933, etching, 20x15cm
British Empire panels, House of Lords, photograph FLewis
Lucy Brangwyn (from a photograph)
Brangwyn in The Jointure garden, photograph
Drawing of intended museum in Tokyo
James Chesterfield Brangwyn, photograph (p109)
James Branwyn signwriting, Townsville, 1913, photograph (p111)

FOREWORD

Still salty from the last swim of our seaside holiday, my three sisters, Virginia, Joanna and Susan and I sat high up on the long cracked leather-cushioned seats along each side of the back of the 'Barouche', our hybrid Rolls Royce and Bedford shooting brake. The huge car had been adapted as an ambulance in the war, but Father used it for transporting the inn signs he restored. Mother waited in the front. We were parked in South Street just beyond the yard of the Ditchling Press with its pounding machinery giving a heartbeat to the peaceful village. Opposite was The Jointure where the famous artist Sir Frank Brangwyn had lived. It was August 1956 and he died on June 11.

We had stopped to offer our condolences to his housekeeper Lizzie Peacock. The Jointure appeared dispirited, as houses tend to do when their owners die. Dust covered the railings and the thin privet hedge and the paint on the once-glossy black front door had faded. It was opened cautiously. My father bent forward and exchanged a few words, then beckoned to us to follow him into the house.

The welcome from Lizzie Peacock, Brangwyn's housekeeper, was quiet and uneffusive and the entrance hall was cool. A contrast to the elegance of the added Georgian façade of the house, the hall was dark and somewhat spartan, a mixture of Tudor and Arts and Crafts. Scrubbed wooden stairs rose up immediately against the left-hand wall but, somewhat incongruously, their straight strutted banisters were polished. They continued along an unusually narrow passage around the stairwell leading nowhere except to the window above the front door. Overhead hung an open-work Art Nouveau-style brass hall lantern designed by Brangwyn himself. Ahead a long passage led straight through the house to the garden door opening into a brick, triple-arched loggia. From this a path led onwards, lined with espaliered apple trees, to the western boundary of the garden, presenting us with an impressive vista.

We had been there before. Father, the artist Crosby Cook, was a familiar visitor. He had called regularly on Brangwyn during our annual summer holidays in Bexhill. By then Brangwyn was in his eighties and only Father was invited to see the master. Mother would stay in the kitchen with Lizzie and we children would be shooed out into the garden so we never met him.

Father's first job on leaving the Royal Academy Schools was as a young apprentice to the Avenue Press in Drury Lane. There he worked as a runner carrying proofs to and from Brangwyn's studios at his London home, Temple Lodge and The Jointure in the country. When Crosby's father died, the Avenue Press, under the direction of Reginald Praill, took over the family printing works which was part of the Cook soap manufacturers. Praill printed the bulk of

Brangwyn's graphic work, his war posters in particular. Brangwyn would discuss with Father the details of the printing process, swiftly brushing in preferred washes of colour, strengthening or lightening parts of the design and scribbling comments on the proofs. After the war they remained friends.

At the Royal Academy Schools, Father married a fellow student, the portrait painter Elizabeth Porteous. Due to some archaic regulation married women were not permitted as students, so when their first child Virginia was obviously expected 'Miss Porteous' was asked to leave. Since the Second World War was imminent, they moved out of London to The Forge in Wood Street Green in Surrey and there a second daughter, Joanna, was born. Crosby continued to work for the Avenue Press, gradually progressing to designing his own posters and other graphic work. When he was called up into the Air Sea Rescue service and served in a minesweeper off Northern Ireland, he produced accomplished watercolours in the hours of waiting between emergencies. I was born in the thick of the war in 1941 and Susan was born just as peace was declared.

In the 1950s Father won a prestigious prize for an inn sign design and, in protest against the loss of traditional and heraldic images to standardised commercial logos, he took up the job of restoring signs to their original designs, working primarily for Friary Meux all around southern England. Elizabeth shared the work, mainly painting the faces and hands. He did the bulk of the pictorial work and became skilled at brush-lettering, gilding and varnishing. It was 'a Forth Road Bridge job', he said, because as fast as he collected the signs, restored them and delivered them back in good condition, the first signs would once again need repair. Often he was asked to work independently and his original signs can be found the length and breadth of the country. He used to joke that he exhibited his work in the largest gallery in Britain, Britain itself.

Now Brangwyn was dead. Lizzie Peacock let us in. She looked weary, still wearing her customary long blue housekeeper's dress and hem-length pinafore, her long white hair pinned as usual into a bun. Her face, once plump, had grown thin and her knobble-knuckled hands were testimony to the lifetime of hard work she had devoted to Brangwyn. She welcomed us into the large kitchen, with its brick walls and floor, where an almost industrial-sized black gas cooker reigned. As Father and Mother commended her for her unfailing care for Brangwyn, especially in his last days, Ginny, Jo, Susan and I slipped out into The Jointure garden.

Where once it was neatly mown and weeded the grass had grown so high that it brushed the gnarled outstretched lower limbs of the espaliered apple trees. It was easy to lose our way as we explored the maze of paths leading through wooden gates into orchards and a walled vegetable garden where smoke seeped from a large mound of fresh bonfire ash. Over the top of the overgrown foliage towered the large twin wings of the red brick house with its arched buttresses and large metal windows. To the north rose the steeple of the Saxon church and to the south lay the Downs, their rounded sun-baked flanks, then mostly free of scrub, defined by the sweeping shadows of the clouds. The clang of a bell called us back again. Lizzie had allowed Father to pull the iron bell which Brangwyn designed to hang outside the studios to summon his assistants back from similar reveries.

We ran up to the long top lawn which was flanked with large clay oil jars. There Lizzie, Father and Mother waited by a large blue and gold painted metal armillary sphere, fashioned by Brangwyn and pinned to a stone plinth he had carved. The plinth, the sphere, the ornate metal scrollwork supporting the bell, the fragments of statuary built into the walls, the roughly drawn patterns in the cement between the paving stones–all spoke of his love for his home. I realised with a sudden pang that this could be the last time that I would be there.

A month or so later, however, Father received a telephone call from Mr Massey, one of Brangwyn's executors, asking if he could please call on us at The Forge that very day. Father was unavoidably busy in the studio but, meanwhile, Mother entertained him by showing him around. At lunch the conversation was largely about Brangwyn and Father's admiration for his work and only then did Massey explain the reason for his unexpected visit. He was having problems. The Jointure was for sale but Lizzie refused to allow anyone in to view it. Brangwyn had wanted to endow the house as a home for artists or, failing that, as a home for children, but it had proved complicated and the idea had to be abandoned. Now Lizzie had decided that our family of artists and children fitted the bill. Massey too had satisfied himself that we would be suitable custodians of The Jointure. Would we consider buying it?

Our home, The Forge in Wood Street Green, Surrey, was a comfortable old tile-hung house overlooking the large circular green that gave the village its name. It had a good garden and outhouses, including the old forge itself where the leather bellows remained intact and could be pumped by a long wooden pole topped with a cow's horn. Father had converted the disused British Legion Hall beside it into a substantial studio. In all it was quite a desirable property. Being near Guildford it was also within easy commuting distance of London. Massey estimated that its potential value would, coincidentally, match just the sum they had in mind for The Jointure.

The next time we arrived at The Jointure it was in the autumn of 1956 and, incredibly, we were soon to own it. We drove in through the yard gates and entered through the kitchen door. Massey met us and showed us round the labyrinth of rooms. Some furniture remained; cupboards appeared to be full and books and rolls of paper lay on the shelves. In the huge and lofty studios easels stood about and unpainted canvases and lithographic stones leant against the wall, an impressive plaster cast of Michelangelo's Taddei tondo filled a high alcove above the fireplace. The executor waved his hand at it dismissively. I assumed that we had agreed to pay for some of the contents but the executor explained that Lizzie had decreed that all that remained should be entrusted to us because we were to guard Brangwyn's heritage and home. Lizzie had moved next door to an adjoining cottage bequeathed to her by Brangwyn. It was named Temple Lodge after Brangwyn's first home in Hammersmith, where Lizzie first came to work for him and his wife Lucy. There she kept her own counsel and we rarely saw her.

We were entranced as we explored the rooms previously forbidden to us. Nearly all of them seemed to have been used for his work. They seemed colourless, dingy and gaunt. The only evident signs of comfort or relaxation were in the small parlour or 'morning room' to the left of the hall. The Tudor dining room with its ancient dark stained beams was, nonetheless, redolent of past conviviality. It remained much as Brangwyn had left it. Except for his favourite Spanish, metal-studded and leather-slung, armchair, the chairs were the rush-seated ladderbacks made to his own design. The refectory table had gone. Brangwyn prized it because he had acquired it from his friend, the artist Napier Hemy. One wall was almost entirely taken up by a plain dresser designed by him for his own use. Backing on to the kitchen chimney was a surprisingly small fireplace surrounded by narrow, green, vitreous tiles and a wooden mantle with sectioned panels. There were no radiators anywhere in the house and the few logs that the little fire could have accommodated would hardly have warmed the dining room to any degree. A large window with a deep, red-tiled, window-seat looked over a side lawn to the south, a false window mirror directly opposite it confused the eye. Two arches flanked the fireplace: one contained a linen press and the other an arched door leading down steps into the sunnier kitchen.

The Jointure was so named because it was once a farm adjoining Wings Place, commonly called Anne of Cleves's House, and was part of her jointure, a legal term referring to the parcel of land or a settlement, made between her and Henry VIII following their divorce.

Brangwyn was sensitive to the different periods apparent in the house. In the 1920s he added two large wings, providing a new kitchen and bedroom to the south and two studios to the north, but by using similar proportions and his own subtle embellishments he blended them harmoniously with the original Tudor building. He formed the first studio by gutting what may have been either an adjoining cottage or a barn or two-storied stable. The steel girders stretched across the empty space were left bare. The brick walls were painted a warm white and the floor was covered in parquet. Near the door to the street a substantial donkey

14

stove had a surround of delft tiles, their prettiness emphasising the general lack of built decoration. However, no doubt, colour would have abounded from his paintings, plates and pots. Long lines of paint spatters indicated the place where his huge murals had been positioned.

The second studio was an entirely new building. Here the warmth of wood prevailed throughout, with a plain planked floor and timber cladding on the steel joists and pilasters of its construction. Tall metal windows faced south, because Brangwyn deplored the tradition of painting by the evenness of north light. A smaller log-burning stove stood in a large open stone fireplace, and set into this was a loving emblem cast in concrete, displaying F&LB, his own and Lucy's initials entwined together. Above this studio was yet another studio in a loft. With typical inventive practicality this had floorboards hinged like a door so that tall canvases could be worked on above and below without disturbing them. We were excited by a small window looking down to the first studio from the level of its rafters, offering irresistible opportunities to spy on those below and startle them with comments from aloft. From there his assistants would, we were told, call down for their master's instructions or to request materials.

The huge stark rooms, with their lingering smell of turpentine, welcomed me. I found them familiar and homely. As a very small child I had spent hours in my parents' studio while they worked. There I would be drawing, always drawing, or poring over their red leather-bound collection of *Punch* and their black Phaidon books on famous artists. Now Brangwyn's studios reminded me of the etchings of Rembrandt–and indeed Brangwyn's own, being immensely high and dark and lit by shafts of light streaming in through tall 'Flemish' windows.

Leading off the first studio through a low door was Brangwyn's air-raid shelter and, beyond that, his workroom. But the main access was through a room Brangwyn used as a private chapel, which still had wartime blackout material at the window. Beyond that was the large sitting room he used as a workroom. It had a massive oak-beamed inglenook which Brangwyn rebuilt with simple square brick alcoves for logs. Over the hearth Brangwyn mounted a copper hood into which was impressed his F&LB device. This room too had been used as a workroom. In the centre stood a high wooden worktable, designed by Brangwyn in a stark but beautiful, almost Japanese style. With typical practicality Brangwyn had it pegged together so that it could be easily dismantled. This room opened onto the hall. Was it is a real memory or was it imagination that there as a small child I had glimpsed Brangwyn briefly? He was wearing a tweed three-piece suit, several safety pins attached to the waistcoat, and the carpet slippers he wore indoors. He wore stout ankle boots or clogs outside. The light from the road-facing windows lit his full head of white hair and beard as he came through from the chapel to greet

Father. True or not, this image remains in my mind as a symbol of the presence of Brangwyn that has pervaded my life.

For once my parents allowed me, as the elder of the two daughters still at home, to have first choice of bedroom. Never before had we had rooms of our own and I didn't hesitate. The room on the left at the top of the stairs had three windows. Two looked eastwards over the road and the other looked down on to the 'ladies' lawn' and south to the Downs. It shared the same square dimensions of the morning room below which, as the smallest, warmest and most comfortable of the living-rooms, had a feminine charm. Perhaps it had been Lucy's domain. Light and completely plain, 'my' bedroom had pale ochre walls, an uncarpeted wooden plank floor and a small fireplace over which Brangwyn had placed a simple wooden shelf. I relished its simplicity and privacy–but waited anxiously for Susan's protest. To my relief she was equally excited about the room she had chosen. It had promising possibilities afforded by the lumpy-walled deep cave beside the huge chimney which rose through it from the sitting room below.

Sue's room had belonged to Lizzie and mine to her son Edgar. Opposite Sue's room was a bathroom looking west across the top lawn, but, further down the corridor was an alarmingly cavernous, gaunt, dark lobby, that was, to us, undoubtedly haunted. It seemingly had no purpose. All it did was link through to the upper section of the first studio.

This enclosed space had been filled in between what had once been two outer walls and an open alleyway from the street to what would then have been a farmyard instead of gardens. At some earlier stage it was used as a shop and, for a while, a doctor's surgery.

The only light in that area came from a small window opening onto the flat roof of Brangwyn's air-raid shelter and a window, curtained in Virginia creeper, which overlooked the Ditchling Press on the other side of South Street. The 'far' bathroom was eventually constructed in half of the frightening space, but the rest remained open to the rafters and presented something of a challenge, night and day, especially since my parents painted it a dark mushroom colour. A fine Brangwynesque wooden door, with one of his elaborate iron latches, opened off the lobby onto a little balcony, where Lucy had sat embroidering while her husband worked below. A trap door opened from it allowing access by ladder only. There was a reason that he wanted her near by but not actually in the studio and that was–I later learned–she was addicted to drink. A man in ostler's clothes was seen occasionally in the first studio. When I lived in the studios in later years I heard footsteps in it so often that, at first, I took no notice when burglars broke in.

Brangwyn's bedroom door was immediately opposite the top of the stairs and, for safety, a gate, matching the banisters, could be swung across and latched shut at night. He had carved two roundels in it. One, on which he carved the F&LB insignia, could be opened from inside, allowing Brangwyn to peer down at whoever might arrive at the front door. His room was as large as the Tudor dining room below and both had disappointingly small fireplaces. It also had a large south-facing window with square rolled iron catches to his own design. A nearby niche served as his altar and it still contained three precious objects, a cross, a figure of St Francis and a tiny ancient clay *pietà* which had long been in Brangwyn's possession. It was the room in which he died and over the fireplace still hung the oil painting he kept close to him. It is of Lucy looking over a canal bridge in Bruges. With it was the photograph on which it was based. It shows him standing where he had placed Lucy in the painting and he is looking across to where she stands on the opposite side. Small boys stare up at the unknown photographer, but in the painting Brangwyn, probably later, substituted some more flamboyant figures, which do not marry with the quieter style of the rest. A dark and puzzling painting, it has the resonance of his own affection for it.

Jo stayed in 'Sir Frank's room' when she came to visit us from her married life in Cornwall and we used it generally as a guest-room. Mother and Father chose the large light room beyond, supposedly Lucy and Brangwyn's bedroom. After her death Brangwyn used it as his Sunday studio and for smaller graphic work and writing letters. It had the same dimensions as the huge kitchen below and like that had large metal windows looking south to the downs and west over the garden. It had an adjoining dressing room which Father decided could be halved to accommodate a new bathroom. This room was reached from the stairwell by a strange, open, half-corridor, half-bedroom, that we called 'the Bulge' where Brangwyn's visitors were surprised to have been offered a bed.

Changes would have to be made but as much as the building work upset me it excited me. A corridor was formed through 'Sir Frank's room' as it became known. This led towards the niche and then turned right and sharp left to the main bedroom. Sir Frank's door was set back into a new stud wall and now overlooked this dogleg. The Bulge could thereby be enclosed as a bedroom for Netty, Jubilee Jeanette Turner, our treasured housekeeper.

Like so many other women at that time, Netty and Lizzie both mourned soldiers killed during the war. Though she usually shared the same stalwart disposition as Lizzie, Netty was dismayed at the prospect of leaving The Forge and taking on the huge kitchen and maze of rooms at The Jointure. She was nervous of losing her way and, in protest, kept her hat on for the first three days. However, she was happier when the kitchen was refitted with new cupboards and work surfaces and two big Belfast sinks (with a stool provided so that she could reach over them.) It was painted a sunny yellow and a comforting new dark blue Aga was installed, but it was still large and draughty. Eventually a room within a room was built in it to provide her with a small sitting room.

Netty was the small, but reliable, rock supporting the household. The morning began early with the rattle of coals as she cleaned and set the fires. Our frocks hung stiffly in our cupboards from her starching; her cooking skills were in the finest tradition and her practical wisdom gave us all stability. Sue and I used to eat an earlier supper, separately from our parents and afterwards would crowd into her snug parlour to watch her black and white television while she knitted christening shawls as fine as cobwebs for Jo's babies, the first grandchildren to arrive.

The house filled up with builders and gradually a sunnier family home was opened up. The big drawing room became elegantly formal, the morning room a comfortable everyday sitting room. The dining room remained unchanged. Off the studios, the front wall of Brangwyn's integrated bomb shelter was glazed with an unfortunately inappropriate, but very enjoyable, concertina-opening metal window. It provided a sunroom that could be used as an open portico with access on to the top lawn. The garden was reclaimed from the overgrowth and Mother filled it with new shrubs and flowers, colour and fragrance. George Blackstone, the gardener, marshalled the vegetable garden back into ordered rows as neatly as he iced cakes for our celebrations. He pruned the fruit trees and ran chickens and a pig in the orchard. The modernisation was, in the main, respectful and much remained unaltered. The original smell, darkness and sense of mystery remained, especially in the huge attics running the length of the Tudor house and in the musty cellars. There Brangwyn's extensive wine racks still contained bottles. They looked promising on our arrival but, to our disappointment, turned out to be his supply of Malvern water.

Brangwyn's presence pervaded The Jointure despite the changes and was the background ambience to my own work. It was caught in the strength of his arched buttresses, the details of his wood carvings and metalwork and in the wittily entwined numerals and quickly sketched caricatures that he drew into wet plaster to mark the date of building work. His additions and alterations were characteristic of his art as much as his drawings, paintings and etchings. Every single part was integrated by his strong sense of design and decoration. It was already familiar to me. A small lithograph of street urchins clustered round an ice cream-vendor's cart hung in our nursery at The Forge and through it, as a small child, I came to know his vigorous but sure line, his well-balanced composition and his sense of fun. Later, in The Jointure garden, Susan dug up the broken pieces of the stone on which it had been drawn.

Father and Mother steadily promoted Brangwyn, allowing those who were interested to visit The Jointure. They regularly put on small exhibitions of his work and, in 1967, their larger, commemorative show at The Jointure played a significant part in Brangwyn's centenary celebrations. The Fine Art Society and the William Morris Gallery in Walthamstow loyally staged important shows in London, but, in the main, the exhibitions took place out of town, chiefly in Cardiff and Brighton. Unfortunately the retrospective engendered little interest of consequence and did little to repair the poor reputation which had beset Brangwyn since the Thirties. This was caused by the rejection of his major project, the British Empire panels, designed as a decoration for the Royal Gallery at the House of Lords, which toppled him from his position as a leading member of the British avant-garde. This was undeserved and caused by a post-First World War collision of conflicting artistic and political opinions.

In 1967, in the climate of Pop and abstract experimentation, Brangwyn's work was still out of step. Figurative art, drawing and technique were then generally disparaged. At this point I began to consider Brangwyn seriously and felt keenly about the injustice to his work. What was it that made his work so distinctive and recognisable? What had influenced it? How could someone so well connected be deemed a recluse? Why did one critic accuse his work of being too dark and another of being too colourful? What was his story? How had someone so famous, and so undeniably good, have been all but forgotten? Because the first retrospective brought him no real revival our family hopes became set on another retrospective in 2006 to celebrate the half-century since Brangwyn's death.

When Father retired my parents converted the loft studio into an open plan flat for themselves. It had a range of windows in the roof with an extensive view of the Downs. The main house was let to a variety of friends, then to Ginny and next to Susan with their families. In 1989 Father died. Mother lived in The Jointure studios for a while but, in 1994, moved with Susan down to Cornwall where sister Jo already lived. I was by then divorced and footloose so Mother asked me to move, temporarily, back to the flat to look after the house as it was put up for sale. Before marketing it, however, Ginny and I tried our best to preserve Brangwyn's former home intact, for use by the village and for the nation. We staged an exhibition of his work and publicised The Jointure's availability and for a while it seemed the house and Brangwyn would have an ideally suitable fate.

Ditchling Museum is housed in what had been the village school. When it opened in 1985 it mostly displayed a collection of historical interest pertaining to the village's Saxon and medieval origins. But, by 1994, it began to focus on the Arts and Crafts identity the village acquired in the early years of the twentieth century. Although the pretty village had attracted artists and craftsmen earlier, Ditchling became celebrated from the mid-1900s when the sculptor Eric Gill, with others, who had formed a coterie around the London home of William Morris in Hammersmith, moved to the village. This group included Edward Johnston, the innovative calligrapher, Hilary Pepler, whose St Dominic's hand press led to the present day Ditchling Press and Brangwyn himself. The museum's curator, Hilary Bourne, came to the exhibition in The Jointure and decided to seek funding from the then new Heritage Lottery to relocate the existing museum into the larger and entirely appropriate premises.

For over four years the family delayed the sale of the house and lent its support to the museum's bid. Hilary appointed Peter Holliday as chairman of the project. Peter was an art historian, a retired teacher and an expert in typography and the work of Edward Johnston. Because of my particular knowledge of Brangwyn and the house, Hilary formally asked me to assist him.

Peter and I, with the rest of the museum team, worked with increasing enthusiasm as we answered the questions asked by the HLF officials. We presented them with the full scope which the proposed museum could offer. We outlined, in particular, how the return to pure handcraft, as practised by the Ditchling artist-craftsmen, made a significant, international contribution to the development of the Arts and Crafts movement towards Modernism and could be successfully demonstrated, through display, exhibitions and conferences. The medieval principles from which the Arts and Crafts practitioners drew their inspiration and which underlay the ethos of the Ditchling artist-craftsmen were firmly entwined with the collection of local history at the museum so all could have been happily integrated.

Although it was Brangwyn's former home the principle was that no one artist would be singled out for precedence. Initially Brangwyn's work was seen to be at odds with Gill's, but deeper study revealed the philosophical unity between them, Johnston, Pepler and the others who joined the 'Ditchling' group and gave the museum its prevailing concept.

Nearby, at Firle, Charleston Farmhouse was overcrowded by visitors eager to see the decorative work of the Bloomsbury Omega Workshop's artist-craftsmen in their domestic setting. The success of this venture in displaying an alternative but associated branch of the Arts and Crafts movement encouraged the South-East tourist board and other local authorities to support the Ditchling museum project. They realised the important educational and recreational opportunities the project offered, as well as the possibility of preserving The Jointure as a whole. Plans were drawn up for a complete refurbishment of the house and garden and so it was allowed to run down. As part of the museum's proposed opening celebrations it planned to stage the 2006 retrospective Brangwyn exhibition on which my parents and, after them Ginny and I, had worked.

The reasons for its failure are as difficult to pinpoint as those that defeated Brangwyn's own generous, but doomed, visionary schemes. Human nature and bureaucracy inevitably played their parts. The final blow came with the change of government in 1997 when the promised Lottery money was withdrawn to be spent instead on Millennium projects. The family was left with a somewhat neglected house and garden once again for sale. However, the museum project had served to emphasise Brangwyn's importance to art history as well as to Ditchling. Interest in him was kindled from new enthusiasts. These Brangwyn revivalists urged us to continue with the work towards the 2006 retrospective, despite the abandonment of the museum project. So Ginny and I set ourselves to the task in earnest. At that point Libby Horner arrived at The Jointure, having chosen Brangwyn as the subject for her PhD. With members of the Brangwyn family, Paul Liss, Rachel Moss, Libby Horner and others, we formed a small committee and helped to bring the retrospective to successful fruition.

Following the collapse of the project and the death of Hilary Bourne, Ditchling Museum remained in the old schoolhouse and reorganised its collection within its existing confines. Increasingly, however, visitors asked for an account of Brangwyn as a private man as well as a public figure. So, in view of my in-depth and personal understanding of his work and his former home, I was asked to write this biographical study.

INTRODUCTION

No artist surpasses him in design, virility of treatment or colour. None has more courage in tackling a subject on a colossal scale Joseph Simpson [1]

In 2006 it has, as ever, proved challenging to all those who study or write about Brangwyn to encapsulate his work concisely. He was an artistic loner and purposely evasive, an artist and designer who continues to stand apart from the vagaries of fashion. He deliberately avoided being overwhelmed by any of the many influences he explored and, at his maturity, he emerged as a major British artist of rare independence and vitality. As a result he presents the art world with a conundrum as to how his work should be classified and, in the past, it has proved difficult to market. But, nevertheless, it sold prolifically in his lifetime and maintains an increasingly strong position in the present-day saleroom.

His prodigious talent grew from his childhood spent largely in his father's ecclesiastical workshop in Bruges. His democratic philosophy and much of his subject matter was influenced by the beautiful city in which they lived and the work of the Belgian painters. In London he had the good fortune to attract important mentors, chiefly Arthur Heygate Mackmurdo and William Morris and, in Paris, Siegfried Bing.

He worked ceaselessly throughout his life. His oeuvre was massive and it is probable that no artist before or since has matched his phenomenal multi-medial productivity but his versatility was underpinned by sound technical excellence and in each of his disciplines he proved himself a master. In this respect he can be considered the natural successor to Augustus Pugin and William Morris.

His gifts were truly remarkable. He adapted himself almost too easily to a wide range of styles and media. He avoided and even scorned, formal art school training, but his innate talent allowed him to assimilate new styles and techniques with ease. His energy and enthusiasm was such that it sometimes ran away with him towards over-ebullience and the work became hurried, but his confidence, courage and, above all, his individuality attracted early attention and rewarded him with considerable fame and fortune.

He proved himself able across an astonishingly wide field. He was a painter in oils and watercolours, an etcher, lithographer, wood-engraver, illustrator, designer of stained glass, mosaic, carpets, metalwork, furniture and ceramics. He illustrated books, magazines and designed posters. He was an architect and interior designer and an innovative and celebrated muralist. In his fine art he drew on tradition but to this he added invention. His applied art anticipated Modernism and while his influence upon the twentieth century is palpable it is largely underrated. He didn't rest upon the success he achieved and was compelled to follow his star.

Each of his disciplines is worthy of detailed study. The total sum of his work is incalculable because he produced many hundreds of etchings, watercolours, oils and drawings. As a result of his extraordinary fame much of his work probably remains hidden in private homes. Despite his celebrity he maintained a modest view of himself as a jobbing artist and his alliance with the working man is evident.

Throughout his multifaceted life Brangwyn maintained a rare integrity. He was, as Vincent Galloway writes in his preface to his book on Brangwyn's oils and murals.

…like one of these 'nova' stars that appear from nowhere and upset all calculations with their size and brilliance.[2]

As his life was bound by his art, so his art was bound by his personality. He was a man of contrasts. Despite his distinguished career and international recognition, he shunned publicity and society, allying himself with the outcasts of society, beggars, cripples and refugees. His giant ambitions were devoid of self-aggrandisement. He had innate wisdom but no sophistication, instinctive artistic judgement but no formal training, high intelligence but little education. He was without guile or malice and was generous, industrious and energetic. Though famous and extremely well connected he was almost a recluse. His blunt approach concealed his sensitivity and he played down his intellectual proficiency.

For two thirds of his long life, the consistently high standard that Brangwyn sustained in both the fine and applied arts brought him international acclaim and from 1900 to 1930 he was lauded as the foremost decorative British artist. The injustices that beset his work following the scandal of the rejection of his 3,000-square-foot British Empire panels for the House of Lords would have broken the spirit of a lesser man, but Brangwyn's artistic élan was indomitable. He continued to work until the end of his life, though fashion turned away from him and the critics ignored him to the extent that he was not included in the books and exhibitions to which he was relevant. As a result, his contribution to the chapters of art history was, for too long, overlooked. However, contemporary critical reassessment has brought him increasing recognition as an artist, craftsman and designer, worthy of British pride. At his death the critic of *The Times* was typical of contemporary evaluation when he wrote:

What stands out is his ability to produce designs that are adapted to their scale, an aptitude so rare among British artists that it may account more than anything else for his great reputation abroad…What struck one most was his combination of imagination and severe practicality.[3]

Had he died at the height of his fame he would have been saluted with greater praise. In 1904 C Lewis Hind, the critic of the *Evening News* wrote:

I dare assert that in the twenty-first century Mr Brangwyn will be reckoned as one of the chief forces of our time. He is entirely himself, bold and original and his work has the decorative quality, the sense of pattern, that has always marked the Masters.[4]

THE GOTHIC REVIVAL

Art is individuality added to tradition *Brangwyn* [1]

When Brangwyn was born in Bruges in 1867 his father, William Curtis Brangwyn, ran a thriving ecclesiastical atelier at 24 rue de Vieux Bourg (now 30 Oude Burg) an imposing house close to the centre of the city and in the lee of the cathedral of St Salvator. A spacious courtyard to the rear of the house accommodated a substantial workshop where embroidered vestments and other church accoutrements were, in the main, sent back for sale in a Baker Street shop in London.[2] There too, although he was not fully qualified as an architect, Curtis ran an independent architectural practice.

In 1861 Curtis was working as an architect's assistant in Scarborough and Eleanor Griffiths was a housemaid for the rector in Llyswen but by 1863 they met and she was pregnant. Editha was born in 1864 and they married in England in 1865. After they moved to Bruges they produced a second daughter Hélène in 1866 in 20 Rue des Pierres (now Steenstraat.) Their third and fourth children, Frank (1867) and Phillipe (1869), were born in rue de Vieux Bourg and Cuthbert (1875) and Lawrence (1878) were born after the family moved back to London in 1875.

Frank, christened Guillaume François Brangwyn, was born at 10.30 am on 12 May 1867 and his life was immediately centred on the workshop. His biographer, Philip Macer-Wright, records that his cradle was placed under a worktable and, when he was old enough, he was given small jobs under the supervision of the other assistants.

Brangwyn's first memories were of '…a lovely enclosed garden surrounded by high walls' where there grew 'a beautiful tree filled with rich red flowers'. Over the walls he could see 'the gables of the town, and from the belfry of the Cathedral rang the bells … bells, bells, all joyous around and above me. My mother told me I played with old bottles and pots. No doubt this was the beginning of my love of pots. Then I used to run in and out of the workshops that were filled with men embroidering the rich vestments and banners. Here I suppose was born my love of colour and textiles.'[3]

During his nine years in the city Curtis enjoyed a close involvement with the Flemish cultural, religious and architectural resurgence. His philosophical inspiration was derived from Pugin and the Gothic Revival and he had worked for G E Street, the ecclesiastical architect who built the Law Courts. Street was one of the principal interpreters of 'neo-Gothic' Victorian medievalism. T E Collcutt, Philip Webb, William Morris and the architect Richard Norman Shaw all, at one time, worked in his office, which thus became a forcing-ground for the Arts and Crafts Movement. Curtis nevertheless continued to work in the neo-Gothic style. In Bruges he was responsible for the reconstruction of the Benedictine Monastery of St André and he worked on the St Julian Hospice and the psychiatric hospital at the former church of St Michael. He also refurbished St Basile and worked on the town hall in Kruibeke. His most prestigious commission was to design a reliquary and carry out much of the painted decoration in the Basilica of the Holy Blood in the centre of Bruges. These architectural projects involved the use of tapestry, stained glass, furniture and mural painting.

Curtis was the first and the most important influence on Brangwyn. However, the city and the Belgian painters also left a strong impression on him in the first years of his life. In 1944 he added a personal appreciation of Belgian art to William de Belleroche's account of his meetings with him in his book, *Brangwyn Talks*.

Belgian art has always rested on the life of the soil, home and domesticity. Its honesty has taken the form of a realistic outlook on life, happily free from the grosser forms of doubt and pessimism, that permits a true picture of people in their natural environment. The Belgian artists have excelled in revealing the drama and beauty of the simplicity of daily life, or what passes for the commonplace to men without vision. In no work is this fine flavour of domesticity more strongly shown than in the pictures of Van Eyck, Brueghel and their contemporaries. Even Rubens and Jordaens in those grandiose flights into mythology kept close to the earth.

In this he perhaps reveals the source of the simple humanity underlying his ouevre, his alliance with the working man and his abhorrence of the social aspects of the art world. Certainly, as in Brueghel's paintings, his work teems with human activity.

Brangwyn did not have particular artistic ancestry. Curtis came from generations of farmers named Brangwin, based in Long Crendon, Buckinghamshire. He changed his name to Brangwyn when he converted to Catholicism. One relative, Noah Brangwin, exhibited at the Royal Academy in the 1850s. Curtis's wife Eleanor came from Llanstephan in Radnorshire.

On his return to London in 1875, Curtis designed Hastings town hall in Sussex and worked on the schools of the Grocers Company and the offices of the Board of Works at Greenwich. In 1879 he produced a scheme for Yarmouth town hall and designed a pulpit for Canford Church in Dorset. Later Curtis and Eleanor separated and Curtis lived out his last years working in Cardiff. Phillipe worked as an interior designer in Canada as did Cuthbert in America. Lawrence became a carpenter and a publican. Little is known as about Brangwyn's continued connection with his family but there is no evidence of disharmony.

Frank displayed a precocious artistic talent. His favourite occupation was to copy the engravings of Charles Degroux, who, much in the spirit of Millais, Holman Hunt, and Ford Madox Brown, depicted the trials of the under-privileged and promoted the noble work ethic. In 1875 Curtis moved his family back to the then rural outpost of Shepherds Bush. He took a house at 19 Richmond Gardens and in 1877 moved to 30 Grange Gardens. Since the Brangwyns were Catholics, Frank was sent to the Catholic kindergarten nearby, but he was never happy in the class-room and frequently escaped to explore and sketch the countryside, especially the banks of the Thames, teeming with boats and all kinds of characters. Brangwyn later said that this was his true education.

Sketching was an unusual occupation for a young boy, but for Brangwyn it was a passion as undeniable as life and breath. One day he came upon an artist at work on a painting of the river and, watching him, a new world opened up for him. Some years later this same artist, Napier Hemy, became his friend.

Westminster Grammar School was the next imprisonment. However, as they travelled together on the morning train, Curtis often failed to alert Frank to get off at the right station and so the boy would habitually avoid school. Instead he would spend the day helping his father in his architect's office at 6 John Street, Adelphi, off the Strand.

THE ARTS AND CRAFTS MOVEMENT

The more modern artist is also the more medieval artist GK Chesterton [1]

When not working with his father Brangwyn would draw and paint around London. Legend has it that Arthur Heygate Mackmurdo, the renowned designer and architect, came across him painting at his easel in Oxford Street and, immediately recognising his potential, befriended him. Curtis had advised his son to visit the London art galleries and, it is also said, that there Brangwyn was 'discovered' by Harold Rathbone. It is possible that, since Curtis moved in the same circles as these eminent figures, he effected the introductions, but both artists encouraged Brangwyn to study at the museum and their help proved influential.

Rathbone was a pupil of Ford Madox Brown, a 'highbrow' and a resolute traditionalist. Brangwyn later described him as 'a queer bird, with intent eyes and spectacles, bright yellow tie and flapping arms'.[2] Rathbone set him to copy the drawings of Dürer and Donatello's bas-relief, 'Christ in the Sepulchre' (a plaster cast of which Brangwyn later kept by him in his studios). Rathbone advocated the use of finely outlined, exact drawing and close-toned painting. However, his was a limited viewpoint, unsuited to Brangwyn's ebullience and energy.

In Mackmurdo Brangwyn found a lifelong friend. Mackmurdo was a friend of Ruskin and a seminal figure in the circle surrounding William Morris. In 1882 he founded the Century Guild and its magazine, *The Hobby Horse*, anticipated the late nineteenth century's enthusiasm for art publications. The furniture he designed and produced at the guild was to prove an important influence on Brangwyn's own designs. Mackmurdo's attempts to introduce the young Brangwyn into society circles failed dismally. Painfully aware of his lack of formal education and ill at ease in society drawing rooms, Brangwyn would retreat with his sketchbook to some far corner of the garden or conservatory. Nevertheless Mackmurdo spent much time with his protégé in the galleries and museums, giving him invaluable education in art history and techniques. They shared a particular enthusiasm for the frescoes of Mantegna, which were on display at the South Kensington Museum and Brangwyn copied them in tempera.

Selwyn Image, one of Mackmurdo's friends, also took a keen interest in Brangwyn's education. He was a clergyman-turned-artist who became Slade Professor at Oxford. He accompanied Brangwyn on long evening walks around London, giving what amounted to a monologue of his erudite opinions on a wide range of topics and learned observations on all they encountered. Brangwyn readily absorbed all he was taught and Image later admitted that his pupil outstripped him in natural talent and achievements.

Most importantly Mackmurdo introduced Brangwyn to William Morris, and in 1882, at the age of 15, he began work in the Morris workshops, where, by coincidence, Napier Hemy was a fellow assistant. Brangwyn's early experiences in his father's studio had equipped him with the necessary skills. He was already versed in the production of tapestries and stained glass and, through his copying, had well-developed co-ordination of hand and eye. He could transfer Morris's designs with precision onto squared-up canvases for tapestries and the wood printing blocks for wallpapers and fabrics. This exacting work served to strengthen Brangwyn's compositional stability and afterwards, before beginning a picture, he would always draw a small version of it in a square or rectangle to test the balance and chiaroscuro.

Brangwyn was at home in the workshop and learned important lessons about the care of tools and the safe use of ladders and scaffolding. Later, when he ran his own studio he demanded the same strict routine as practised by 'the master'. John Ruskin's theories informed both Pugin and Morris and therefore Brangwyn. Degroux had instilled in him a deeply felt respect for the working man and he was sympathetic to Morris's socialist principles. Morris preached that it enlivened and refreshed all aspects of art to work in many media and that an artist could remain true to himself across a broad spectrum. Brangwyn never strayed from this precept and worked concurrently on the fine and the applied arts all his life.

THE NEWLYN SCHOOL

I have never painted with such directness as on those fortunately rare occasions when I have worked at sea, and I have carried large pictures right through to the last stages in smithies, stable sheds, and amidst all sorts of queer surroundings Stanhope Forbes

Had he been older, and had family responsibilities, Brangwyn could easily have become trapped as an assistant to Morris. He was to work with Morris, on and off, until Morris's death, but he knew instinctively that he had more to learn in the wider world. After two years he found that the work ceased to challenge him, so, in 1884, inspired by an etching of 'The Old Barbican Gate at Sandwich' by Charles Holloway, which he saw in a shop window, he set off to find adventure there. For some months he earned a modest living by selling his work, painting shop facias and signs, and the names of boats on their hulls. But then, owing money to the landlord of the Admiral Owen with whom he lodged, he 'shot the moon' and signed on as a crewman with the *Garibaldi*.

Little is known of the extent and timing of his voyages at this point, but a painting called 'A Bit on the Esk near Whitby' was exhibited at the RA in 1885. In later years he related that in 1886 he travelled steerage to Cornwall on the *Waterford Packet* and disembarked in Falmouth.[1] From there, carrying all his equipment on his back, he walked to Mevagissey. The pretty harbour with its whitewashed cottages and busy fishing boats was, he said, 'a sight that knocked me silly'.[2]

Brangwyn admitted to having been distracted from his painting there as he spent too long hobnobbing with the farmers and fishermen and too long, also, in the arms of a fisherman's daughter called Katie Chesterfield for whom he developed a youthful passion. The result was that in October 1886, when Brangwyn was 19, she bore him a son. Brangwyn had no money and feared that entrapment in marriage would curtail his career, so he worked his passage back to London and took a studio there.

The boy was not acknowledged as his son. He was named James Chesterfield and was brought up by his grandparents, Joseph and Grace Chesterfield and his aunt, Edie, in Mevagissey. He emigrated to Australia in 1909 and, it seems, remained in ignorance of his illustrious father until 1915.

In London Brangwyn moved into one of the cheap, run-down Wentworth Studios in Manresa Road in Chelsea, at that time an unfashionable area of London. There he shared food, paint, models and adventures with other poverty-stricken artists. His co-tenant was AD M'Cormick and in adjoining studios surrounding a yard were Frank Short, Jacomb Hood, Nelson Dawson, William Llewelyn, JJ Shannon, Cecil Lawson, Stirling Lee, and the Toft brothers, Alfred and Alfonso. He joined the Royal Naval Volunteers with Short, who became a lifelong friend. They divided their time between gunnery drills and other naval exercises and painting, either in the studio or on trips to the coast to find marine subjects and, in Brangwyn's case, to fraternise with the fishermen and sailors.

It is clear from Brangwyn's paintings that he returned to Cornwall in 1887 and 1888, so one hopes that at that time he supported his son as best he could. It seems, however, that, as the boy grew older, Brangwyn did not maintain any contact with him and it cannot be proved that Brangwyn supported him financially when he was able to. In later life Brangwyn spoke of his remorse at having neglected those he loved and, presumably, his abandonment of his son was a major reason for secret and sincere regret and soul-searching as to whether he had sacrificed others for his own career. His art was, however, a compulsion that could not be denied.

Money was generally in short supply and art materials were consequently scarce but, fortunately, two benefactors appeared. The first was Harriet Barnett, a benevolent and artistic friend of Mackmurdo's, who had heard of the promising young artist. Brangwyn became her protégée. Like Mackmurdo's, her attempts to include him in her social gatherings failed, but she was not discouraged. She bought his work and arranged commissions from her friends. However, she prudently kept back substantial portions of the payment and invested it in consols. Sadly, when he closed the account during the First World War, the sum represented a small fraction of the value of the work.

More practical help came from Frederick Mills, or Old Sugar as he was known. He was a generous man and had lucrative links with a sugar plantation. He was the head of Newman's, a supplier of art materials in Soho where Brangwyn bought his paints. Taking pity on Brangwyn's poverty, Mills offered to finance him on another trip to Cornwall to be repaid with the work he would bring back.

The paintings Brangwyn produced at this time were muted. While he was not actually one of the Newlyn School, he adapted to the naturalism and narrative qualities of their work. He produced several distinguished paintings in Cornwall between 1887 and 1890 which were equal to any the School produced and led to some critical confusion as to whether or not he was one of their number.

COLOURIST

The destiny of art is to transmit from the realm of reason to the realm of feeling *Leo Tolstoy* [1]

In 1890, holed up once more in the Manresa Road studios, Brangwyn soon became impatient to travel again. Working outdoors in Cornwall he felt the first dissatisfaction with the sombre tones of his palette. The impact of the French Impressionists also affected his tonal range, but their effect upon him was psychological as well as pictorial. They liberated him by giving him the impetus to break rules and follow his own vision. As he said, 'There is a mysterious something in colours which I can only describe as "life".'[2]

He remembered that his painting 'Waterlogged' was bought by the skipper of a cargo boat and, tremulously, called at the man's London home. To his delight he was told that there was a vessel leaving shortly for the Black Sea and he could travel as a passenger and repay the skipper with his paintings and drawings, the arrangement he had enjoyed with Old Sugar.

After putting in at Antwerp the ship sailed towards the Bosphorus and, one dawn, arrived off the coast of Constantinople which, in the hazy light of the rising sun, appeared to Brangwyn as 'a city that lay shimmering like a pearl in a silver sea'.[3] This critical experience remained with him for ever and transformed his artistic vision.

In 1890 Brangwyn made three voyages under the auspices of his skipper friend, all the while bringing home works which began to receive acclaim.

The paintings were exhibited at the RA and the Institute of Oil Painters, the New English Art Club and the Grosvenor Gallery. The critics described him as 'an artist of promise, a precocious talent, a painter of technical skill'. One of his more important oils, his large narrative marine painting called 'Funeral at Sea', was shown at The Society of British Artists in 1891 and, at the Paris Salon later that year, it was given the Place d'Honneur and awarded a medal.

On a trip to Spain in 1891 he fully explored colour and chiaroscuro. His companion was Arthur Melville, a highly accomplished painter and leading member of the Glasgow School. His example further encouraged Brangwyn's trans-formation. Brangwyn picked up Melville's technique as quickly as a magpie seizes bright objects and their work is at points indistinguishable. With Melville Brangwyn developed a broader, looser brushwork and brighter colours and by deepening his shadows he accented the contrast of his sunlit areas. The critics, who were used to his close-toned paintings, received the dazzling new works that Brangwyn brought home with caution, but the work led to a venture funded by TJ Larkin who had a Japanese gallery in Bond Street. He had staged a successful exhibition of especially commissioned paintings of India, and in 1891 he asked Brangwyn and another travel-inspired artist, William Hunt, to paint their impressions of South Africa.

The scenes that engaged Brangwyn on his travels were forever more to provide his subject matter. As a child he was deeply impressed by the working men whom he had found toiling in gloomy but picturesque poverty in the paintings of Millet and the engravings of Charles Degroux. In South Africa, however, they danced as they worked, treading grapes in the blazing sunshine of the Cape. The foliage he had worked into formal patterns for Morris's fabrics was replaced with depictions of real flowers and fruits and his canvases became filled with exoticism and abundance.

Two paintings exemplify these changes, 'Funeral at Sea' exhibited in 1890 and 'The Buccaneers' of 1892. The first painting has a static solemnity.

It portrays a narrative shipboard scene, restrained in mood, with all usual activity put aside for a moment of reverence. The naturalism is exact, the paint delicate and almost monotone so close is its range. In contrast, the second painting, a view across the bay at Puerto de los Pasajes in Spain, heaves with movement. It shows a crowded boat rocking in a sea painted a rich dark Prussian blue. A large red flag flutters above a swarthy band of battle-scarred pirates and the distant shore shimmers with intense heat. While also being narrative it is daringly opulent and original. The brushwork is vigorous and the paint thickly laid in, the dark heads and hands of the men are sharply defined against their bright clothing, and the rhythm of the composition holds sure across the huge canvas.

'The Buccaneers' was exhibited at the Grafton Gallery in 1893. Shocked by his change of style the British critics wrote in fulsome disapproval, '….garish and aggressive'–the *Manchester Guardian*; '…a war cry of *fin de siècle* barbarism'–the *Pall Mall Gazette*; 'slap dash'–the *Saturday Review*. The magazine *Truth* perceptively declared that it was 'more like a mosaic pavement than a picture,' thus unconsciously acknowledging its latent decorative qualities. Unlike his fellows, the critic in the *Spectator* was enthusiastic about Brangwyn. Reviewing Whistler's 'Study in Red' he wrote, 'This picture reminds me of Mr Brangwyn, the juicy qualities of whose work Mr Whistler reproduces so well.' Whistler was then 59 and Brangwyn 26. In fact Brangwyn's use of impasto and his speed and energy were not at all similar to Whistler's approach. However, Brangwyn's later interior decorative schemes, in which he used warm grey backgrounds, elegant Japanese motifs and gilding, show Whistler's influence.

A few weeks after it had been slated in London, 'The Buccaneers' was exhibited at the 1893 Paris Salon. There it caused a sensation. The Parisians accepted his shift of mood with rapture. While in England the critics remained divided in their opinion of the young artist, the French accepted him as the leader of the British avant-garde. The carpet was worn threadbare in front of the painting and fashion that year promoted a 'Brangwyn red'.

He attracted the attention of Seigfried Bing who commissioned him to paint an exterior frieze for his innovative new venture, Le Maison de L' Art Nouveau in Paris. Through this Brangwyn became established internationally.

ART NOUVEAU

It is a sobering fact; Art Nouveau was the first great international style since the Middle Ages (and the last of course) to which Britain made any perceptible contribution *Sir Lawrence Gowing* Observer *5 July 1969* [1]

There were moments earlier in history when British art was fashionable and influential abroad, but none proved so important as that initiated by Ruskin and the Pre-Raphaelites which was disseminated by Morris and others into the Arts and Crafts movement. Morris promoted his socialist-inspired ideal of eschewing the banality of mass-manufacture in favour of the individuality and beauty of hand-wrought work. Ironically, however, he in fact engendered a fashion for work by illustrious designers, such as Mackmurdo, Charles Robert Ashbee, Walter Crane and Charles Rennie Macintosh, that commanded prices only the privileged could pay. But their naturalistic style was recognised on the continent as Le Style Anglais and the trend spread rapidly on the continent where it became even more ornamental and curvilinear. It was known as Jugenstil in Germany, Modernista in Spain, Stile Liberty in Italy and Art Nouveau in France.

In 1895, Brangwyn's painting 'The Miraculous Draught of Fishes' was exhibited at the Paris Salon and received great acclaim. That summer, aware of his growing reputation in France, Seigfried Bing asked him to paint an external frieze, one hundred and eighty feet long, for his new gallery Le Maison de L'Art Nouveau at 22 Rue de Provence, Paris, as well as two internal panels, Music and Dance for the entrance hall. Working alongside Fond Louis Bonnier–Bing's architectural advisor– in conjunction with Victor Horta and Henry van de Velde, brought Brangwyn into the company of the Paris *connaisseuse*.

With no previous experience of working on scaffolding, out of doors, Brangwyn completed the frieze successfully and at top speed because Bing wanted to open the shop by December. He executed the mural freehand, working in all weathers, literally *en plein air*. The exterior decoration consisted of two long painted bands running the full length of the two-sided corner building, one directly beneath the eaves and the other below the upper windows. He divided the frieze into sections separated by thin verticals and linked the whole design with flowing horizontal lines. This interplay between the vertical and horizontal became a repeated device. The upper section displayed a series of oriental craftsmen. The lower showed figures intertwined with vines, foliage and scrollwork and the whole was punctuated with stencilled ornamentation. He thus developed a technique which formed the basis of his future mural work.

In his experimentation several influences can be seen. His stylised designs were outlined in blue and the colour was laid on in isolated patches. This is indicative of several elements in his training. It echoed the outlined drawing he learned from Rathbone and his work lining-in designs for textiles and wallpapers for his father and for Morris. He left clear areas of colour to be painted separately as if they were to be embroidered or printed. This had a practical purpose: it enabled him to carry individual pots of colour up the ladders to 'fill in' separate areas rather than mixing colours on a palette. The stylised forms, chalky hues and processional figures were inspired by the Mantegna murals and by the prevailing influence of Puvis de Chavannes.

The murals were painted on canvas and adhered to the wall through *marouflage*, a process in which powdered white lead mixed with copal oil and turpentine was spread in a paste on both the wall and the back of the canvas. To seal the paint he used Keim's process, a method in which earth pigments are dissolved in distilled water as a painting medium. When the work is dry, it is sprayed with a hot solution of waterglass, or stereochrome, made of silicic acid and potash.

In contrast to the exterior friezes his two interior panels were painted in oil and, though more traditional than the exterior style, hinted at the curvilinear forms and rich colouring that typify Art Nouveau.

Following Brangwyn's success with the murals, Bing commissioned him to design articles for sale in the gallery. These ranged from furniture, ornate metal lamps, carpets, ceramics, painted fans and enamelled jewellery. With Emile Gallé and René Lalique he also produced glassware for Tiffany. Ashbee, Macintosh and Mackmurdo and other British artist-designers had dealings with Bing but not as consistently as Brangwyn did. In the main Bing chose to show the work of continental and particularly French artists whom he selected as being exponents of the new art. These included the painters, Edouard Vuillard, Georges Seurat, Pierre Bonnard, Eugène Carrière, Camille Pissarro, Henri Toulouse-Lautrec, Anders Zorn and Paul Signac, the sculptors, Auguste Rodin, Emile Bourdelle and Constantin Meunier. Rodin became a particular friend to the young Brangwyn who was still only in his late twenties.

Brangwyn was commissioned, with Bonnard, Vuillard and Toulouse-Lautrec, to design stained-glass windows, a craft he had learned from his father and Morris. In his opaline and multi-veined glass Tiffany exploited the natural irregularities of the medium. The lead work was used sparsely and the sections of glass, kept as large as possible, let in the maximum amount of light. This open style influenced the stained glass windows that Brangwyn went on to produce throughout his life. Eventually Bing gave him commissions for whole interior schemes including the furniture, fabrics and carpets.

Carpet-designing particularly interested Brangwyn. Working for Bing and his associate, Julius Meier-Graefe, he moved away from the busy floral-based ornamental carpets produced by Morris, Voysey and Walter Crane, towards larger, simpler and more open designs. Although he too used nature-based themes, his carpet designs were abstract and flat-patterned. He was familiar with the carpet weavers of Belgium and France and with the Turkish and Persian carpets that he had seen on his travels. The tones he used harmonised with the restrained mood of his wall colourings.

While working for Bing and Tiffany, Brangwyn put into practice the experiences gained from his father and Morris. He learned with ease and fascination the methods and technical limits of each different craft. This equipped him for his future multi-disciplined career, but he stayed true to the precepts of the Arts and Crafts movement. He believed, like Morris, that the craftsman must stay true to the nature of his materials and that form must follow function. His work in his father's architect's office taught him that architecture is the framework for all embellishment; that murals, furnishings, windows and colour, while being both practical and decorative, must be unified with the built space. Morris declared that it was as important to make:

'…a proper pot or pan as a cathedral' and that 'if one designs a pair of shoes one must be able to walk a hundred miles in them.'[2]

In Austria the architect Otto Wagner eschewed the contortions of Art Nouveau in favour of a return to Morris's purer adherence to the nature of materials. His pupil Josef Hoffmann's view on furniture-making was that:

'The designer should respect the straight fibres of the wood' and not make 'curves on top of curves. Art must be useful as well as simply decorative.'[3]

The work Brangwyn produced for Bing and Tiffany shows that he too sought to keep unnecessary surface decoration to a minimum rather than rely on the sinewy elaboration used by other exponents of the style. He became more attracted by the simpler method being explored by the Austrian artist-designers.

In the 1890s the Kunstlerhaus Exhibitions in Vienna that showed the work of leading British Academicians including Frederic Lord Leighton, Hubert Herkomer and Lawrence Alma-Tadema, had begun to be regarded as outmoded. The writer Hermann Bahr thought they had become a mere 'market place or bazaar'.[4] In 1897, Hoffmann with Josef Maria Olbrich and Koloman Moser set up a separate group, the Vienna Secessionists. Their meetings were chaired by Gustav Klimt and given respectability by the 85-year old watercolourist Rudolph von Alt. Their philosophy echoed Brangwyn's because Klimt's aim was to promote the interaction between art and life, 'We recognise no distinction between High art and Minor art or between art for the rich or art for the poor. Art is common property.'5

Brangwyn was a founder member of the Secessionists whose exhibitions were also supported by Rodin, Puvis de Chavannes, the Belgian Symbolist Fernand Khnopff and the Russian artist Wassily Kandinsky, who became an enthusiastic admirer of Brangwyn's work. He particularly admired Brangwyn's use of 'complementary' colours such as scarlet and royal blue or more often orange and cerulean blue. The German architect Walter Gropius, founder of the Bauhaus in Weimar and Dessau, and the composer Schoenberg both drew inspiration from the group. The British artists involved were Whistler, John Singer Sargent, Walter Crane and the Glasgow Four, Charles Rennie Macintosh, his wife, Margaret Macdonald, her sister, Frances McNair and her husband, Herbert. By 1909, however, Brangwyn was the only remaining British member. He could have easily continued his lucrative association with Bing and Tiffany but he was slightly out of tune with Art Nouveau in France. He may have felt that, once again, he was in a cul-de-sac, as he had been when working for Morris and with the Newlyn painters. Possibly he sensed that a fashion of so bright a flame would quickly burn out, but, whatever the reasons, he gradually withdrew from his liaison with the gallery. However, by the turn of the century, he had acquired a wealth of knowledge and experience and had money in the bank.

DECORATOR

I am a decorator. My problem is how to make a church or a house, or a
room, look warmer and happier, to complete what the architect has left
incomplete *Brangwyn* [1]

Brangwyn had escaped from marriage to Katie Chesterfield when he was 19. At
23 he proposed to the sister of a fellow-artist in Chelsea and had been turned
down by the girl's father because of his penniless state and lack of prospects.
Now, however, with plenty of 'tin' and artistic recognition, he felt the need for
stability, a house, a studio and a wife.

On January 28 1896, at St George's Register Office in Hanover Square, the 28-
year-old Brangwyn married Lucy Ray, a 26 year-old nurse, the daughter of a painter
and glazier. They rented rooms for a while. Lucy returned to her nursing and
Brangwyn continued to work intermittently with Bing. Marriage did not
immediately cure his wanderlust as he had hoped it would and, in 1896, leaving
Lucy in London, he travelled to Assisi and then Venice, which enchanted him. His
response to the great Venetian painters inspired a number of majestic oils that are
among his finest works. His Venetian series alone establishes him as a formidable
painter. Inexplicably, however, and certainly undeservedly, the 1897 Royal Academy
Summer Exhibition relegated his painting of Venice, 'The Dogona', to the upper
rails. The following year 'The Golden Horn' was also ignominiously 'skied', eliciting
a protest from a critic in *The Spectator*, 'There are dozens of sleek mediocrities one
would willingly banish to the skyline to make way for such a breezy piece of
shipping and great clouds as Mr Brangwyn's.'

'Sleek mediocrities' there were indeed. The Victorian era clung on at the RA.
Brangwyn's work simply knocked the majority of the works into the shade and he
was punished for it.

Annoyed by the treatment he was receiving from the RA, Brangwyn found
other outlets for exhibition, particularly abroad. However, in 1904, as his reputation
grew stronger and he was awarded honours, the RA reconsidered and elected him
an Associate member. The critic of the *Morning Post* wrote:

> If ever the Academy selected a young genius who is marked out for greatness,
> Mr Brangwyn is the man—as foreign countries have already recognised.

As a flood of new commissions poured in Brangwyn realised that a large and
permanent studio was urgently required. Lucy went house-hunting and in 1900
fell for Temple Lodge in Queen (now Queen Caroline) Street in Hammersmith. It

is an elegant Georgian house with large rooms, a cavernous basement and a large square garden to the rear. It also had an adjacent 40-foot shed which could be adapted for use as a large studio. It was ideal and they decided to rent it.

Brangwyn enthusiastically set about adapting and furnishing his first real home. He painted the walls of the drawing room an elegant warm grey, to set off his display of paintings, pots and antiques. New furniture and other items were swapped in exchange for his own paintings, a practice learnt in the Manresa Road studio days. He did not design new furniture for the house or subject it to his overall style as he could have done. Instead he remained sensitive to its historical identity. Lucy may also have had a strong say as to the furnishing, but the house became an elegant and eclectic mixture of items, harmonised into a whole by Brangwyn's natural artistry. Lucy used one of the bedrooms as a private sitting room and Brangwyn opened a window from it into the studio below so that they could keep in contact with each other.

Brangwyn had been at the hub of artistic and social activity in Paris at a time of tremendous change and dynamism and at the outset of their married life Lucy and he were congenial hosts. By all reports their Sunday afternoon receptions at their new home were delightful and well attended, often by some of his fellows at the Royal Academy who would customarily do the rounds. When it was warm enough, croquet would be played in the large garden that Brangwyn had transformed with exotic and colourful planting.

Soon, however, Brangwyn's huge workload caused him to become increasingly homebound. While he was happy to receive visitors at Temple Lodge the formalities of society occasions alarmed him. Privately he made lifelong friendships, especially with the group of friends with whom he founded the Chelsea Arts Club in 1891: Whistler, Phil May, Frank Short, William Walcot, Sir George Clausen and Sir William Richmond who lived close to Temple Lodge. Sir Alfred East was his closest friend. When he was in serious financial straits in 1902 East rescued him by buying his painting 'The Cider Press'. Thereafter his commissions kept him solvent and he died a wealthy man.

William Morris died in 1896 but the area surrounding Kelmscott House, his London home overlooking the Thames at 26 Upper Mall, Hammersmith, continued for a while as one of the centres of the Arts and Crafts movement. A group of artist-craftsmen had gathered there to live in adjacent houses and to put into practice the ideals of the Master. Thomas Cobden-Sanderson lived at 1 Hammersmith Terrace and Emery Walker at No 7. They had co-operated in Morris's revival of the hand press and the lettering arts. They were involved with his pioneering Kelmscott Press and in 1900 they set up their own Doves Press. In 1905 Edward Johnston, the calligrapher, moved to 3 Hammersmith Terrace and Douglas (later

Hilary) Pepler already lived at No 14. In 1905 Eric Gill, the sculptor, letter-carver and calligrapher, moved to a house and workshop in the next street, 23 Black Lion Lane. Johnston, largely self-taught, was invited to teach calligraphy at the Central School of Arts and Crafts by William R Lethaby. Lethaby was an important influence in the development of Morris's Arts and Crafts ideals towards the concepts of an emerging Modernism. He taught that, to achieve perfect unity in craftsmanship, mind, skill and materials should be inseparable. As Lethaby was mentor to Johnston, so Johnston became mentor to Eric Gill.

Pepler was a Quaker and such was his philanthropy that he set up the Hampshire House Workshops in Hogg Lane for local workmen and, later, for refugees from the Great War. There he staged art exhibitions to which Gill, Johnston and other artist-craftsmen, including Brangwyn, contributed. This tightly knit group was younger than Brangwyn and were more acquaintances than friends. He was too busy with numerous important commissions to concentrate on typography and hand presses and had evolved his own sturdy, ragged and individual calligraphic style. He might have gained a great deal, socially, had he attended the Art Workers' Guild and other gatherings but his career needed no social boosting. Work took precedence over such meetings, over his guests and even over his wife. There were several other reasons for his habitual avoidance of social occasions that were full of 'deep-water swells'. Having been to sea his language was sometimes somewhat salty and could affect his conversation inappropriately. All his life he would say, 'I must give up this bloody swearing'. He habitually ended his sentences with a robust rhetorical 'what'. He felt that his lack of education was a hindrance and from his childhood he had always felt more affinity with the workman than the 'toff'.

Lucy was in charge of the household but as their financial situation improved she took on a maid-of-all-work called Lizzie Berry. It was a busy and happy household until Lucy suffered a miscarriage and was left unable to bear a child. This was an enduring disappointment to her and Brangwyn and must have compounded the regret that Brangwyn would surely have felt about his unacknowledged son. Brangwyn and Lucy's relationship continued as one of close and amiable companionship but Lucy was not equipped to take a real interest in her husband's work, though he thought her a good critic, and she began to feel neglected and bored. When, in 1908, they did get away together, to visit Brangwyn's old haunts in Bruges, Lucy broke her ankle. On her return she soothed her pain with strong drink and gradually became an alcoholic. This carried, at the time, such a social stigma that it put paid to any entertaining and largely confined Brangwyn to the house, cutting him off from society even further.

In order to boost their finances the Brangwyns took in a Japanese lodger who had married an English girl. He was one of the first men to be permitted by the Japanese to settle in Britain. Through him Brangwyn made the acquaintance of several notable members of the Japanese embassy, including Kijoro Matsukata who had come to Europe to collect western art. Enthusiastic about Brangwyn's work he became one of his wealthiest patrons and amassed such a collection of the finest paintings by Europe's leading artists, including much of Brangwyn's best work, that in 1918 his father, the Marquis Matsukata, offered to finance a museum in Tokyo in which to house them. Moreover this was to be designed by Brangwyn and named the Brangwyn Museum.

Having decorated his own house, Brangwyn received an interesting commission from Sir Edmund Davis, a South African mining millionaire, to redesign a music room and a main bedroom at his home at 11-13 Lansdowne Road, Notting Hill. This commission resulted from the work he was still doing for Bing and it was his first chance to do his own complete design scheme. It involved new panelling and wall colourings, painted decorations and lighting, ceramics, carpets and furniture. The result was more Whistler than Morris or Bing. He used elegantly subdued tones as a background for a painted frieze in the spacious music room and smaller panels in the bedroom.

He produced furniture that was close in concept to that of Mackmurdo. Mackmurdo believed that it was vital to future design that craftsmen should harness rather than spurn the machine and Brangwyn shared this view. The uncompromisingly rectilinear structure of his furniture stayed faithful to the wood–generally cherry–and was softened by the pliant curves of metal handles and hinges. At other times his designs were hand made, using peg jointing. Often it was 'flat-packed', a practicality employed earlier by Pugin. In all his room designs he delighted in adding mischievous utilitarian elements, concealing cupboards in the panelling, hiding drawers in the mantelpiece, and even a secret telephone. Larger pieces could be taken apart for 'a good scrub' and ornament was confined to inlay so as not to catch the dust. Pollard & Co made the furniture in 1900 but the designs were so innovative that they were exhibited in 1930 as contemporary.

Having successfully completed the décor for Davis, Brangwyn was invited to dine, but declined, apparently saying, 'You would not invite your plumber, so why me?'

MURALIST

The mural painter is not only a painter but a poet, historian, dramatist and philosopher *Walter Crane* [1]

The mural painter is also required to be an acrobat, carpenter and interior designer. By the mid-19th century the tradition of mural painting, which had continued without interruption on the Continent since the Reformation, had, in Britain, largely lapsed. The Gothic Revival brought renewed interest in 'wall decoration' and, in 1840, the House of Commons set up a Select Committee to promote the inclusion of fine art in the rebuilding of the Houses of Parliament. A Royal Fine Arts Committee was also formed, chaired by Prince Albert and run by Charles Eastlake, Henry Hallam and Lord Mahon, with the Tory prime minister Sir Robert Peel in close consultation. Their aim was to set up a British School of High Art but their controlling influence upon the artists caused friction.

The areas of the Houses of Parliament chosen for decoration were the Poets' or Upper Waiting Hall, the Peers' Robing Room and the Royal Antechamber. Since early Italian murals were then in vogue the committee requested the use of fresco as the preferred medium. This proved to be disastrous. Fresco requires the artist to work on small sections of a mural each day. Lime-resistant pigments are mixed with water and as they dry they fuse with the plaster surface of the wall or panel and become permanent. This method is fine for hot dry countries because the plaster dries quickly, but in England it proved unsuccessful. Fresco was totally unsuited to the damp atmosphere of the Thames-side building. The panels were mostly painted on slate but, despite having air spaces behind them, most of them flaked, discoloured and mildewed and by 1850 had to be removed.

Ten years later, however, Prince Albert, who held great sway on the committee, decreed that the Royal Gallery at the House of Lords should be decorated with twenty-one murals painted by his favourite artist, Daniel Maclise. Maclise refused to use fresco, preferring waterglass. Protected from any interference from The Royal Fine Arts Commission by his royal patron, Maclise produced only two enormous paintings, 'The Death of Nelson' and 'The Meeting of Wellington and Blücher at Quatre Bois', when the Prince died in 1861. The RFAC immediately cancelled the project, ostensibly on the grounds of cost, but in fact their initial enthusiasm had waned. Disheartened, Maclise watched as his waterglass faded and he died in 1870.

1895 marked yet another renewal of interest in murals. Group projects in public places were encouraged for artistic and educational purposes, and to promote patronage for the arts from both public companies and private individuals. Just before he began working for Seigfried Bing in Paris Brangwyn learned that Lord

Leighton, the President of the Royal Academy, in conjunction with the Gresham Committee, was looking round for 24 leading artists to paint separate large panels in the Royal Exchange in London.

As a child, Brangwyn had seen his father painting decorative murals in the Basilica of the Holy Blood and St Michael's in Bruges. He was also familiar with Leighton's murals and those of George Frederic Watts. His own first effort was at Mackmurdo's behest. In 1886 he was commissioned to paint a design by Herbert Horne on the drawing room ceiling of Pownall Hall in Wilmslow for the Boddingtons, the brewing family, therefore the idea of mural painting appealed to him.

Watts had been involved several mural projects including the ill-fated Westminster Hall fresco project in 1853. Whether by luck or judgement his own fresco stood up well compared with those of others and since then he had enthusiastically 'taken up a crusade against bare walls'.[2] He had been 'keeping an eye on Brangwyn's paintings' whose 'broad masses of colour' he felt were 'ideal for fresco'[3] so Brangwyn turned to Watts to ask him to recommend him for the scheme.

He was delighted, if somewhat nervous, when he was invited to visit the prestigious artist at his home at Little Holland House, an occurrence 'which he found so daunting that when Phoebe (the maid) opened the door he forgot his name'.[4]

Afterwards Watts wrote to Briton Rivière:

Young Frank Brangwyn (the best eye for grand effects and colour out I think) came to see me to ask if I could help him to get a space on the walls of the Exchange which he is willing to cover without pay… We were much taken with the young fellow who has been a sailor I think before the mast & still has the sailor's roll. I am out of everything & can do nothing but you might speak a word for him, he has more originality than most, & it won't do for the Academy to let the best men slip.[5]

The artists who became involved included Edwin Abbey, William Yeames, Stanhope Forbes, Ernest Crofts, William Wyllie, Andrew Gow, E Albert Cox, Solomon J Solomon, Sigismunde Goetze, Henrietta Rae and Ernest Normand. Despite Watts's recommendation Leighton turned Brangwyn down on the grounds that, although his work was admirable, so young an artist could not undertake work of such size and importance. However, in 1899 when Sir Thomas Devitt of the Skinners Company offered to commission a panel for the hall, his chosen artist was Brangwyn.

Brangwyn's subject was commerce. Neither Devitt nor Brangwyn were happy with the historical idiom and instead chose modern commerce. However, such was Brangwyn's decorative sensitivity that his contemporary scene blended seamlessly with the other paintings. He built on the theme of craftsmen he had employed in the Maison de L'Art Nouveau and showed muscular dockers unloading a ship in the Pool of London. The figures grouped in the foreground provide a dark frame thereby concentrating attention on the distance. The arched tops of the panels had given the other artists some problems but Brangwyn overcame the difficulty with ease. He used tall cranes to provide vertical interest, leaving space for an open sky. The other artists depicted events in history and, apart from that of Forbes, their works were painted in the late Victorian neo-Pre-Raphaelite style based on easel painting. Brangwyn's was the only one fully to consider decorative unity and he was careful to retain the symbolic element to prevent the panel from becoming too pictorial.

'All colours must have the same carrying power–or retiring qualities, so that one feels the wall,' he advised. 'Even if the background might have distance, the colour and tone keeps it from looking like a hole in the wall.'[6]

The panel was painted in oil on canvas and to enrich his foreground he foolishly took the advice to use bitumen which has a tendency to darken, but he swiftly reverted to more stable pigments and in his later murals frequently used tempera. Leighton had used a method called 'spirit fresco', a laborious method imitating true fresco, but using dry plaster and pigment bound in gum resin, white wax, oil of lavender, copal varnish and turpentine. Mural techniques were then still experimental. The Royal Exchange was the first place in Britain where *marouflage* was used and French workmen had to be called over to give technical advice.

The artist Joseph Simpson referred to the Royal Exchange scheme in an article for the *Weekly Dispatch* in 1923 entitled 'Art in the business place'. He declared that:

> One artist, Brangwyn unquestionably, should have been selected for the whole work. Had that been done we'd have seen paintings that are part and parcel of the wall's surface. The Royal offers us no more than a picture gallery, only one or two (artists) have understood the difference between an easel painting and a decoration.[7]

In 1902 he received the commission that brought him full public recognition and secured his election as an Associate member of the Royal Academy. It was to supply eleven panels for the newly renovated banqueting chamber of the Worshipful Company of Skinners in Dowgate Hill, built in 1668. Historical subjects were chosen. Brangwyn's work succeeded triumphantly. He combined the grandeur of the Venetian masters with exuberant Colourist freshness.

His assured technical and compositional skill provided a sure basis for his rich imaginative expression. The patina of his vigorously searching brushstrokes was never over-polished. The monumental grouping of his robust figures and objects never became static and was refreshed by airy passages. Unlike the similarly anecdotal history paintings of his contemporaries, he avoided solemnity, sentimentality, rigidity and over-finishing. As DC Konody, the art critic of the *Daily Mail*, wrote when the panels were unveiled in 1909:

> He seems to belong to a dead race of Titans. His creative energy seems boundless and knows no concessions to vulgar taste. Every picture …is a defiant challenge: Take me as I am or leave me… What all his work has in common is the supreme breadth of handling–the reduction of all objects in nature to the simplest, most summarily generalised forms. Form–or rather the distribution of masses of light and dark in the right place and in the right quantities–and colour, rich and sonorous, are the materials with which Mr Brangwyn constructs his pictures.[8]

In 1908 Devitt instigated another large commission. This was a ceiling decoration for the luncheon room of Lloyds Register of Shipping in Fenchurch Street, for whom Brangwyn had earlier painted two fine oils, 'Queen Elizabeth Going aboard the Golden Hind' of 1903, and 'Blake's Return after the Capture of the Plate Ships' of 1907. The ceiling required ten rectangular panels and one large central panel. Brangwyn was concentrating on the still incomplete Skinners Hall murals and the panels show a measure of distraction and repetition. Nevertheless they were powerful paintings and expanded his theme of the working man. Unfortunately the images of sweating dockers were not quite the dainty decoration that the members of Lloyds would have preferred when dining. Before they were installed in 1914 they were exhibited at the 1913 Ghent International Exhibition and there their impact was applauded. Lloyds approved the delay because it was good advertising for the company. The ceiling remained in place for fifty years but the paintings darkened and were eventually removed during renovations.

Wyndham Lewis was to lambast Brangwyn in his magazine *Blast* as an outmoded Edwardian but he failed to recognise that he had in mural painting forged the way to Modernism.

Another landmark in Brangwyn's burgeoning career as a muralist was an important commission to decorate the British Rooms at the 1905 and 1907 Venice international exhibitions, later the Venice Biennale. He produced painted friezes and designed benches and plinths. In these rooms each country displayed its best contemporary artists, and this further established his reputation internationally.

RH Kitson, a director of Kitson and Co in Leeds, a firm of locomotive manu-facturers, became a friend as well as a client. He bought Brangwyn's murals from the 1905 Venice Biennale and presented them to Leeds City Art Gallery. Later he also presented Leeds with two important oils exhibited at the Royal Academy in 1908, 'The Rajah's Birthday' and 'The Return of the Messengers from the Promised Land'. He then commissioned Brangwyn to undertake new decorations for the apse of St Aidan's, a city church in Leeds. Brangwyn had painted a large section of the hemicycle before coming to the conclusion that the polluted atmosphere in Leeds would affect his paint. He covered the cost of the wasted work himself and offered instead to carry out the mural scheme in mosaic, a material that can be easily cleaned. He used tessarae of a synthetic vitreous compound which was cheaper than pure Venetian glass but just as durable.[9] With real originality his mosaic design featured a procession of devotional figures on each side of the chancel steps leading up to the altar. It covers an area of 300 square feet and, including the entire apse, is thought to be one of the largest mosaics in Europe.

In 1910 Kitson also asked Brangwyn to design a dining room for his villa, Casa Cuseni, in Taormina in Sicily. For this Brangwyn used the traditional local medium of fresco. While he was there he visited Messina which had recently been devastated by an earthquake. It was possibly his first encounter with the aftermath of disaster. He was deeply and lastingly affected by the plight of the people. Later, when he came to design his recruiting posters for the Forces during the First World War, he drew on his experiences at Messina because he had no first-hand contact with the front line.

WORKS ON PAPER

> The fresco-painting of the bill-sticker is likely, so far as I can see, to become
> the principal fine art of modern Europe *John Ruskin* [1]

The enlarged studio at Temple Lodge enabled Brangwyn to install a large etching
press. Mackmurdo had encouraged his earlier attempts and it was a medium entirely
suited to his sure but lively draughtsmanship, his compositional skill and dramatic
chiaroscuro. Brangwyn's artistic identity can perhaps be seen most clearly in his
etchings. The line is entirely his own, unadulterated by assistants except in the
printing process. In no other medium does he maintain such faultless consistency.

When Brangwyn began etching the main exponents of the medium were Sir
Francis Seymour Haden, Alphonse Legros and James McNeil Whistler but their
plates were needled with a fine delicate line. Whistler thought that 'a huge plate is
an offence'.[2] He believed that an etching plate should be small, in sympathy with
the needle used to engrave it. He overlooked the fact, however, that it is the acid
that determines the strength of the line rather than the needle. Sickert's prints
were more robust but are still frail beside Brangwyn's. Legros gave him some
practical instruction but Brangwyn wanted more from the medium and, characteristically, he subjected it to experimentation. He used very large zinc plates and,
occasionally, bit them on site. Sometimes, in the studio, he allowed the acid to bite
them almost to destruction. The resulting prints have wonderful strong, wide,
and velvety lines. The ink is often given a warmer tone with the addition of burnt
sienna. It takes the greatest skill to maintain such a quantity of ink in the furrows
and keep the non-etched areas clean. In some areas he accepted foul biting to add
to the texture, and the etchings have richness often said to equal that of
Rembrandt's. With larger runs he was assisted by the expert printers Arthur Covey
and Edward Trumbell and later Frederick Goulding whom he considered to be
the most skilled since he had worked with both Haden and Whistler.

Brangwyn used an innovative device to add overall tone to some of his larger
prints. Before printing he placed a thin sheet of buff or warm grey coloured
paper on top of the inked plate, between it and the thicker sheet of white base
paper. In the printing process the pressure of the etching press severed the toned
paper along the edges of the metal plate leaving a white margin. It is unlikely that
glue was used to bind the two sheets of paper together because it appears that the
pressure in the grooves of the deeply-etched lines was enough to cause adhesion.

Etching technique aside, Brangwyn has proved himself to be one of the great
etchers of architectural subjects. His etchings have a majestic sense of scale which
critics have frequently compared with Piranesi. While they show no evidence of

labour and maintain overall liveliness, the drawing is sure; each vertical is upright and each horizontal level and, although they are swiftly drawn, every detail of his buildings, artefacts and machinery is accurate and would pass the scrutiny of the builder. This scrupulousness can be traced back to Brangwyn's training in his father's architectural office. His architectural understanding of the buildings he portrayed gave his work structure and authenticity. In fact his work in all media is soundly based on sure technique and preparatory study which allows him a deceptively careless freedom of expression.

His etching of 'Santa Maria della Salute' was awarded the Grand Prix at the Milan Exhibition in 1906 and thirty etchings, shown at the Barcelona International Exhibition in 1907, were awarded a diploma.

At this stage of his life he worked intensively on mural commissions, private easel paintings, watercolours, etchings and projects in other media. With astonishing adroitness he was able to work in many different styles, scales and media at one and the same time. This trait confused the British critics who believed that versatility showed a lack of seriousness.

In the early 1900s Brangwyn quickly gained a respected position in the print world. In 1903 he was made an Associate and Fellow of the Royal Society of Painters and Printmakers. From its foundation in 1908 he was an active member of the Senefelder Club, becoming its president in 1917, and he founded the Society of Graphic Arts in 1920 which regularly exhibited at the Royal Institute Galleries. Feeling the need to become more directly involved with a new generation of students he set up the London School of Art in 1904, conveniently near to Temple Lodge in Stratford Road, Kensington. It became known as 'Brangwyn's'.

In this venture he was joined by John MacAllan Swan, a sculptor and fellow Academician. Arthur Covey, his assistant from Chicago, and William Nicholson were both lecturers. Brangwyn was an enthusiastic teacher but tended to impose his style upon the students. The painters Algernon Newton and Nina Hamnett were pupils at the School of Art and the latter described how he would draw or paint on their studies 'unintentionally transforming them into lively examples of his own work'.[3]

He also taught etching at the school and one student was the renowned potter Bernard Leach. Leach was brought up in Japan and arrived in England in 1906. He joined Brangwyn's etching class in 1908.

Brangwyn was an authority on Japanese ceramics and had a distinguished collection of them at Temple Lodge. He himself threw pots occasionally and was later to design ceramics commercially. Brangwyn's links with the Japanese may have brought Leach and him together and possibly Brangwyn's passion for Japanese pottery sowed the seed of Leach's later interest in them. Leach returned to Japan in 1909 and taught etching, his own etchings being notably 'Brangwynesque'. He took examples of Brangwyn's drawings and etchings to Japan where they were copied extensively by the wood-engraver Yoshiro Urushibara. Leach was also inspired by the Arts and Crafts movement's enthusiastic return to craftsmanship, as taught by Brangwyn, and found his full expression of it in Japanese raku pottery.

Brangwyn could not resist a challenge and some grand diversions included the coronation of George V for which Brangwyn designed street decorations, scenery for a pageant on the Thames and settings for the Chelsea Arts balls. Such was his ability, curiosity and confidence that he rose to every challenge. He knew it was a fault, saying that if someone had asked him to lay a railroad across America he'd probably have attempted it. Once Douglas Fairbanks Junior contacted him from the United States to ask if he would be the artistic director on a film he was making about pirates, but Brangwyn turned down the offer without hesitation saying that 'trying to show off a flat-chested, spindle-shanked, lipstick-star was not my cup of tea.'

Neither, it seems, were mayoresses. Although he was an able painter of faces he avoided society portrait commissions after an occasion when he was asked to paint the mayoress of Bath. Overwhelmed by her imposing presence and her expectations of the portrait, he repeatedly failed to get a likeness. For successive sittings he draped his unsuccessful attempts mysteriously behind a cloth, but, as the moment of the expected unveiling approached, he gave up, took a photograph and persuaded his friend Cecil Rae to finish the head for him, confining himself to an exuberant Brangwynesque background. Fortunately the lady was satisfied with her 'Brangwyn', but thereafter he limited himself to painting informal portraits of his friends.

He once received a royal commission—but turned it down. Celebrated artists and craftsmen were invited by Queen Mary to decorate and furnish her dolls house at Windsor Castle and Brangwyn was asked to provide a miniature mural. He replied, thanking the Queen but jokingly replied saying

If you want me to paint the front of the palace… I'm you're man, but I have not the physical strength nor the ambition to cope with such a work as you have paid me the honour of asking me to carry out.[4]

He enjoyed making small woodcuts. They were not just a medium he used for illustrations and *ex libris* bookplates, but were a form of relaxation. Shaw Sparrow recalls him doing them on holiday for his own enjoyment and when ill in bed. The ragged marks of the woodcut suited his vigorous line and he chose the medium for his humorous Christmas cards, which were much prized by his friends. During his lean years he had supported himself by producing illustrations for art magazines such as *The Studio* for which he painted monotone figurative oils emulating photographs and showed his tonal command. Although speedily produced they were finely detailed. This practice continued throughout his life as a lucrative sideline. He used linocut less frequently and usually for commercial purposes.

He produced a large quantity of watercolours, painted primarily for his own enjoyment. In these his expressive and spontaneous response to landscape is unleashed. Some have the quiet control of a Cotman and some are wildly flamboyant, but they are, without fail, supported by his able brush-drawing and compositional and architectural structure. They may be small in scale but they are large in conception.

He was ideally suited to lithography. He drew directly onto the stone rather than use a tracing of the design and he used a snakestone eraser as a means of adding highlights and texture to dark areas. It was his favourite of the printing methods.

> Lithography is the only (printing) medium in which you can let yourself go…express yourself exactly as you feel…the only medium in which an artist can have his drawings reproduced without any deterioration in his work. It is the first of all the graphic arts–gives back truly all that the artist puts on stone.[5]

Had it not been for the First World War Brangwyn might have experimented further with lithography as fine art. As it was, the bulk of his work as a lithographer was taken up with the production of posters.

Certainly the First World War proved the 'power of the poster'. In 2000 Margaret Timmers and Ruth Walton presented a fine exhibition with that title at the Victoria & Albert Museum, showing examples from the museum's important collection, which had benefited from large donations by Frank Pick and Reginald Praill.

Like Morris and Klimt, Frank Pick aimed to bring good design back into everyday life. Pick was dissatisfied with the paucity of good graphics in the commercial world and selected artists and designers of stature to produce posters of the quality he sought. Brangwyn and Edward McKnight Kauffer were the first artists to be commissioned by Pick to produce posters as a form of art. Strangely Brangwyn was not chosen as an official war artist. In 1918, the writer Arnold Bennett, who was on the Imperial War Committee, wrote to his friend Thomas Bodkin,

> I have succeeded in turning down all RA painters except Clausen. Some feat, believe me! Yes, I have even turned down the inevitable Brangwyn.[6]

Although he had not been officially selected Brangwyn was among the most productive and well-known practitioners of war posters. Some of these were highly charged and shockingly graphic, showing a surprising latent violence that hints at dark elements in his psyche. However, this intensity of feeling probably reflects his profound affinity with the troops and the plight of the country. Artistically, they led him towards sentimentality and caricature. His stature as a major artist became dangerously associated with values which would inevitably soon be swept away but the posters were extremely effective. As usual, Brangwyn fitted the job to its purpose–without thought to the market.

Another reason for the posters' success is that the images are strengthened by text. In all his graphic work, instead of leaving the printers to add the standard typefaces, Brangwyn used his own very distinctive brush lettering and this integrates with the drawing and unifies the whole. Brangwyn's lettering is robust and jaunty. He frequently uses 'dwarfing'–a technique of reducing the size of some subordinate letters to fit the space and this gives his text typical informality and liveliness.[7]

Other war poster artists were William Nicholson, Augustus John, Charles Shannon, Charles Ricketts, William Rothenstein and Edmund Dulac but, unlike Brangwyn, they are not remembered for their posters. In the main they avoided such deep emotional involvement; they portrayed air and sea battles with the emphasis on the pictorial rather than the political and so retained their artistic integrity.

His war effort was initially a recruiting mission and a call to arms, but its effectiveness affected him personally. The Kaiser reputedly put a price on his head and, whether or not it is true, Brangwyn certainly believed it and this gave him another reason to be reclusive. When Reginald Praill closed the Avenue Press he left some of his collection of Brangwyn material to my father. This included a small notebook in which Brangwyn had listed his posters. Beside 'Put Strength into the Final Blow, support War Bonds' Brangwyn has written 'Bayonet. Price on FB's head–also Will Dyson.' While he took the threat seriously, Brangwyn was more deeply affected when a poster he produced for the American Navy encouraged his nephew in America to join up and, tragically, he was killed within a few days. Brangwyn was stricken with guilt, feeling that he had lured not just his nephew but his fellow men into conflict and horrific widespread slaughter. He found himself in an agonising dilemma and his normally optimistic confidence was knocked. Such was his high profile, however, that he was unable to duck out without consequence. He persuaded himself that the defence of life and liberty was good reason to continue but he was forever troubled by his decision.

Praill gave Brangwyn his most diminutive commission, an assignment shared with Edmund Dulac. This was for a set of stamps depicting the work of the Red

Cross, printed by Praill and sold by Associated Newspapers (proprietors of the *Daily Mail* and the *Evening News*) in aid of the British Red Cross Fund. After the war Praill continued as Brangwyn's printer and friend and, with William Orpen, George Clausen, Sir David Young Cameron and Augustus John, Brangwyn was asked to produce publicity posters for several railway companies. Among others, he produced splendid views of Durham and Berwick for the London North-Eastern Line, and 'The Curzon Street Depot at Birmingham' for the London-Midland and Scottish Railway Company. In 1936 he produced a poster for the London Underground showing Southwark Cathedral.

At the Millennium opening of the Tate Modern a room was devoted to Pablo Picasso's studies for his painting 'Guernica'. Accompanying them was Picasso's statement:, 'What do you think an artist is? ...painting is not done to decorate apartments. It is an instrument of war, for attack and defence against the enemy.'[8]

This quotation was illustrated, not by a Picasso drawing, as one would expect, but by Brangwyn's poster in aid of funds for the Republicans in the Spanish Civil War and, seen in context with Picasso's work, the eloquence of their expressionism is complementary.

DITCHLING ARTIST-CRAFTSMAN

> There is no philosophy of art other than the doing well of a job for a given purpose *Brangwyn*[1]

Weighed down by the moral dilemma presented by his war poster work and exhausted by the gruelling demands of his huge workload, Brangwyn became ill. In 1917, after five days of Zeppelin raids on Hammersmith he packed up his work on three lithographic war posters commissioned for the publicity department of the United States Navy by an old pupil Lieutenant Reuterdahl and approved by Admiral Sims then resident in Britain. With Lucy, he retreated to Ditchling, a village near Brighton in Sussex, to finish the work and convalesce. He rented Coombe Down Lodge, a cottage at Coombe Wood, from a friend, Major Percy Garratt. It was safely sheltered from bombs on the north flank of the South Downs beneath Ditchling Beacon but, ironically, was destroyed in a fire after the war. Eventually, as London continued to be bombarded, Brangwyn decided that he would 'give up the game in London' and, needing a house with more space for wartime self-sufficiency, they looked round for a local 'potato patch'.[2]

The house the Brangwyns found lies at the heart of Ditchling in South Street, a short step from the crossroads at the centre of the village. It appealed to them both and they decided to buy it in 1918. On 27 November that year, Lucy wrote to their friend Mr Lane about the return of a walking stick he had left behind and added, 'We have practically bought a fine little old house down here which will keep us busy with the alterations for some time. It is called The Jointure House.'

The Jointure was so called because it had been apportioned to Anne of Cleves as part of the settlement when Henry VIII divorced her. The term 'jointure' is a legal term referring to lands jointly owned by husband and wife following a separation. The rambling Tudor house presents a Georgian façade to the road and has gardens stretching westward at the rear with panoramic views of the Downs. An adjoining cottage or barn was also bought and gutted to the roof to provide a lofty studio. It was the first house Brangwyn had owned and he set about altering it with renewed energy. 'I compulsively put brick on brick,' he wrote to a friend, 'throwing up an arch here and a buttress there.'[3] In restoring the house he also restored his spirits. In 1919 he was also cheered by his promotion from Associate of the Royal Academy to full Royal Academician. Needing a 'diploma work', he bought back his painting, 'The Market Stall'.

In Ditchling he renewed his friendship with some of the group of artist-craftsmen with whom he had become acquainted at Hammersmith. Gill, who was born in Brighton, had settled in Ditchling in 1907. Johnston followed him in 1912 and Pepler had arrived by 1915. Brangwyn was particularly close to Pepler. He wrote the preface to one of the St Dominic's Press books—the *Ditchling Drawing Book*, printed by Pepler in 1920. In 1950 he drew a lithographic portrait of Pepler with himself in the background. It was used in the third edition of Pepler's book, *The Hand Press*, shortly before his death in 1951. Whether Pepler influenced Brangwyn's decision to move to Ditchling is unknown, but certainly the Arts and Crafts centre that the village was becoming would have attracted him. During the Second World War, when the south coast was threatened and he had a fancy to move away, he chose to move near another enclave of the Arts and Crafts movement—the Ashbee workshops in Chipping Campden in Gloucestershire. He bought Dover's Court in 1940, but never lived in it.

The First World War had destroyed many things beside lives and buildings. It altered perceptions of social structure, upset moral stability, and, in time, unleashed a fierce rejection of the values of the Edwardian era. Morris's utopian dream of creating a happy world of fulfilled and happy craftsmen evaporated since so many of the craftsmen themselves were killed. Lost with them were many of the traditions of craftsmanship handed down through the generations and today the need for their specialised skills is still felt. Although the artisans themselves were depleted, a few groups of artist-craftsmen had 'retreated to rural outposts to live a simple, almost primitive life and revive the aesthetic of pure handcraft in a spirit of defiance against industry and mass production'.[4] They based their lives on Morris's precepts, but in developing their craftsmanship they became vanguards of Modernism. Prominent in this exodus was CR Ashbee's Guild of Handiwork in Chipping Campden, Gimson and Barnsley's in Sapperton and Godfrey Blount's in Haslemere. In Ditchling, Gill, Pepler and others were moving towards the foundation of the Guild of St Joseph and St Dominic.

The roots of the Guild lay partly in the postwar mood of artistic discovery reflected in Roger Fry's exhibition, 'Manet and the Post-Impressionists'. This opened in a flurry of excitement and dissent at the Grafton Gallery in 1910. It included works by Gill, Fry and Rothenstein but, more importantly, by Matisse, Cezanne, van Gogh and Gauguin. It was the first time the French artists had been exhibited in Britain and the exhibition was intended to challenge English conservatism. It succeeded. Henry Tonks, Sir William Richmond, Charles Ricketts, Wilfrid Blunt and others scorned the paintings. Augustus John, a protégé of Tonks, was at first restrained by his loyalty to Tonks but finally visited the exhibition. Gill widely reported that John thought it a 'bloody' show[5] but, on the contrary, Augustus was enthusiastic about it. Commendably he later encouraged his friends to buy the first few van Goghs to be purchased in Britain.

In Hammersmith Gill, Johnston and Pepler lived closely as families and spent much time together in deep philosophical discussion. Likewise Gill, Roger Fry, Jacob Epstein, William Rothenstein, Ambrose McEvoy and John would meet regularly at John's Chelsea studio and discuss utopian dreams far into the night. One materialised and, soon after the exhibition, it took them to Asheham House near Firle in Sussex. Their intention was to buy the house and work together forming an artist's co-operative to circumvent the dealers and realise their ideals independently, in a rural setting. They strode about on the Downs around Firle Beacon planning a contemporary Stonehenge to be sculpted by Gill and Epstein as a burial ground for the group. Rothenstein wrote enthusiastically to Gill, 'Save a little corner for me and you shall carve on it, "Here lies one who loved more than he was loved." '[6] John thought it should also be a temple, an idea that expanded into the formation of a totally new religion. Clearly the whole concept was precarious. Jokingly John described Gill's aim for it as 'a neo-Nietzschean cult of super-humanity under the sign of the Ithyphallus.' Epstein's part in it was to be 'realised by an apotheosis of himself on a colossal scale, blowing his own trumpet' and his own preference was for it to be a 'rehabilitation of the earth-mother'. What Fry and McEvoy's contribution was to be John did not record, but Gill and Epstein's view of John was that he was 'quite unmanageable'.[7]

The Asheham dream might have been an impossible venture but in it may have lain some of the seeds of the Guild of St Joseph and St Dominic. It certainly led to the Bloomsbury Group activities at Charleston Farmhouse. When the artists abandoned Asheham, Fry still saw opportunities in the house and suggested to Virginia Bell and Leonard Woolf that they should rent it after their marriage in 1912. They in turn encouraged Virginia's sister Vanessa, with Duncan Grant, David Garnett and others, to rent nearby Charleston Farmhouse from which to do war work and to continue the work they had begun in Bloomsbury for the Omega Workshop.

Despite immediate appearances, closer examination reveals that there are fundamental principles shared between the Omega workshops, the philosophy of the Guild and Brangwyn's beliefs and aims. All of them stem from the Arts and Crafts Movement.

Previously in Hammersmith the Morris acolytes, Johnston, Pepler and Gill had 'discussed endlessly a way of life which could be free and whole–a self-determined life in the country'.[8] In Hammersmith Johnston and Gill were also preoccupied with the revival of calligraphy and the reformation of the lettering arts for modern use. Johnston produced his seminal guide, *Writing and Illuminating and Lettering*, in 1906, to which Gill added a chapter on inscriptions in stone. Douglas Pepler established his hand press as part of the Hampshire House workshops. Brangwyn continued to work on and off for Morris until Morris's death.

When they settled in Ditchling the work of all the artist-craftsmen was continued. By then Gill was working as a sculptor as well as a letter-cutter and for a while Epstein joined him, using a high street garage as a sculpture studio. Gill, Pepler, Johnston and Epstein, but not Brangwyn, spent many hours walking and talking together along the Downs, which provide a majestic and timeless backdrop to the life of Ditchling. Although the First World War intervened, the idea of a religiously based community of artist-craftsmen in Ditchling continued to grow and soon afterwards came into being as the Guild of St Joseph and St Dominic, which was built on Ditchling Common to the north of the village. It consisted of a series of workshops clustered round a chapel.

In Hammersmith Pepler printed Cobbett's *Cottage Economy* through the Westminster Press, run by Gerald Meynell and this was popular reading at the time. The concept of going back to the land at the Guild was influenced in part by Father Vincent McNabb. A Dominican prior from Hawkesyard Priory, McNabb was an anti-liberal Distributist influenced in his turn by Hilaire Belloc's *The Servile State*. Together their aim was to live out in practice the medieval Thomist principles of St Thomas Aquinas and to seek God communally within a stringent, craft-based, religious life. Gill and Pepler converted to Catholicism. Pepler stopped calling himself Douglas and instead used his second name Hilary. Johnston's loyalties were with his wife Greta who came from a family of Scottish Presbyterians.

The ethos of handcraft prevailed at the Guild. Each craftsman owned his own tools and the shared use of them was discouraged to preserve individuality in mark-making. Power tools were in the main found to be inappropriate in method, and so mechanisation was discouraged. The Guild attracted, among many others, David Jones and Desmond Chute. Epstein, despite his affinity with Ditchling, drew away from them.

Brangwyn and others in the village mistrusted the evangelical and politicised demonstrativeness of Catholicism as practised at the Guild. He believed religion and sexuality to be private matters, so much so that his Catholicism was conducted in the downstairs room at The Jointure consecrated as a private chapel. He refused to use the word 'creation' in reference to his work saying,

'Lay into a job, do an honest, truthful piece of work and let The Creator do the rest.'[9]

Gill had a different viewpoint regarding the Creator. 'Remember you are making a real thing not merely a picture of a thing…It is in this sense that we are made in God's image. For we are really creators.'[10]

Brangwyn relied on his instinct rather than his intellect and tended not to waste good working time analysing and philosophising. Conversations round his table revealed his enquiring and informed intelligence but he would robustly dismiss such attributes. He advocated modesty and felt that work should be done to the highest standards, meaningfully and for the love of God rather than for gain or self-promotion and here Gill agrees.

> The love of God means that work must be done according to an absolute standard of form; the love of our neighbour means that work must be done to an absolute standard of serviceableness. Good quality is therefore twofold: work must be good in itself and good for use.[11]

David Jones who found solace at the Guild, echoed Brangwyn and Gill when he said, 'Do as good a job as you can, take a humble and reverential attitude and God will do the rest.'[12]

Edward Johnston attributed special importance to the object and the work itself. He said, 'Things are His Will,' and 'we are ourselves God's tools'.[13] His dictum, 'Look after Truth and Goodness and Beauty will take care of itself,'[14] was a byword at the Guild.

From the beginning Brangwyn agreed with Mackmurdo that 'the craftsman is essential to the industrialised world'[15] and was concerned that the tradition of handcraft should inform the use of the machine with good design appropriate to its practicality. Likewise, Johnston opined, 'Unless the design arises out of the actual construction of a thing it is reduced to the level of extraneous ornamentation.'[16]

Only Catholics were permitted to work at the Guild. This policy eventually led to some altercation. First Pepler found it necessary to employ a non-Catholic at his press at the Guild, then he found it necessary to use power-operated presses. Neither of these issues was acceptable at the Guild, so in 1937 he moved his St Dominic's Press to premises opposite The Jointure, renaming it The Ditchling Press.

Johnston quite quickly found the physical hardships of self-sufficiency at the Guild too tiring and time-consuming, his wife Greta did even more so. Johnston could not, like Pepler, convert to Catholicism, so, in 1920, after what he called 'a gentle schism'[17], Johnston and his wife bought Cleves, a small house in the village, next to their first house, Downsview. There he grew vegetables and kept chickens, for pleasure rather than subsistence, constructing an ingenious system of pulleys which allowed him to open the chicken coop in the mornings from the comfort of his bedroom.

Gill had an unconventional sexual philosophy which was not restrained by the usual social mores and, although this was not shared with the rest of the Guild members, they, unfortunately, became associated with it. Money and land ownership caused friction within the community. In his autobiography Gill put his abrupt departure from the Guild in 1924 down to his need for a more secluded and private workplace, away from the publicity that he and the Guild had begun to attract. However, privately, the split between him and others in the community was more complex but it was kept publicly obscure. Gill left abruptly for Capel-y-ffin in Wales, followed soon after by David Jones. The Guild continued without Gill, but in continuation of his best ideals, until 1989 when it closed. Work from the Guild was collected together at an exhibition at the Gillian Jason Gallery under the poignant title 'A Lost Idyll' in 1989.

Charleston Farmhouse continued as a hub of artistic and literary activity until the 1990s. After World War II Grant and Bell painted nearby Upper Berwick church with murals and, as in the farmhouse itself, almost no surface was left unadorned. Unlike Brangwyn, their approach as decorators was to apply paint extraneously rather than integrating it appropriately with the setting, but this audacity gave their work its charm. In their pottery and paintings their joyous disregard for formality is more akin to Brangwyn's own approach to his work and his ceramics and tile designs are notably similar. As he said, 'I am a decorator'.

ARCHITECT

…an artist among architects is as rare as an architect among artists Herbert Furst [1]

When Brangwyn moved into The Jointure he was excitedly distracted from his gruelling daily work regime by his plans for rebuilding and alteration. He sought to keep his Arts and Crafts-style additions in keeping with the existing Tudor building, much as Morris had done at his country house, Kelmscott Manor in Oxfordshire. When furnishing the house he relied on an antique dealer called FE Fitness, but as time went on, his requests became more and more homely. He wrote Fitness copious letters listing the objects he required, 'A bulldog pup and some garden seeds, 3 pairs of soft indoor shoes and a barrel of the best ale for my friends,' were just a few.[2] For clarity he characteristically illustrated his requests with amusing and descriptive illustrations.

He did not employ an architect, preferring to work directly with a local building firm, Stennings, and often drew plans and details on walls near the work in hand. Some of these were uncovered in later alterations. The new studio proved too small and dark so an extra section was added with a tall Flemish-style north window. The door to the street was joined to a tall window above and both could be removed to allow large canvases to be carried through.

The Brangwyns continued to rent Temple Lodge because Lucy preferred to be with her friends in London and the home with which she was familiar. Brangwyn attempted to entice her to The Jointure by placing loving embellishments in the details of the woodwork and on the walls, the recurring theme of their intertwined initials, L&FB, set around a sacred heart and cross. He also carved a wooden mould of the reversed image and a cast concrete block of the design was set into the walls of any new building. Eventually a pattern emerged whereby Lucy joined him at The Jointure for the summer and Brangwyn spent the winter months in London. In the first studio a small gallery was fixed at an upper level, linking through to the upper floor of the domestic wing. There, as in Temple Lodge, Lucy could sit and embroider and be part of her husband's working life and he, Lizzie and the assistants could keep an eye on her 'illness'.

As more and larger mural commissions were undertaken in The Jointure, Brangwyn added another studio overlooking the garden. The third, a loft studio with floorboards that hinged back to accommodate tall murals, had a small internal window at the height of the rafters to allow assistants to call down for instructions and materials.

A matching domestic wing incorporated the spacious bedroom Brangwyn used as a Sunday studio. It had the best views in the house overlooking the garden and the full sweep of the Downs. To the west the two windmills, Jack and Jill, still punctuate the skyline. Jill is still working. Her gently circling sails must have reminded Brangwyn of Belgium. To find a house with such a view was surely a crowning delight to his artist's eye. Windmills, like bridges and ships, were favourite subjects and almost hallmarks of his work. On a scrap of paper he has written:

> Man in his efforts to harness the forces of Nature has produced two beautiful wind-driven contrivances, the sailing ship and the windmill. The one defying the ungovernable fury of the sea; the other stemming the tide of the mighty wind with its frail fingers.'[3]

Lizzie had left the Brangwyns in December 1909 when she married Francis Joseph Peacock, but he enlisted as a soldier at the outbreak of the First World War and was killed in 1914. Lizzie then returned to work for the Brangwyns as Mrs Peacock, bringing with her a baby son, Edgar, whom the Brangwyns all but adopted, paying for his schooling and giving him a home.

The new spacious kitchen Brangwyn built at The Jointure, directly below the Sunday studio, did not please Lizzie at first because it replaced her cosy Tudor lean-to, but a larger room and stove were required to feed the household's growing number of assistants.

The first was Arthur Covey, an American who had trained with Karl von Marr in Munich and, having become aware of Brangwyn's growing reputation in America, came to Temple Lodge to work with him. He helped out with classes at the London School of Art and wrote four major articles on Brangwyn's works for *The Studio* magazine. An accomplished artist in the Brangwyn mode, he returned to work on murals in America and helped to promote Brangwyn's work there. Another American, Edward Trumbell stayed two years and later also pursued a career as a mural painter in the United States, eventually becoming director of the mural programme at the Rockefeller Center. Trumbell was less influenced by Brangwyn than Covey and this is evident in his work which is stylised in the Art Deco manner. Trumbell was succeeded by Allen Tupper True, who also stayed for two years, and Elijah Albert Cox who stayed for ten. After them another American, John J Murphy, an illustrator and printmaker and sometime portrait-painter, was taken on. The assistants who helped at both Temple Lodge and at The Jointure were the English artists, Frank Alford, Laurence Bradshaw, Reginald Lewis and two Americans, C Peter Helke and Dean Cornwell. Later Brangwyn was assisted by William Stewart, a scene-painter who, after Brangwyn's death, had a life-tenancy of The Jointure garden studio. Most faithful of all his assistants was Kenneth Center, a fine artist in his own right who settled in Ditchling. Both Center and Lewis helped with the British Empire panels.

Brangwyn's output during the war years was formidable. Besides producing a large number of propaganda posters he completed murals for Lloyd's Register of Shipping, for the Panama Pacific International Exposition in San Francisco, and for the Cuyahoga County courthouse in Cleveland, Ohio. The mosaic murals for St Aidan's church in Leeds were also finished and Brangwyn added further stained-glass windows to some earlier designs he had installed at St Mary's, Bucklebury. He designed a private billiard room for Horton House with an innovative table which avoided all the usual bulbous and heavily ornate characteristics and was, instead, sleek and modern, restricting all decoration to inlay.

An architectural scheme for the proposed Brangwyn Museum and Kyoraku Bijutso Kwan or Sheer Pleasure Arts Pavilion to be built for Kijoro Matsukata on a site near Tokyo shows what he could have achieved with a major architectural project. Sadly the site was later destroyed by an earthquake and the plan was abandoned. It is clear from his detailed drawings however that the building would have been approached from the point of view of an artist, with an artist's under-standing of the light and space necessary for the purpose of displaying works of art. In designing the museum Brangwyn used his experience of construction learned through his father's architectural work, and from his building and adaptations at The Jointure. Sympathetic to the oriental culture he added subtle elements drawn from Japanese principles of architecture but the large, quadrangular building had a contemporary, almost Roman, simplicity. A lofty entrance hall, flanked by galleries, led to a cloistered ambulatory with open rounded arches sur-rounding a sunken Japanese garden with a central ornamental fountain. With a colour scheme playing around with shades of his favourite warm grey, it had promise of being a place of restful peace.

Because of his wife's alcoholism and the rigid timetable in the studios, Brangwyn hardly socialised, but he had contact with other accomplished artists and craftsmen in the village. Ethel Mairet lived at Gospels in Beacon Road. She moved to Ditchling in 1917 from the Ashbee workshops in Chipping Campden, where her husband Philip Mairet worked for Ashbee as an architectural draughtsman. Her house was indeed a beacon for those seeking to study her revival of hand-loom weaving and natural (or vegetable) dyeing. This interest was fostered by her first marriage to the architect and philosopher AK Coomaraswamy. In 1902 they travelled to India and Ceylon where she was inspired by the weaving and dyeing techniques practised there. She welcomed these as an antidote to the commonly used, industrialised, *jacquard* loom with its pre-set punch card, methods which, with synthetic dyes, had prevailed in England since the 18th century. She and Philip built Gospels, an

Arts and Crafts house, incorporating the weaving rooms. In Ditchling Philip worked primarily as a builder. Those Ethel taught at Gospels included the Ditchling weavers Valentine Kilbride, Petra Gill, Elizabeth Peacock (not Lizzie Peacock), Marjorie Kendon and Hilary Bourne who, with her sister Joanna, founded Ditchling Museum in 1985. Among other notable artists in the village were the painters Louis Ginnett, Knighton Hammond, Ethel Rawlins and Charles Knight, the distinguished watercolour painter.

Between 1920 and 1903 Bernard Leach and Shoji Hamada worked together in their studio at St Ives, exploring the origins of English medieval pottery. Leach was influenced by the Japanese raku potters and they, in their turn, were inspired by the Arts and Crafts philosophy which Leach brought back to them from his training with Brangwyn. The collaboration was somewhat circular because the Arts and Crafts movement was influenced by the Japanese. In 1921 Leach and Hamada came to Ditchling to visit Brangwyn and his fellow artist-craftsmen. Hamada was profoundly affected by all of them, but by Ethel Mairet in particular; she presented him with one of her husband's hand-woven suits which he later wore at his wedding. Hamada came to Ditchling again in 1929. This time he brought with him the distinguished Japanese potter Yanagi Setsu who bought copious amounts of hand-dyed and woven material from Ethel and 60 yards of tweed from Valentine Kilbride, at his workshop at the Guild. The notes Yanagi took back about the natural dyeing and weaving process informed the burgeoning folk art movement in Japan. In the summer of 1936 Leach came back to Ditchling and camped with his wife and dog in a chalk pit on the Downs.

Although in 1941 he became actively involved with a protest against a large development proposed for an extensive tract of land near Ditchling, Brangwyn favoured the building of sensitively integrated housing within the village. Besides The Jointure properties and the cottage he left Lizzie, which she later called Temple Lodge after the Hammersmith house, Brangwyn owned Nos 1 and 5 Lewes Road, East End Farm in East End Lane and No 5 in Beacon Road. In memory of Lucy he built almshouses at No 53 East End Lane, naming them The Lucy Brangwyn Homes. Brangwyn's buildings can be identified by their characteristic Brangwyn-esque details and by the cement cast of his and Lucy's initials. In 1927 a tract of land was acquired to the south of The Jointure and work began on the building of a garage. Brangwyn wrote urgently to Albert Rowley of the Rowley Gallery: 'For goodness sake get down here and rescue me from this monstrosity'.[4] Mysteriously the garage owner pulled out and Albert built a house on the existing foundations. He lived there with five of his ten children.[5]

Brangwyn protested vigorously when a local builder called on him to ask if he could give Brangwyn's name to an estate that he proposed to build just north of

Two-master off Tenedos (now Bozcaada) Turkey, 1890, oil, 37x 45cm

Funeral at Sea, 1890, oil, 206x234cm, *Glasgow City Council*

Buccaneers, 1892, oil, 206 x 231cm, *Brian Clarke*

Carpet, 'Plants', woven by Templeton & Co for 1930 Pollard exhibition, 287x269cm, *Musea Brugge, Groeningsmuseum*

Ceramics, Royal Doulton,
Harvestware 1930-40

Ceramics, Royal Doulton, 1930

Lucy on a Bridge in Bruges, 1908, oil, 43x53cm

Lucy and Frank Brangwyn on a bridge in Bruges, 1908, photograph

Skinners Hall Panel, The Granting of their Charter to the Skinners Company by Edward III, 1 March 1327, oil, 285x305cm, *The Worshipful Company of Skinners*

The Sawyers, 1904, pencil, 38x30cm

'Peace', poster, 26x50cm

Preliminary drawings for 'Peace', 15x12cm

Swansea panel, South-East Asia, 1926-1933, oil and tempera, 600x390cm, *City and County of Swansea*

Ditchling Beacon, watercolour, 1946, 38 x40cm

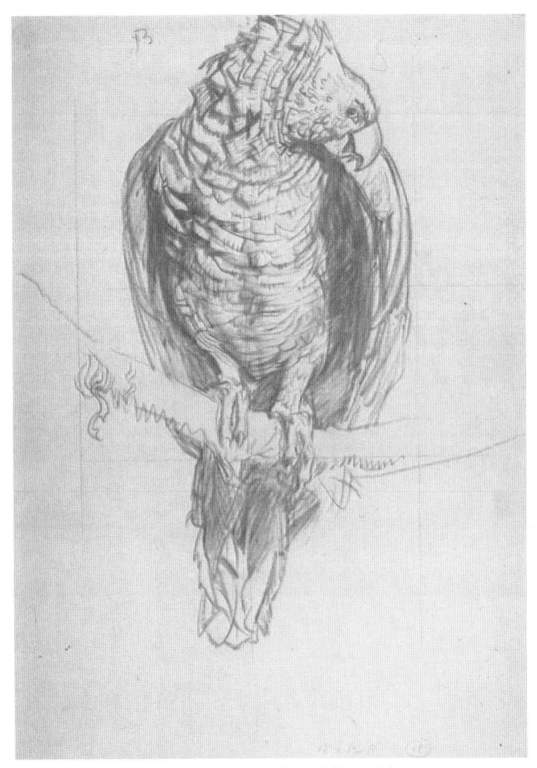

Parrot, sanguine, 43x31cm, *City and County of Swansea*

Rhinoceros, pencil and sanguine, 49x74cm, *City and County of Swansea*

Black Mill at Winchelsea, pen, pencil and wash, 50x65cm

The Jointure house and studios
The Jointure from the garden

The Jointure hall and stairs (June Buck/*Country Life* picture library)
The Jointure dining room (June Buck/*Country Life* picture library)

The Jointure drawing room with Roger the dog, ink, 12x15cm
The studio door, 'The first stage on the road to the Hotel Arents', ink,
13x18cm

The Ice-Cream Vendor, lithograph, 17x15cm
The Crossroads, Ditchling, ink, 15x20cm

Dressing table, Pollard & Co, 1930
Bedroom, Pollard & Co, 1930

A Good Harvest at Ditchling, 1946
'A good westerly wind to Mrs Peacock's joy', 1944, ink, 20x22cm

'Buy War Bonds', poster
'Spain', general relief fund for the women and children of Spain, poster

Old Bridge at Rome, 1921, etching, 30x35cm

Brangwyn working on a
stretched canvas

Brangwyn working at a
lithographic stone

73

Installing the British Empire panels, 1933, etching, 20x15cm

British Empire panels, House of Lords, photograph FLewis

Lucy Brangwyn (from a
photograph)

Brangwyn in The Jointure garden,
photograph

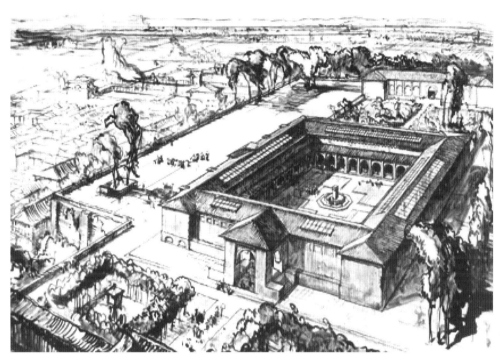

Drawing of intended Brangwyn museum in Tokyo

Brighton at Withdean. However, after the builder persuaded him of the social need for well-designed and affordable houses, Brangwyn became interested enough to help with the designs. The estate today boasts Brangwyn Way, Brangwyn Avenue, Brangwyn Drive and Brangwyn Crescent and also Peacock Way–after Lizzie.

The Ditchling residents rarely saw Brangwyn, but on occasions he would ask them to bring their children to pose for drawings, mainly for his murals. He was remembered for occasionally opening the studio door and asking people to come in off the street if he required a model urgently. Stennings, his and our local builders, joked that they spent more time posing for him than building. The well-known Sinden family, Leon, Joy and Donald became frequent models and can identify themselves in the murals. Brangwyn also used photographs. Sir Donald recalls the photographic sessions with Brangwyn and his father Alfred Sinden, a local chemist. From 1931 Alfred took many of Brangwyn's photographs and developed the plates himself.

The use of photography was by then no longer frowned upon. It was sanctioned by many earlier painters. Vuillard, Degas and Walter Sickert in particular show the influence of the camera, showing figures half out of shot and in poses which could not have been sustained for long drawings. Brangwyn used only his own landscape snapshots for his etchings and watercolours but for the photographs of models in the studio he used professional photographers. Brangwyn himself set up the poses. It was a device to speed up the mural painting process and to ensure accuracy. The resulting prints were squared up and copied onto canvas by his assistants and Brangwyn would then swiftly complete the work. Joseph Simpson, knowing that Michelangelo allegedly took two days to paint a double lifesize figure, asked Brangwyn how much time he had taken on one fifteen foot high. Brangwyn replied that he had, 'knocked it up in less than a day. Once I get my cartoons enlarged on to the canvas I just eat it up.'[6]

Joy Sinden became one of his regular female models. While the naked torsos of muscular workmen are almost a trademark of his industrially-themed work, he used the female nude less frequently. This has led to unsubstantiated suggestions of homosexuality. The fact that he sublimated his female nudes might in fact suggest the opposite, their scarcity giving them added frisson. In his smaller works nudity appears intimate and private and appears to be a testimony of his respectful and wholesome appreciation of unclothed women as real people rather than as depersonalised objects. It is often said that, in his paintings, he paid equal attention to his naked ladies' contours as to his well-rounded melons. This is true in the sense of the painterly consistency he maintained across his canvases, but not true with regard to the sensuality of his portrayal of pearly female flesh. In this he has affinities with the Flemish painter Rubens and the Venetian masters. It is interesting that in the British Empire and the Rockefeller Center murals, both large public spaces, his nudes lack this intimate sensuality and are somewhat overstated.

Brangwyn's official dealer was D Croal Thompson. He specialised in the Barbizon artists and staged a well-received exhibition of Brangwyn's drawings at his gallery Barbizon House. Building on this success he hired 184 Queens Gate, a grand mansion in London and, in 1924, presented a fuller exhibition of Brangwyn's work, the largest one-man show by a living artist ever held in Britain. Matsukata lent works awaiting shipment to Tokyo. The Fine Art Society lent 151 etchings as well as other paintings and drawings. Private owners and museums were equally generous. Despite the fact that the majority of Brangwyn's works were dispersed around the world, it was a huge exhibition, displaying 470 pieces in all his different disciplines. The prime minister, Ramsay MacDonald, opened it to a distinguished audience and his speech showed some understanding of Brangwyn's motivation.

'I candidly confess to you that I love passion, I love colour, I detest materialism,' he announced and declared that Brangwyn was a great democratic artist whose work 'symbolised the fundamental and eternal verities and the struggles of humanity.'[7]

The critics were equally laudatory. They congratulated him particularly on his understanding of the different qualities of each medium. An article in the *American Magazine of Art* published a rather too all-encompassing overview.

Brangwyn has kept pace with modern thought and has let it influence him without running away with him. The elements of Cubism can be discerned in his lithographs and etchings of ships and guns and Futurism has not entirely been ignored by him, though he has chosen his own way of presenting movement. While his interest in labor is that of a creative socialist, that Impressionism and Post-Impressionism too have had an influence on his palette is clear from the range he has and the fluency of his brush, far beyond anything of pre-Impressionist days, or of his own early period. He is an artist who does not stand still, indeed his advance is steady. He gives ample evidence of *plein air* observation of nature and of deep study of light and shadow. He gets figures, living and moving, from mere touches of pigment even as Whistler did, but with greater fiber. I do not think, as a figure painter, that his drawing reaches to the great heights of medieval foreign masters or of Greek and Assyrian sculptors, but he does reach more nearly to their mountain tops than any has done in modern times. Few living artists can compete with him in the many crafts he practises with such colossal mastery and energy. In landscape he certainly goes far beyond medieval or classic painters.'[8]

At the last minute Brangwyn funked the grand opening, giving in to his resistance to social occasions, and his shyness verged on the impolite. However, there is no evidence that this caused offence. It may, on the contrary, have added to his mystique.

Displayed in the exhibition were drawings for a set of Stations of the Cross commissioned by a friend in France, the artist Théophile Steinlen, to be distributed among the churches whose own Stations had been destroyed in the war. This was followed in 1922 by a request from a Father T Ryan, an Irish missionary, to paint a set of Stations for a leper colony at Westford near Pretoria in South Africa. Brangwyn chose to depict the scenes in modern dress and portrayed the soldiers at the crucifixion in contemporary uniform. This caused some consternation but Brangwyn protested that the great religious paintings had always used the costume of their time and added, 'Do people imagine that the world's supreme tragedy should be painted in the style of a Christmas card?'[9]

A series of mural panels for the chapel of Christ's Hospital in Horsham was one of Brangwyn's longest assignments. The school was designed and built by Aston Webb and E Ingress Bell in 1902 and the commission came through Webb. The murals were begun in 1912 and were not completed until 1923. The theme chosen was 'the mission and expansion of Christianity, beginning with the Acts and leading to the conversion of our islands and foreign missionary work.' Brangwyn rarely left his work empty of people and at Christ's Hospital the whole mural is filled with figures. The chosen medium was tempera, which was by then available in tubes. It was painted on canvas *marouflaged* to the walls. He used a light pastel tone, drawing on his earlier work done in the style and coloration of the French Nabi painters with whom he had associated in Paris at the turn of the century. The title of each panel, lettered in gold, provides a linking ribbon of royal blue to harmonise with the furnishings in the chapel. Mindful of his captive audience of boys, Brangwyn lent mischievously towards caricature in the figures, an element to which generations of pupils have responded.

On 2 December 1924 Lucy died of bronchial pneumonia. Brangwyn was devastated. Despite her alcoholism, they had maintained a strong partnership. As a widower he had opportunities to express the sexual side of his nature but was discouraged by a priest who, no doubt, reminded him of the fact that he had once before betrayed his faith. This struck deep. Brangwyn became remorseful and used his work as a vehicle in which to express his penitence.

THE BRITISH EMPIRE PANELS

When critics are divided the artist is at one with himself Oscar Wilde

In 1906 the First Commissioner of Works, Lewis Harcourt MP, formed a select committee to report on the unfinished decorative condition of the Palace of Westminster. Where Prince Albert had earlier sought to decorate the private royal areas Harcourt saw an opportunity to bring art to the people by commissioning murals for the publicly used East Corridor. Harcourt's committee included Sir Edward Poynter, then President of the Royal Academy, John Singer Sargent and William R Lethaby and Lord Carlisle, the amateur artist and patron of Burne-Jones and Morris. The artists involved included Frank Salisbury, John Byam Shaw and Henry Payne. They produced a successful scheme taking its lead from Holbein's 'Ambassadors', acquired by the National Gallery in 1901. The East Corridor project ran concurrently with Brangwyn's Skinners Hall murals and both projects achieved a rare moment of harmony between patron and painter.

Subsequent mural schemes, commissioned by the government, were bedevilled by political control and issues of propaganda which were imposed upon artists, inhibiting their freedom of choice. Sigismund Goetze's murals for the Foreign Office, painted between 1912 and1920, had to be altered, not for artistic reasons but because they did not match postwar ideals at odds with those prevailing when the project was commissioned. Moreover, contemporary artists thought Goetze's classical style to be old-fashioned.

A commemorative Hall of Remembrance was envisaged in 1918 to be built in a garden on Richmond Hill. Sargent, Paul Nash, Stanley Spencer, William Orpen, Henry Lamb, William Roberts and Wyndham Lewis were commissioned to provide images from the First World War but, whereas Goetze's murals were considered out of touch with reality, their paintings were deemed too graphic. The Hall was never built and the paintings were consigned to the Imperial War Museum.

The infighting between the advocates of classical, traditional and modern art continued to seethe and the situation was repeated in an ensuing proposal for state murals in St Stephen's Hall (1924-27). While not being directly part of the Palace of Westminster, the hall comes under its aegis. Sir David Young Cameron was in charge. He was a member of the British School at Rome, for whom the Italian Renaissance artists are exemplars. This time it was stipulated that depictions of war were not acceptable. Once more the panels were to be history paintings depicting significant incidents in parliamentary life. Sir Henry Newbolt and William Whitley, later to become chairman of the BBC, came in as advisors and were assisted by the historians GM Trevelyan, Albert Pollard and CH Firth.

Predictably the avoidance of modern references went directly against the views of the avant-garde. Apart from Charles Sims's lively painting of the signing of the Magna Carta, the rest, by artists such as Sir Thomas Monnington, William Rothenstein, Vivien Forbes, Colin Gill and George Clausen were seen as outmoded. When they were unveiled in 1927 Herbert Furst, (who admired Brangwyn greatly) said that they had '…no living so to speak…all the subjects seemed remote and hardly in contact with the present at any point'.[1]

This artistic and political see-saw remained unresolved and it was into this potential hornet's nest that Brangwyn blithely stepped when he accepted his largest commission, one that was to occupy him for seven years and change his life.

In 1924 there was growing impatience in the House for a memorial to commemorate the losses sustained by the peers in the First World War. A sculpture by John Tweed was commissioned to fill an alcove in the Royal Gallery. It was to be funded by the peers. The great benefactor and member of the Guinness family, Lord Iveagh, was approached by the Lord Great Chamberlain, the Marquis of Lincolnshire, and he agreed to donate a commemorative mural scheme to fill the entire chamber. Brangwyn was chosen to execute this commission. Sixteen wall spaces were to be filled in a hall one hundred and ten feet long, forty-five feet wide and forty-five feet high, three thousand square feet in total. The sum offered was £20,000 and a contract was drawn up. To avoid state interference, terms were agreed whereby Brangwyn was answerable to Lord Iveagh alone and his murals were to accommodate and harmonise with the two very large paintings by Maclise depicting Nelson and Wellington that would remain *in situ*. This presented Brangwyn with a seemingly insuperable problem but, characteristically, he does not appear to have been daunted by it. Instead he was hugely enthusiastic, believing that the project could be the crowning achievement of his life's work.

Brangwyn had not so far encountered political pressure and he did not expect it. He had been put forward for the Hall of Remembrance, but was busy with other commissions and, for the same reason, he was not involved in the St Stephen's Hall murals. He was used to having a relatively free hand and, since he always sought to meet the requirements of the client while remaining sensitive to the architectural environment of any of his murals and interiors, he had, on the whole, maintained cordial business relationships in his commissions. Complaints were usually due to his tendency to be late in finishing and delivering commissions. His reaction to the Royal Gallery was that it was 'heavy, bilious and stuffy'.[2] Brangwyn intended to design something which would both integrate with it and refresh it.

He produced a large quantity of very beautiful finished work for Iveagh and Lincolnshire's first theme, depicting scenes from the First World War. They complemented Maclise's paintings in tone and subject, using soft grey blues, ochres and pale pink and have Cubist elements in their structure which would possibly have found favour with all parties. Only its subject was debatable. Lord Iveagh thought images of conflict and death might prove politically questionable. Brangwyn found the 'blood-and-khaki' aspect depressing. It was dangerously provocative for Iveagh to choose an artist who had produced some of the most graphic images of war in his posters and Brangwyn, who felt deep remorse about the effect of his posters, was not inclined to repeat them.

Next Iveagh and Lincolnshire turned back to the plans Sir Charles Barry had recommended for the Royal Gallery. He, with Pugin, was the architect of the Houses of Parliament and thought that the walls should be decorated with 'a gorgeous enrichment of matter more allied to the College of Arms than of Arts.'

Brangwyn's second design was therefore heraldic and comprised of the family trees of all the peers. But this idea was quickly also abandoned by Brangwyn and Iveagh because it presented endless problems with genealogy and, at over 3,000 feet long, might prove repetitive and boring.

Finally Brangwyn and Iveagh settled on the first component of Barry's suggestion and indeed produced a gorgeous enrichment of matter with a new scheme harking back to Morris wallpaper. As such it was in complete sympathy with Pugin and Barry's architecture and the decorative style of the period in which the Houses of Parliament was built. Brangwyn designed an arrangement of massed figures and foliage, reminiscent of tapestry and Morris's fabric and wallpaper designs. Instead of the earlier blue coloration of the war theme, which might in the end have proved more acceptable, Brangwyn settled on a bright array of colours to reflect the dapples of coloured light which would travel across them from the high stained-glass windows. These repetitive, light-toned murals were designed to fill the spaces on the end walls entirely, but left the space around Maclise's paintings clear, to preserve their prominence.

It was intended to be a celebration of the triumph of life and peace over warfare and death, the regeneration of the fraternity of nations and nature's recovery after destruction. It was Brangwyn's emphatic plea to the politicians to strive for peace rather than war. Privately it was his statement of personal atonement. In tune with the current political enthusiasm he was encouraged to portray the glories of the Empire, which he chose to do with an array of exotic plants, animals and figures. The timing of the choice of subject coincided with the establishment of the Empire Marketing board in 1926 and reflected the current political emphasis on the value of the plentiful products from the Dominions.

The murals became known as the British Empire Panels, but, for Brangwyn, the work was not confined by that theme. For him the message was eternal. It presents an ideal paradise with echoes of Pre-Raphaelite fantasies, but it was portrayed with a thoroughly modern emphasis and even strayed towards the current preoccupation with the primitive. He accommodated traditional painting and at the same time drew on the Symbolists. He also adopted the flattened linear qualities of the Nabis. The work incorporated all the influences he had assimilated, starting from his first experiences in his father's workshops. Despite these the work is wholly unique. The amount of work done in preparation for the mural is astonishing. He went to extraordinary lengths to solve all of the problems, even to the extent that he made painted copies of the stained glass windows and the pilasters.

He used a light pastel range of colours because the hall was dimly lit through an upper range of dense stained-glass windows. With such a vast area to cover he could not have sustained the more detailed and painterly method he used for the Skinners Hall and Lloyds Registry of Shipping murals. He therefore used a flat-patterned, stylised and highly decorative approach enabling him to maintain consistency of colour and leaving clear areas to be filled in by his assistants, the technique used by those who embroidered the altar-cloths and tapestries in his father's workshop. His design, though dense, was nevertheless well grouped and featured images of importance at strategic points in the Gallery. It was optimistic, joyful, generous, totally well-intentioned and full of Christian idealism.

The studios at Ditchling became busier than ever. His assistants were numerous. They included Reginald Lewis, Dean Cornwell and Roger Bland, the son of Iveagh's secretary. Scatalo, a scene-painter from La Scala in Milan, proved instructive in the preparation and support of large canvases. William Stewart, also a scene-painter, joined the team. In 1928 Kenneth Center arrived. He left in 1941 to serve in the war but settled in Ditchling and remained a close companion until Brangwyn's death. Villagers came in and out to model for him as well as John Stenning, the local builder, and Marco Alfrate, an Italian chestnut-seller. 'A massive negress'[3] was engaged as a model and she arrived with a tribe of children. They were persuaded out of their clothes and, once out of them, the children refused to put them on again and ran naked in the garden and village, to the consternation of Lizzie and the neighbours. Brangwyn made visits to the zoo and to botanical glasshouses producing working drawings worthy of Dürer, and by 1927 the work was well ahead of schedule.

But at that point came catastrophe. Lord Iveagh died. Lord Lincolnshire stepped in to take charge, but he too died. Lord Iveagh's son, Rupert Guinness, then took over but, without his father's firm patronage and Lord Lincolnshire's control, Brangwyn's work became a target for bureaucratic wrangling. Having been kept literally out of the picture the Lords asked to see sketches. Brangwyn hotly replied that, after two years' work, he was well past the sketch stage and reminded them that their request was outside the terms of his agreement. In fact the Royal Fine

Arts Commission needed to see the work. They were asked to make judgements on other matters in the Royal Gallery and could only do this in context with the proposed murals. A member of the RFAC was dispatched and instructed to arrive unexpectedly at the Ditchling studios, but Brangwyn refused him entry. Brangwyn worked on for three more years, resisting interference, until 1930, when one end wall was complete. Only then did he consent to display the work, but on condition that it was installed in its proposed position in the Gallery.

As a result the Lords were predisposed to disapprove the work. They were perplexed and nervous when faced with such exuberant and colourful paintings and so called upon the Royal Fine Arts Commission for their views. Unfortunately for Brangwyn they were once again in thrall to the classically-inspired British School at Rome.

In its report to the Clerk of the Parliaments the RFAC was mindful that Maclise's paintings should have precedence because the Royal Gallery had come to be known as the Waterloo Chamber after one of their titles.

> The commissioners fear that Mr Brangwyn's paintings will not harmonise with their surroundings. While his paintings are brilliant in colouring, fertile in invention and full of fancy in their luxuriant variety and treatment, their insistent motives ill-accord with the Waterloo Chamber; the large paintings of tropical flora and fauna flanking the War Memorial and the historic cartoons would appear inappropriate.

What is probable, however, but was, no doubt, inadequately explained, is that what they were all looking at was under-painting. Brangwyn was a perfectionist as an interior designer and had they been finally fixed in place it is very likely that, if they failed to harmonise with the rest of the gallery and the paintings by Maclise, he would have toned down the brightness with a glaze. They would then have been varnished. This had not, and could not have been done at the stage at which they were judged. As Brangwyn knew full well, it is dangerous to show clients uncompleted work.

The RFAC also felt that the panels had little relevance to the Empire. To a degree the Empire would have been of nominal significance to Brangwyn, who was more probably inspired by his love of travel and his sympathy with the countries he depicted, but it was nevertheless apparent. However, his determination to portray the integrated multicultural benefits of international co-operation suggests that he would have been opposed to overbearing imperialism.

The ensuing battle is recorded in Hansard, the parliamentary record, as well as *The Times*. William Rothenstein was a member of the commission and opined that

Brangwyn's 'robust and full-blooded art is not of our taste today and is unsuited to Pugin's Gothic interior. Pugin is not of our taste today and Brangwyn's is not in tune with it.'

His reasoning was entirely ill-informed because Brangwyn's work originated from the Pugin and Morris tradition of wall decoration. Moreover, his statement was contradictory–but it held sway. James Bolivar Manson, then director of the Tate Gallery, was another supporter of the classical idiom. He was chairman of the RFAC and was equally decided in his opposition to Brangwyn. 'We don't like Brangwyn,' he declared. 'He is not a painter. Wields a big brush but can't paint.'

The views of the avant-garde were, of course, also influential. Where the Lords and the RFAC thought him too modern, he was categorised by the Post-impressionists and Cubists as a traditionalist and an academic. He was thus refused for being too modern for the traditionalists and not modern enough for the Modernists. Assailed by opposing views the work had no chance.

Lord Salisbury valiantly supported Brangwyn. He acknowledged 'the mortal blow' it would inflict on the artist who had done the work in good faith and had obeyed the terms of the agreement. Lord Melchett also spoke up for him, although the grounds for his defence were also incorrect.

> It seems an unfortunate thing in this country that when you get a combination of a generous donor and a great artist the result always is rejection and a snub for their work… Anyone who knew the great work of Mr Brangwyn would know that he would not be able to produce pictures that would harmonise with and hang next to the work of Maclise. That could have been decided before anything was done at all.

Brangwyn's friend, Selwyn Image, wrote to *The Times* saying that it was quite usual to be startled by a piece of new decoration and that in time the Lords were likely to look more favourably upon it. He advised that it was a mistake to expect an artist to stick completely to the style of a past period. But it is clear that he didn't trust Brangwyn's ability to blend with the Maclise paintings when he said:

> That [Brangwyn's designs]…would not and could not be… of a piece with [Maclise's work] must, one imagines, have been plain from the start…for Mr Brangwyn is an artist of vital originality, whose work has been before the world these 30 years and more…

Both Melchett and Salisbury suggested that any decision should be delayed until the work was finished and on the walls. This view was also supported by a

letter from seven Royal Academicians: Sir Herbert Hughes Stanton, Sir William Orpen, Sir William Goscombe John, Sir George Clausen, Sir John Burnett, Sir Aston Webb and Sir Arthur Cope.

Even Walter Sickert wrote to *The Times* insisting that the work should be finished and left for at least six months to enable proper considered judgement to be made. He warned that one should 'treat the contemporary artist as a potential classic.'

It was all to no avail. The murals were rejected but, although they had no destination, the project was not cancelled. Instead, in accordance with the contract, Brangwyn was required to finish the work before payment of £7,000 would be made. He agreed to this, hoping that, once finished, they could be reconsidered. This involved three more years' work, making seven years in all. The rejection did indeed deal his reputation a mortal blow, as Lord Salisbury predicted.

Had Lord Iveagh not died it is very likely that the murals would have been installed. Brangwyn had skilfully designed his murals to suit the space and, over time, they would have, no doubt, have proved to be more than just suitable. It is probable that, after a while, they would have been seen as an admirable and unique statement of hope for international peace.

But was there more to it? By 1930 the government, which had applauded the Empire at the start of the commission was less enthusiastic. Britain was by then torn between the Empire that it could not afford and the desire for trading links. The British Empire Exhibition at Wembley, opened by George V in 1924, was so popular that it was reopened in 1925, but it still lost money. Worse, it became something of national joke. The debts caused by the First World War were, by then, beginning to bite and industrial strife led to the General Strike of 1926. The British Empire Board was heading for closure in 1933. Was Brangwyn rejected because his murals were considered too politically influential and was it that the political message was not appropriate rather than the murals themselves?

Brangwyn had taken on an almost impossible task and fulfilled his part in it admirably. The world at large, however, only understood one thing, that the indomitable Brangwyn had been toppled from his pedestal.

Lord Crawford and Balcarres, the chairman of the mural commission, wrote in a letter to Lord Peel bemoaning his lack of authority in the business.

…the muddle of the House of Lords affair, what with one committee and another and the Lord Chamberlain bedevilling the whole business, has been a source of lamentable confusions.

But for Brangwyn it was serious. Such was his fame that his 'failure' was of

87

enormous public interest. In 1846 Benjamin Robert Haydon, who had conceived the idea for the decoration of the Palace of Westminster, was driven to commit suicide when the committee did not deign even to include his work in the applications. After his notorious rejection Brangwyn forged on, driven by his unquenchable thirst for work, but his reputation was severely and unfairly affected.

The critics abruptly turned their backs on him. This attitude was maintained for the rest of his life and for too long afterwards. Other state mural artists had suffered rejection from the Palace of Westminster and earlier mural schemes had, on several occasions, been abandoned by the government. These rejections did not resound in art history, but the House of Lords debacle was such a cause célèbre that it brought a complete halt to future state commissions. The Royal Gallery walls are still covered in John Crace and Co's brown and gold wallpaper, a sombre and safe background to Maclise's paintings. As Degas said, 'The English see with their ears.'

The Marchioness of Lincolnshire, the widow of the Lord Great Chamberlain, and whose son, Lord Wendover, was killed in the war was so distressed by the decision that she wrote to the *The Times*.

> Fifty-five peers voted against the acceptance of Mr Brangwyn's pictures. The voting was cruel on the part of the noble Lords–cruel to the memory of our very generous and kindly friend, Lord Iveagh, his 'father's son', cruel to Mr Brangwyn who gave of his very best and whose wonderful conception was to have formed a beautiful setting to the House of Lords memorial…cruel also to the Mothers and to the Wives who have waited patiently [for a memorial which] would have lived for ever, merging with the fragrance and joyousness of the youth of those who died.

There was some small compensation for Brangwyn when he was awarded the Albert Medal of the Royal Society of Arts. The Duke of Connaught, Queen Victoria and Prince Albert's eldest son, presented it to him in 1932. But he may have recognised the irony in the honour. Maclise was Prince Albert's choice of artist for the Royal Gallery and, after Albert's death, had had the majority of his project rejected as well.

When the panels were finished they were held in trust by the Iveagh estate and remained rolled up at Kenwood House until the *Daily Mail* offered to exhibit them at the 1933 Ideal Home Exhibition. After some deliberation, Lord Iveagh considered this would be an opportunity to show the murals to the public and might help in the difficult task of finding a suitable venue for them. The panels retained their integrity, despite the inappropriate setting but, when fully lit, the brightness of the colours caused comment. When they were displayed in the Royal Gallery their brightness was not put forward as being among the reasons for their rejection. This emphasises the point that, even though the mural had not received a final toning down, Brangwyn took the conditions presented by the dim lighting into careful consideration. At last Brangwyn could see the work complete but whether or not he chose to view them is not, as far as I know, recorded. The exhibition led to an offer of £40,000 from an American collector, but Iveagh was loath to let them go abroad. Fortunately the city councils of both Cardiff and Swansea expressed an interest in acquiring the work of the Anglo-Welsh artist. Finally Swansea was chosen because the city's new Guildhall was in the process of being built and could be adapted to fit the panels. With a generosity equalling his father's, Lord Iveagh presented the murals to Swansea. The vast room in which they were hung was named The Brangwyn Hall and opened on 23 October 1934 by the Duke of Kent.

Brangwyn did not attend. He wrote to Macer-Wright who did.

No doubt you have seen that the panels have been given to Swansea. They have a very fine building and the panels will look very well there, but it is not the place for which they were designed so they will not be seen as one would have wished. I wish I were going with you, not because of the show, but because it would be delightful to visit certain places nearby with you.'[4]

It is admirable that the panels remain in Britain and, although they are much prized in Swansea, it is at once clear that they are not shown at their best at the Guildhall. Without the strong delineating structure of the Royal Gallery they hang disconnected, their tapestry and wallpaper effect is lost, as is their significance as a war memorial. Brangwyn had used pastel tones to compensate for the gloom of the Royal Gallery and these are unsuited to the airy lightness of Sir Percy Thomas's 1930s architecture. Brangwyn had already proved himself as a highly sensitive interior designer, so he was understandably disheartened by the unsuitability of their new setting. He felt that his reputation had been compromised. He did not attend upon them when they were installed and therefore failed to attune them to the requirements of the building and its light, as was his normal practice. In the last years of the work, when the murals seemed to have no destination or purpose, he clearly lost heart and allowed the work of his assistants to prevail. The work of less able hands is now more clearly visible, being closer to view and brightly lit.

Nevertheless Brangwyn was not idle. He had finished the job despite his disappointment and, except for the plants, did not repeat any images throughout the vast series of canvases. He had not hurried or skimped in any way. Despite the drawbacks, the panels retain their joyousness and are sustained by Brangwyn's imaginative optimism and his extraordinary skill. They are effective in a way that Brangwyn did not intend. Seen at closer range than would have been possible at the Royal Gallery, the hugeness and density of the murals continually surprises, revealing new figures and creatures, much as Brangwyn would have discovered in the tapestries and embroideries in his father's workshop. Animals suddenly appear from behind plants, and half-hidden birds almost sing. The more familiar one is with the murals the more they come to life. The quality of endless discovery gives them magic and mystery. They resound with his love and hope for mankind and are a plea, not just for peace on earth, but for the care of nature's delicate balance.

Brangwyn presented Cardiff with the first panels on the theme of war and he presented the Guildhall with his preparatory studies for the later panels. These are also displayed at the Brangwyn Hall and include some of Brangwyn's finest drawings. The hall is used for all sorts of activities, even boxing contests. But it is perhaps at concert performances that there is the best opportunity for reflective observation of the murals, when his visionary world is enhanced by musical accompaniment. The panels can be seen by a wider public than would have been possible at the Royal Gallery and, though his name has been largely forgotten elsewhere, it rings out from the Brangwyn Hall.

APPLIED ARTS

The future of design is to maintain an alliance between the artist and the businessman *Herbert Furst* [1]

During the seven years the Empire panels took to complete Brangwyn had undertaken other commissions. In 1925 he completed work on murals for the Missouri state capital, Jefferson City, USA which had taken ten years. He also designed a stained-glass window for St Winifred's, Manaton in Devon.

Pollard & Co, for whom he had previously produced furniture designs, staged an exhibition in October 1930, showing ostensibly new room schemes in which Brangwyn had designed everything–décor, carpets, lighting, glassware and ceramics, even the ashtrays. In fact these designs were those he produced in 1900 after working for Seigfried Bing. They therefore predated those of other designers in the exhibition, including CR Macintosh. Thirty years later, they were received as thoroughly modern. The critic of the *Scotsman* wrote:

> In the application of art to utility Mr Frank Brangwyn RA has decidedly and successfully entered a new field. His designs for furniture and many other household requisites…are notable both for their novel conception and for their ingenious handiness. Executed in rare woods from many parts of the world and departing considerably from orthodox ideas, some of the exhibits, though certainly beautiful, may in their unusual appearance prove too modern for some tastes; but women will find in many of them those common sense ideas which before they may have seen in their minds but never in shops. It is this combination of art and craft which makes this exhibition unique.

The *Architectural Review* was puzzled by the designs which they saw as 'modern yet somehow not modern', a criticism that Brangwyn had heard before.

In 1928 Brangwyn was delighted by a commission to produce pots and tableware for Royal Doulton's standard ware. These were also included in the Pollard exhibition. The director of Royal Doulton, Charles Noke, was looking for fresh ideas that were less formal than their other ranges and Brangwyn could certainly supply informality. His tableware was inexpensive and colourful and although the pieces were industrially manufactured they retained a hand-thrown appearance. His designs were faintly impressed on the clay in moulds and then freely painted by hand by workers at the factory. This input from others was deliberate on Brangwyn's part; he wanted the hand painters to enjoy personal involvement with the process and, by doing so, each piece could be given individuality.

There were several different styles of geometrically-patterned Royal Doulton earthenware, but his Harvest Ware is the most representational, depicting decorative sheaves of gourds, grapes and cherries. He also designed more traditional Mediterranean-style pots and jugs which were hand-thrown by the Ashtead potters. He never allowed any of his designs to be manufactured without understanding the medium first. He threw his own pots and made prototypes of his own furniture. He made the iron armillary sphere in his garden and carved the stone pedestal himself. His sketchbooks show page after page of his experimental ideas.

1930 was a busy year. As well as dealing with the Pollard exhibition Brangwyn was asked to design the setting for the Chelsea Arts Ball on an Egyptian theme. He enjoyed this diversion again a few years later when the theme was the Champagne Age. More importantly, that year he produced an unusual and very elegant design for the first-class dining rooms of the luxury liner the SS *Empress of Britain*. Notable artists were asked to design other rooms in the ship. Edmund Dulac designed the smoking room, John Lavery the ballroom, Charles Allom the lounge, PA Staynes and AH Jones the entranceway and, intriguingly, William Heath Robinson the nursery and cocktail bar.

Brangwyn's dining chairs were square and geometrically strutted, but the seats were upholstered in a pattern that was echoed in a larger version on the tablecloths for the tables, both round and square, each with its own square lamp. The carpets reflected the same curving pattern. An octagonal central plinth of plain pale wood echoed a block of oriental-style opaline lights above, each one hung from long strips of mirror. His main decoration was displayed on three 12-foot panels for one end of the room, two panels for a minstrels' gallery and a frieze above the cold buffet. For these he chose an innovative and beautiful technique for which he sought the help of AJ Rowley at his gallery in Silver Street, Kensington.

They devised a method whereby silver leaf laid on gesso formed the base. A design of stylised foliage reminiscent of the British Empire panels was delicately inscribed upon the silvered panel and this was then thinly painted, allowing the silver to shine through. The mural was then varnished, to preserve it and to add a golden glow. Reflected in the mirrored hanging lights the panels must have glowed with restrained elegance.

Rowley had worked with him before on his wood carving projects and, in 1933, Brangwyn designed a carved wooden frieze, showing a stylised procession of workmen, for the exterior of his gallery.

In 1931, while waiting for the fate of the House of Lords panels to be decided, Brangwyn had not been idle. He made 73 drypoint etchings for a book called *L'Ombre de la Croix* published in Paris by J & J Theroux. Between 1927 and 1936 he designed two large commemorative stained-glass windows for Lord Iveagh, one in St Patrick's Cathedral, Dublin and the other in St Andrew and St Peter's parish church in Elvedon, Suffolk.

In the late afternoon in the studio above the kitchen at The Jointure, as the sun set behind the windmills, he continued as ever with graphic work–woodcuts, bookplates and illustrations, also his daily paperwork. The letters that he wrote there to his friends were sprinkled with lively cartoons, robust descriptions and opinions. Center recounted that he never worked in the main studios on Sundays and never finished a job on a Friday. After Lucy's death he used Temple Lodge less and less, leaving it in the hands of a caretaker. In 1935 he finally gave it up. Throughout his life his friends remained constant. The door of The Jointure was always open to the painter Louis Ginnett who would come down from Chichester House in the High Street to talk about his murals on a Sussex theme. These are now displayed in a sixth-form college in Brighton. Hilary Pepler was a frequent visitor. Augustus John called occasionally to collect bundles of hand-made japan paper which Brangwyn received from a supplier they shared and, in 1941, drew his portrait. Lizzie and Kenneth Center kept the house and studios in order and Chatsfield the gardener kept them all supplied with fresh fruit, flowers and vegetables.

THE ROCKEFELLER CENTER

Christ is always being crucified *Brangwyn* [1]

Undaunted by the traumas of the British Empire panels Brangwyn embarked on another large-scale mural project. This too was to prove controversial. The Rockefeller family had built a towering seventy-storey skyscraper in New York, which dwarfed St Patrick's Cathedral beside it and was intended to be a centre of commerce and culture. Three distinguished artists were invited to produce competitive designs for the main lobby. These were Matisse and Picasso, who refused to compete, but Diego Rivera accepted, on the condition that his designs would be unquestioned. Consequently Brangwyn and José Maria Sert were commissioned on a non-competitive basis.

The commission was to represent New Frontiers and the murals were to be painted in monochrome with some lettering. For a while Brangwyn was stumped, but further guidance from New York suggested that it should consist of four panels with the themes:

Man's family relationships
His relationship as a worker
His relationship as a part of government
His ethical and religious relationships

The Jointure studios, tall as they were, could not accommodate the huge canvases so Brangwyn rented a room at Brighton Art Gallery. He later presented the gallery with a set of his etchings in gratitude.

Diego Rivera was a communist and, determined to use his mural for political propaganda, included a portrait of Lenin. This infuriated the Rockefeller family and they insisted that it be painted out. Rivera furiously refused and, when a storm of anti-Leftist indignation broke out, Rivera was dismissed, the mural removed and Sert was asked to supply an extra, replacement, panel to fill the space.

This furore had unfortunate consequences for Brangwyn. His design for the fourth panel was based on the Sermon on the Mount and included the figure of Christ, but the dissenters insisted that if Lenin could not be included then neither should Christ be shown. There was further discussion about Christ's suitability for the Center, given that He had overturned the tables of the money-changers in the Temple. It was then suggested that a Great Light would be a workable substitute, but Brangwyn replied that this representation of Holiness would have equal religious significance. Eventually, though in some trepidation, Brangwyn took no notice of the dispute and included the figure of Christ, but as a back view and in silhouette. Fortunately, in 1934, the Rockefeller family received the murals with pleasure and without comment.

Sert obtained permission to use a rich purple-black and, by comparison, Brangwyn's mural, obediently painted in monotone, appears insipid. He would have far preferred to have used colour but, remembering the problems he had with the House of Lords, he scrupulously complied. He used pale ochre as a mid-tone, with raw umber for the dark areas and a warm white for the highlights.

He was to work on two more mural commissions in his lifetime. The largest, painted in 1935, was a lunette for the Odhams Press building in Long Acre in London which covered an area of approximately 180 square feet. Then, to his delight, in 1937, he was asked to add four more panels to add to those he painted for the Skinners Company thirty years before. He feared that, at 68, he might not be strong enough to undertake the work and he found climbing ladders difficult, but he completed the panels satisfactorily. They had been his first important murals and they proved to be his last.

Throughout his life he was frequently incapacitated by exhaustion brought on by overwork and he suffered from undiagnosed stomach pains and latterly, rheumatism. Towards the end of his life he became hypochondriac, expecting his demise imminently and was daily surprised that he hadn't 'fallen off the plank'.[2]

MUSEUMS

Art should have meaning and message and be accessible to all Brangwyn [1]

Brangwyn was by nature generous. He began to give away his work and his treasures to museums and galleries as early as 1917 but in 1935 he began to sort his affairs in earnest. Walter Spradbury, a watercolourist and poster designer living near Walthamstow, heard about the proposed dispersal and approached him with a suggestion.

William Morris was born at the Water House in Walthamstow and since the turn of the century the local council had made several unsuccessful attempts to turn it into a museum; they had amassed a collection of works by Morris in the process. Spradbury suggested to Brangwyn that his material relating to Morris could be donated to the council to encourage the project. Brangwyn leapt at the idea, feeling it would be a way of repaying the debt he felt he owed Morris. He was equally delighted when he was reunited with Mackmurdo, by then aged 84, who offered to contribute some of his own Arts and Crafts collection. The council was enthusiastic and said that the public health authority, who was using the premises, could be relocated in about three years.

Brangwyn put together a quantity of works by Morris and included some by other members of the Pre-Raphaelite Brotherhood, including Holman Hunt, Millais, Rossetti, Burne-Jones and Ford Madox Brown and some of their contemporaries such as Leighton, Watts and Alma-Tadema. He also added work by his own contempories, George Clausen, Walter Crane, Charles Shannon, Napier Hemy, Arthur Melville and DY Cameron and donated twenty-three of his own paintings. Until the Water House could be vacated the collection was temporarily loaned to the city of Liverpool. Walthamstow Council formally accepted the gift and, in gratitude, named the proposed museum, The William Morris Gallery and Brangwyn Gift.

Without Lucy, Lizzie became the staunch protector of her master, guarding him from unwarranted interruption and running the household to a strict routine. The front door was invariably shut in the faces of uninvited callers, but one who came knocking proved to be an insistent young man. This was William, the 21-year-old son of Albert de Belleroche. His father, an esteemed painter and acquaintance of Brangwyn's, had moved to Rustington and William suggested that the two Sussex-based artists should share an exhibition. Such was Willie's power of persuasion that they agreed and in 1934 a joint exhibition of their lithographs was held at Worthing Art Gallery.

Brangwyn was then engaged upon his third set of lithographic Stations of the

Cross. He was as usual anticipating his death and in penitence portrayed himself among the crowds on the road to Christ's crucifixion. He confessed to William de Belleroche that:

When I think of all the things that I've done in my life I sometimes wonder if I've been saved. That's one of the reasons why I'd like to make up for things. I'd like to paint one or two noble subjects before I die–the Last Supper, the Baptism of Christ–something that would, in a way, make up for the time I've wasted in my life. I only hope that when my hour comes I shall die in piety. Without God I am nothing.[2]

Brangwyn again used a device whereby the main subject is shown in a bright light in the background of his lithographs. The viewer is therefore invited to join a group of onlookers in the foreground. This construction both heightens the emotional involvement of the viewer and focuses concentration on the subject by presenting it through a dark frame of figures.

Most of the edition was printed on paper but three sets were printed on sycamore wood following the experiment of James Richardson of Warminster. This innovative process made the lithography more durable than when printed on paper and removed the need for protective glass. They were reproduced as a book entitled *The Way of the Cross* for which GK Chesterton wrote an introduction. Brangwyn was by then almost 70, the work shows signs of his failing powers and his expressive drawing was occasionally ugly and distorted, but the Stations nevertheless have a powerful intensity of feeling.

Brangwyn was concerned that these lithographs should be housed in religious institutions. He felt it was unacceptable to sell his religious works on the open market. They were therefore presented to Campion Hall, Oxford, and to Brighton Art Gallery. In Brighton an exhibition of the donated work was opened by Hilaire Belloc in 1935. Belloc wrote of his pleasure in '…having this opportunity of telling Brighton people that you are the first artist of our time–which has the great merit of being true.'[3]

Belleroche came up with another idea. He was friendly with Gaspard Lefebvre, a Benedictine monk at the monastery of St André in Bruges, who was editor of the Catholic magazine *L'Artisan Liturgique*. Belleroche's first suggestion, that the Stations should be reproduced in the magazine led to a proposal for an exhibition of Brangwyn's religious art to be held at the monastery. A set of Stations, printed on sycamore wood, was immediately dispatched to them. However the proposed exhibition proved difficult. It would have to be small because only a few areas of the monastery would be available to the public and no women could be admitted.

Brangwyn was excited by the chance to exhibit his work in the beloved city of his birth and had put together a substantial amount of work. He therefore asked if it was possible for the bulk of it to be exhibited nearby in the city. Belleroche went one better. He approached Paul Lambotte, the Honorary Director of Fine Arts for Belgium, and told him that, if a large retrospective exhibition could be held in Bruges, Brangwyn might be persuaded to give his works to the city on a permanent basis. Lambotte, in his turn, built on the idea and offered the Hotel Arents as a permanent Brangwyn Museum.

Brangwyn was overjoyed. The earlier plan for a Brangwyn Museum in Tokyo had come to naught. An earthquake wrecked the site and Matsukata lost the money with which he intended to pay for it.

Brangwyn knew the Arents House. It is part of the Gruthuuse Palace, a beautiful 15th-century building near the church of Nôtre Dame and the Musée Communale. He immediately began drawing up plans and had a firm idea as to its style. He wrote instructions to Belleroche.

> The Hotel Arents will have to be arranged as it were my own home. Not a museum, but a private house where FB has lived. It must have some old pots on the tables, tapestries on the walls and a cat or two sitting by the fireplaces. A few comfortable, solid oak seats should be distributed in the rooms so that the old Bruges folk could come and sit down, smoke their pipes, read the papers— or look at my pictures.

The museum was opened on 29 July 1936 amid much congratulation from distinguished Belgian dignitaries, artists and writers and, to add to Brangwyn's pleasure, he was made a Citoyen d'Honneur of Bruges and a Grand Officer of the Order of Leopold II.

Belleroche continued to make frequent visits to Ditchling and he wrote two anecdotal books, *Brangwyn Talks*, and *Brangwyn's Pilgrimage*. They give a valuable flavour of Brangwyn's colourful speech and lively reminiscences, describing his eccentricities and life at The Jointure. On 29 September 1948 he wrote to Praill telling him of his plans for a third volume though he predicted difficulties with it because he had 'had enough trouble getting him to allow me to publish the life story which is coming out, which is a continuation of *Brangwyn Talks*.'[4] Brangwyn accepted Belleroche's books and gave inscribed copies of them as presents, but through modesty added jocular protestations. Unfortunately these left his friend with a reputation as something of a scrounger and a literary romancer. However, Belleroche's diligent recording of Brangwyn's life is now respected and valued as a vivid account of the artist in private at The Jointure. Belleroche also bought an extensive collection of works by Brangwyn on his own account. This, along with the work which Brangwyn gave him, has in the main been preserved. Belleroche, as well as being instrumental in setting up the Brangwyn Museum at the Arents House Bruges, had connections in France, at Orange in the Vaucluse, and there, in 1947, he opened a second permanent collection of Brangwyn's work.

RETROSPECTIVE

There aren't any opinions on art–or there shouldn't be. Leave it to time, my boy. If a work is good it will be good forever. If it is bad you won't improve it by slanging *Brangwyn* [1]

On the eve of the Second World War Brangwyn made preparations at The Jointure by building two bomb shelters, one in the house and one in the garden. The main shelter was built onto the back of the house. It had a flat roof constructed of reinforced concrete two feet deep. It covered a small area of paving in front of the downstairs chapel, blocking its view of the garden. A door led from the shelter into the first, roadside, studio and it linked the two wings of the house through one of the oldest rooms, the brick-floored dairy, or Pots Room, in which he used to mix his paints and clean his palette.

In 1941 the Water House in Walthamstow was still not available and in fact was not to be ready until 1950. The collection of works destined for the planned Morris Museum was still in Liverpool. Brangwyn considered this to be unsafe and he also thought it would be wise to find a refuge away from the south coast. He therefore bought Dover's Court in Chipping Campden and moved the Morris collection out of danger. The etcher FL Griggs built the house and his widow was allowed to stay on as caretaker. Brangwyn would have liked to move there himself but Lizzie wouldn't budge. His visit to the house was his last trip away from The

Jointure. In that year he was knighted, but declared that he was too frail to attend the investiture.

From then on he never left The Jointure and it became his whole world. His days followed a routine. He rose early and had coffee and medicinal charcoal biscuits for breakfast. He would be in the studios soon after 9 and, with a short break for 'elevenses', work through till about 3. Lizzie would then serve a simple lunch, usually meat and potato pie, or what Brangwyn called a 'playful sausage'.[2] After the meal there would be a short rest and a walk round the garden he found so inspiring.

Only in the last few years did this routine alter. Then, through the pain of his rheumatism, he resorted to rising late and retiring in the early hours of the morning. He was 5 foot 8 inches in height, stocky and full of sturdy Taurean determination. In his youth he was mostly clean-shaven, but later grew a beard to hide what he thought, mistakenly, was a weak chin. His eyes were full of merriment, testifying that his habitual grumbling, particularly about his health, rarely dipped into deep depression. Work was his mainstay and cure. His pencil was rarely out of his hands, even to his last days. He drew continuously, exploring ideas for his work and to record his observations, but he used the backs of bills, old letters or even envelopes, never considering these sketches for exhibition. However, hundreds have been found, framed and prized for their intimate immediacy and humour. For a professed non-intellectual he had a fine collection of books and a wide knowledge of art history.

The Jointure afforded him the space and privacy he needed, where, as he recommended to Kenneth Center, 'one should be free to walk in the garden without one's trousers'. He bought adjoining tracts of land and opened up his existing gardens, forming long vistas, lined with espaliered apple trees. Large earthenware oil jars, which Brangwyn brought back from the Mediterranean, punctuated the path along the 'top' lawn and on a low wall behind them he displayed a collection of smaller clay pots made by Mary Seton, the wife of GF Watts. These were originally made for Sir William Richmond in Hammersmith but had found their way into Brangwyn's garden. He wouldn't have been able to resist them. At the far end of the lawn he planted a large square-sculptured laurel hedge into which he cut an archway. Through this was a cool and secret Italianate courtyard over which presided the bust of Socrates which Brangwyn bought in Venice. It had lain for years in the garden of his friend Professor Antonio Fradeletto, the local MP, who instigated the Venice International Exhibitions for which Brangwyn designed the British rooms in 1905 and 1907. The exhibitions later became the Venice Biennale. The bust originally came from Spalato, or Split in the former Yugoslavia. Fradeletto had found it being used as an anchor with an iron hook inserted into the head.

Brangwyn surmised that it might well have come from the palace of the Emperor Diocletian. There was no doubt that it was Socrates, he said, though the nose was damaged.[3] He allowed ivy to grow over it as a wreath to hide the hook. Socrates's benign gaze was reflected in the mirroring water of a false well made from a large, brick-encased, copper wash boiler from the original Tudor kitchen.

Brangwyn even drew with his stick in the concrete between the flagstones on any new paths, sometimes rippling lines and sometimes flowers. In fresh plaster on new walls he would inscribe the familiar F & LB initials intertwined around a sacred heart and cross, the emblem of his devotion to his religion and his wife. Everywhere in the garden stone cupids, shells and bits of medieval sculpture peeped from the foliage even as his painted figures, birds and animals peopled his murals.

His planting was exotic and architectural with statuesque globe artchokes, palms, acanthus and gunneras. He used his flowers and foliage as inspiration for his murals, particularly the British Empire panels, where among a plethora of plants, rhubarb leaves, sunflowers, convolvulus and daisies from his garden proliferate. His flowerbeds were planted with massed blocks of flowers, lilies, roses, irises and billowing peonies. He loved blue flowers, ceanothus was under-planted with bluebells and wisteria softened the arched buttresses. Long, low retaining walls made of assorted stones, some carved, were punctuated with great mounds of rock plants.

His afternoon tour might result in a posy for the house, the stems cut with the scissors he habitually carried. A local gardener told us that once, when a fruit cage of netting was constructed to keep the birds out, Brangwyn cut a hole in it 'to let the poor buggers in'.

Visitors, if they were to be admitted, were asked to call at teatime and, weather permitting, they would be marched down to admire the orchards and vegetable garden. In the evening he was usually joined by whichever artist had come to live in the garden studio. In the 1920s Brangwyn fashioned the studio from a coach house in the entrance yard and in the war he offered it as a schoolroom for refugee children.

Brangwyn suffered several disasters during the war. In 1939 a depository containing Matsukata's collection of the paintings, destined for the doomed museum in Tokyo, was destroyed in a fire and some of Brangwyn's most important early works were burned. The carved facia of the Rowley Gallery received a direct hit and in 1941, the SS *Empress of Britain* was torpedoed and sunk.

Brangwyn also began to lose old friends. William Walcot in 1940 and Sir Frank Short in 1944 successively lived and died in the Garden Studio. Mackmurdo died in 1942. He lost Chatsfield, the gardener and was bereft when Jock, the mongrel bought as a replacement for his beloved dog Roger, died too. Brangwyn was convinced that he was the next to go, but he had fourteen years left and the postwar years were to bring him yet another prestigious honour.

In 1947, when nearly 80, he produced a series of powerful religious paintings for St Mary's College, Lindthorpe and, in 1950, the William Morris Gallery and Brangwyn Gift in Walthamstow was opened by the prime minister, Clement Attlee.

The Festival of Britain in 1951 was the spark which kindled new and rapid developments in modern art and design. Plastic and nylon, industrially dyed in bright synthetic colours, abounded. The basic principles of the Arts and Crafts movement continued to endure and develop behind the scene but abstract and Pop art prevailed. Brangwyn who, throughout his life, had tried to keep pace with artistic movements finally disapproved. He deplored what he called 'stunt' art. It went against his Arts and Crafts principles when he realised that an artist's motivation was to shock, deliberately to try and change fashion instead of letting the process evolve naturally, to work for fame and monetary gain instead of for love of the work itself. He believed that 'art is individuality added to tradition', but that this is achieved through a regime of industrious work, coupled with the pursuit of technical excellence, and that inspiration comes from the Creator.

As part of the Festival of Britain's South Coast celebrations, the curator of Worthing Art Gallery, LM Bickerton, asked Brangwyn if he would once again exhibit his work. Brangwyn refused, saying, 'I have not exhibited for years as the spirit of the time is against me.' But once again the persuasive William de Belleroche stepped in and 105 works were exhibited, the majority loaned by Willie himself. Sir Gerald Kelly, then President of the Royal Academy, opened the exhibition and took a fresh look at the neglected artist.

> I have a very great admiration for Frank Brangwyn's work, and I regret that he has emulated Achilles in retiring to his tent at Ditchling. He is a difficult man to get at. I have only once been able to get into the presence and that was because we had a mutual friend at Ditchling...but I shall be proud to open an exhibition of the works of a man who will be remembered when we and all our little isms and fooleries have been chucked into the discard.[4]

'Tell him I'm dead.' Lizzie had taken a telephone call from Kelly who was offering Brangwyn a singular honour. Enthused by the Worthing exhibition he decided to use his high office to persuade his fellow academicians to agree to a Brangwyn retrospective at the Royal Academy–the first ever offered to a living artist. This was a real accolade, but when he received the news from Lizzie Brangwyn dismissed it out of hand. This time it was Lizzie who was persuasive.

The more stubbornly he refused the offer, the longer she denied him butter at his table. Finally he relented and, in October 1952, 470 works, a tiny fraction of his life's work, were exhibited in the Diploma Galleries at the Royal Academy.

The exhibition caused a gratifying flurry of interest, but Brangwyn as usual grumbled about it. In a letter to his friend Elinor Pugh, the neice of Mackmurdo, he writes that he thinks it must be a 'silly show, from the catalogue it must be full of rubbish. The best thing is the sketch of our dear old Mack which I had given to the RA.' In the same letter he advises her, 'Never read press cuttings, they are inevitably inaccurate.'[5] The exhibition moved on to Brighton Art Gallery and, shortly after that, was shown at Ferens Art Gallery in Hull. Later, in 1954, the Usher Art Gallery in Lincoln staged an exhibition and that was to be the last in Brangwyn's lifetime. His work was out of step with the Fifties and, within his lifetime, his diminished reputation never fully recovered.

The time had come for a tidy-up. He and Kenneth Center went through all that remained in the studios, making difficult decisions about what should be kept, given away, or put on bonfires. Dover's Court was no longer needed so Brangwyn sold it. Brangwyn had allowed the etcher Griggs's widow to continue to occupy the house and the new owner also, kindly, let her stay there for her lifetime.

What to do with The Jointure itself was the next problem. With typical generosity Brangwyn decided that it should be used as a home for six artists, 'with a parrot to keep them in order'.[6] For a while the Brangwyn roost was ruled by a disagreeable and demanding parrot. Lucy had been particularly fond of parrots and soon after her death Brangwyn and Lizzie were startled when a stray parrot flew in through her bedroom window and perched upon her bed.[7]

Brangwyn set up an endowment on The Jointure. If, for some reason, artists couldn't use the house Brangwyn thought it might be used as a home for children, but neither scheme came to fruition. The sums required to endow The Jointure were large and kept increasing. Fearing that he could not sustain them Brangwyn cancelled the payments. A similar plan for Temple Lodge had failed for the same reason. Brangwyn had rented the house but, before he gave it up, he offered to buy it and present it to the Borough of Hammersmith with a collection of works by notable local artists ranging from Zoffany to Sir William Richmond.

Brangwyn's last years were lonely. His work is crowded with people but perhaps this subconsciously reflects the fact that he lacked the warmth and daily companionship of a family. He wrote to his friend Walter Spradbury that it is 'for me a bit sad to sit by a poor fire' on Christmas day 'and dream of my dear ones gone and all I might have done to make them happy.'[8] This dream probably included Lucy, his parents and siblings with whom he had maintained little contact and probably his son James.

He became superstitious, refusing to pass anyone on the stairs and taking the last two steps at the top together. A gypsy once told him he would die in a fire and thinking that this fearful conflagration was imminent he would rise in the night to check in case logs had fallen from the hearth. In fact it was much of his best work that was destroyed by fire when the warehouse where it was stored went up in flames was during World War II.

Late in life he wrote to Philip Macer-Wright 'I can still do a bit of wild water-colour' and such was the strength of his compulsive drive that, as he grew weak and incapable of daily work, he was constantly troubled that he hadn't done enough. Even though he was probably one of the most prolific of artists ever he was not satisfied. As Picasso said, 'An artist never finishes.' Gertrude Stein said of Picasso, 'He did not set himself the problem of expressing truths which all the world can see but the truths which only he can see'.[9] But the truth when it is expressed can be mysteriously recognised by the world, and the world recognised it plentifully in Brangwyn's work. No true artist ever reaches his elusive vision of perfection and only mediocre artists think they have achieved it. Only the blindness that afflicted his last days halted Brangwyn's quest. Finally, on 11 June 1956, he died quietly in his bed.

The ever-watchful and constant Lizzie remained at his bedside throughout his last days. She wrote to Mackmurdo's niece, Elinor Pugh.

I miss him very much after so many years. He pleaded for me not to let them put him into a nursing home and I promised him he would remain at The Jointure until the end. He did not want a nurse, only me, so I toiled on night and day for two weeks. When he became very ill I had to get a nurse but he called for me. He was a good patient. I know he was happy although in so much pain in his spine and he knew he would pass out at The Jointure, they injected into the spine to help him. I held his hand to let him know it was me. He knew I was very tired and said, 'When I have gone on you must rest and not let anyone worry you.' He said goodbye to me, he clenched my hand and he passed away quietly, but he left everything in perfect order. I lost all my hair through all the worry but it is coming back nicely now. [The] Jointure is sold to friends of Sir Frank's and they are settled in now.[10]

Brangwyn was buried beside Lucy at St Mary's Catholic Cemetery next to Kensal Green Cemetery. At the funeral Sir Gerald Kelly and Humphrey Brooke represented the Royal Academy. Maurice Boulanger stood in for the Belgian ambassador and Professor Valeer attended on behalf of the museums. Edgar Peacock was present with Mrs N Brangwyn and Mrs E Dowling, his sisters-in-law, and Mrs V

Kidd and Mrs W Wright, his neices. All he requested was that some leaves from the grounds of The Jointure should be scattered on his grave. Lizzie put his letters to Lucy in the coffin but, on his instructions, burned all other letters and private papers.

Obituaries hailed him as a grand old man of British painting, a Renaissance artist still working in the mid-twentieth century, failing to recognise the impact he had made on design and decorative art in the twentieth century.

Even when examples of his best work in all media were assembled for the retrospective exhibitions in 2006, assessing it as an entity still remains a challenge. He presents the viewer and critic with a conundrum, refuting any fixed opinion with surprises. What is evident in all his work, in all the different media, is that the freedom he cherished was supported by technique but not stifled by convention nor imposed upon by formal training. He worked with innocent simplicity, generosity and humility, without intellectual dissection or introspective anxiety. He grumbled but was incapable of malice.

For him work was play, as it had been from his childhood spent largely in his father's workshop. This playfulness made his art fresh, radical and vivacious, but it led him towards the grotesque and over-hasty sketchiness. He tended towards the illustrative when it was out of favour, but this grew out of his strong need to communicate. Each achievement led him to another and he experimented with new methods and ideas. To have reined in this enthusiasm would have impeded his momentum. He never settled back on his successes and grew stale. He could have safely continued to produce oil paintings of the quality of the Skinners panels and found a secure position in art history books as an esteemed Edwardian but his nature was too full of curiosity and energy to stay in one mode. The rapid developments of the times, both artistic and national, drove him on. He had experienced poverty and feared it even when he was wealthy. He determinedly viewed himself as a jobbing workman rather than a well-heeled society artist and, as a result, accepted too many commissions and completed them in haste. But, nevertheless, his genius supported them. Such was his control over his innate talent that he never stopped and questioned his ability, only his message. Essentially this was his love of humanity and nature, his abhorrence of the cruelties of war and the importance of working for the love of the work itself, in humility and without self-aggrandisement. His work was his life.

Now the time for twenty-first century reckoning has come. To an extent Brangwyn has been re-accepted as a master, certainly as one of the chief artistic forces of his time, as C Lewis Hind predicted in 1904. His uniqueness is seen as an attribute and his determination not to adhere to the vagaries of fashion a strength. His contribution to the artistic developments of the twentieth century has been recognised by critics as being more pervasive than it appears, or has been acknowledged. His work has, of course, been assessed within the context of his time, but it will outlive opinions of the age and present itself again in later centuries.

APPENDIX: JAMES CHESTERFIELD BRANGWYN

While Brangwyn was in Cornwall in 1886, aged 19, he had a passionate affair with Katie, the daughter of Joseph Chesterfield, one of the fishermen in Mevagissey.

She bore him a son on 2 October 1886 and called the boy James Chesterfield. She didn't, however, register Brangwyn as the father of the child. Brangwyn's strong ambitions and lack of money caused him to abandon his sweetheart and son and he took a studio in London. However, it is evident from his paintings that he was in Cornwall frequently during the boy's first years. His oil painting 'Mending nets at Gorren' depicts fishermen in a boatshed in the village next to Mevagissey. He also painted an unusually charming oil of a woman and a small boy in a rowing boat at nearby Polruan in the Fowey river. Both were painted in 1887. Despite continuing to work in London and abroad, Brangwyn produced paintings of the area until 1890.

In1888 Katie married Thomas Laurence and produced two daughters. They all lived with her parents and her sister Edith in a four-roomed cottage at Cliff in Mevagissey. From 1901, after his grandparents had both died, Edith took the major role in the care of the young James. After 1901 there is—so far—no record found of Katie and Thomas's whereabouts. but James remained with 'Aunt Edie' and spent his childhood in Mevagissey.

Although it appears that he did not know his father was an artist, James went to Truro Art College and won a scholarship to study art in Spain. Nevertheless when he sailed to Australia on the *Oroya* on the 11 February 1909 he stated that his profession was 'labourer'. His grandmother, Grace Chesterfield had a brother, Thomas Davis, who had a farm near Cardwell in North Queensland. In 1908, possibly realising that he was dying, Thomas had made provision for James in his will leaving him his land, which was mostly laid down to timber. James must have known his great-uncle only briefly because Thomas died on 15 June 1909. (He continued to manage the land until the 1950s.)

James found work in Brisbane as an apprentice to a leading firm of signwriters. He excelled in adding pictorial touches to the signs. He became so valued as a worker that, when war broke out in 1914, James feared that his boss, Victor Day, would not let him join up. So, although he had six months left on his indenture he, like his father before him, 'shot the moon', enlisting at Rockhampton, some 450 miles north of Brisbane. He signed up with the Australian Expeditionary Force as James Chesterfield, again putting down his profession as 'labourer', presumably to get Victor Day off his tail.

A few weeks later he married Minnie Hope Ainsworth, a tailoress. The wedding took place on 18 December, in the parish Church of St Andrew, South Brisbane,

James Chesterfield Brangwyn, photograph

and, on this occasion, the surname on the marriage certificate is put down as Brangwyn. His father is named as Frank Brangwyn. Presumably having been told only that Brangwyn was a painter, James assumed he was a house painter because he dignified his father's occupation by entering it, aptly, as 'decorator.' His mother is named as Catherine Elizabeth, which he might have guessed to be the formal name of Kate E Lawrence. Katie was in fact christened Helen Kate and this uncertainty suggests that he was kept in ignorance of his parents' real identity until his marriage. With brown eyes and dark curly hair James inherited his father's looks as well as his talent.

His sudden change of surname necessitated a Statutory Declaration in the army records. Either the Forces insisted on his proper parental origin or it was required for his marriage, but it is probable that it was only at that late point that James made enquiries.

During the war James served first in Egypt in 1916 and then in France, where on 4 July 1918 he suffered a gunshot wound to his left hand. He was invalided to the UK three days later and hospitalised in Birmingham. Minnie travelled to England in 1916 on the last ship to take civilians and stayed at Angle House, East Hill, St Austell in Cornwall.

On his discharge from the army in 1919 James held the rank of lance-corporal. He and Minnie sailed back to Australia on the *Königen Louis*, arriving there on 21 June. Later that year, on 29 December, their daughter Berneice was born. Another girl named Hope was born on 9 March 1922 and Howell (known as Jim) arrived on 26 April 1924.

When James had arrived back in Australia a rival sign-writer to Day was waiting for him on the quayside, but James insisted on honouring the six months that he owed Day. An acrimonious period followed which James fuelled by working to rule.

When he left he set up a thriving commercial sign-writing workshop of his own in George Street, Brisbane. He was joined in the business by his daughter Hope and his son Jim, who eventually took it over.

James had already proved himself a keen artist in Australia. He was an exhibiting member and on the committee of the Royal Queensland Art Society. Besides oils and watercolours he was a fine wood carver and brass worker. James's children and grandchildren also inherited artistic talents but James never divulged the identity of his father during his lifetime. In those days the revelation of illegitimacy would have caused a scandal, for James, for his mother and for his famous father.

After James's death on 26 May 1962 Albert Sherman, a friend from Truro Art School, revealed the identity of James's parents to his children. Albert had also emigrated and James clearly kept in touch with him as a confidant. Albert told them that Brangwyn had been an eminent painter but by then Brangwyn was no longer famous.

It is not known whether Brangwyn told Lucy about his son. If she did know she might have been greatly distressed because, after a miscarriage, she was unable to bear children. This could have been a further reason for her alcoholism. No record has yet been found of Brangwyn having supported James financially. He was poor when James was born but, later, he was generous with his considerable fortune. Rumours of Brangwyn's having a son in the colonies existed. Rodney Brangwyn hinted at the possibility in his book, but only now has the true story been told.

James Brangwyn signwriting, Townsville, 1913, photograph

1867 Brangwyn born at 24 rue de Vieux Bourg, Bruges (now 30 Oude Burg) to Eleanor (née Griffiths, Welsh) and William Curtis Brangwyn (English). Curtis, an architect designer, had worked with GE Street. He had a workshop in Bruges producing embroideries and furniture in the neo-Gothic style, for the refurbishment of churches and other buildings

1874 Curtis Brangwyn moves the family back to London where he works on a number of projects. The family live in 19 Richmond Gardens (now demolished) Shepherds Bush. Brangwyn attends a nearby Catholic kindergarten

1877 The family moves to 30 Grange Gardens (now 27 Minford Gardens)

1878-79 Brangwyn intermittently attends Westminster City Grammar School, but prefers to work in his father's architect's office and to draw in the streets, museums and galleries in London

1882 AH Mackmurdo discovers him and he is befriended by Harold Rathbone. They both give him instruction and Mackmurdo finds him employment in the Morris workshops. Both Morris and Mackmurdo imbue him with the philosophy of the Arts and Crafts Movement

1884 Brangwyn leaves Morris and supports himself by selling his work and painting signs and the names of boats in Sandwich, Kent. Signs on with the *Garibaldi* and sails as a working seaman back to London

1885 'A Bit on the Esk' (oils) exhibited at the Royal Academy. Occasional work for Morris, takes lodgings at 39A Queen Square, Bloomsbury. Spends time in Mevagissey, Cornwall.

1886 'Waterlogged' (oils) exhibited at RA. Paints ceiling at Pownall Hall, Cheshire, to a design by Herbert Horne. Occasional work for Morris. His illegitimate son, James Chesterfield, is born in Mevagissey.

1887 'Sunday' (watercolour) exhibited at RA. Works in Cornwall in the style of the Newlyn School

1888 'Barkstrippers' exhibited at RA. Spends time in Cornwall and London and voyages to Constantinople

1889 'When we were boys together', 'All hands shorten sail' and 'Minutes are like hours' (oils) exhibited at the RA. Rents 4 Wentworth Studios, Manresa Road, Chelsea. Joins the Royal Naval Volunteers

1890 'Funeral at Sea' is exhibited first at the Society of British Artists and then at the Paris Salon. Elected member of the Society of British Artists. Sails to Spain and Tunisia, Turkey and Romania and possibly to Antwerp and the Danube. Leases 14 Trafalgar Studios, Chelsea

1891 First one-man exhibition at Royal Arcade Gallery, Bond Street. 'From the Scheldt to the Danube'. Founder member of the Chelsea Arts Club. Illustrates *The Graphic* magazine. Sails to South Africa with William Hunt, paid for by Larkin, returning by Madeira. Takes No 4 Stratford Studios, Kensington, but keeps 14 Trafalgar Studios

1892 Joins the Japan Society in London. TJ Larkin, Alfred East and Seigfried Bing are fellow members. Exhibition of South African paintings commissioned by Larkin for his Japanese gallery in Bond Street. Illustrates several magazines. Becomes a corresponding member of the Munich Secessionists. Member of the Institute of Oil Painters. Travels to Spain with Arthur Melville

1893 'The Buccaneers' (oils) decried at Grafton Gallery but acclaimed at Paris Salon

1894 Thought to be in Morocco with Dudley Hardy

1895 Paints murals for Seigfried Bing's Maison de L'Art Nouveau in Paris and designs items for sale in the gallery for Bing and Tiffany. 'Trade on the Beach' bought by French government. Medal at Chicago Exhibition. 'The Blood of the Grape' and 'Scoffers' (oils) exhibited at RA.

1896 Paints 'The Dogona, Venice'. Designs carpets and other items for Bing. Founder member of the Vienna Secessionists. 'The Blood of the Grape' (oils) exhibited at the RA. Marries Lucy Ray, a nurse, on 28 January at St George's Register Office. Travels to Venice and Assisi and to Spain with Alfred East. Autumn honeymoon at Longpre in France

1897 Works for Bing

1898 Continues to work for Bing. Gold medal at Munich International Art Exhibition

1899 Designs stained glass for Tiffany. Exhibited at the Grafton Gallery. Continues to design items for Bing

1900 Ceases to work for Bing and Tiffany. Commissioned to design interiors for EJ Davis at 11-13 Lansdowne Road, Notting Hill. Commissioned by

Thomas Lane Devitt to paint a mural for the Royal Exchange with other leading British artists (completed 1906). Leases Temple Lodge in Queen Street (now 51 Queen Caroline Street) in Hammersmith. Entertains Royal Academicians and others. Associates with the group of artists living near Morris's former Thames-side home at Upper Mall, Hammersmith. Exhibits with Gill, Johnston and others at Pepler's Hampshire House Workshops

1902 Devitt commissions eleven murals for Skinners Hall. Awarded Chevalier of the Legion of Honour (promoted to Officier in 1920). Designs billiard room for Thurston and Company. Alfred East buys his 'The Cider Press' to pay off Brangwyn's debts

1903 'The Cider Press' exhibited at the Venice Biennale. One-man exhibition held in Amsterdam. Paints 'Queen Elizabeth going aboard the Golden Hind' for Lloyds Registry of Shipping's chairman's room. Brangwyn starts etching

1904 Starts the London School of Art in Stratford Road Kensington with JM Swan. Arthur Covey and William Nicholson are lecturers. Elected Associate Royal Academician. Alvin Langdon Coburn and Arthur Covey work as studio assistants.

Elizabeth Berry arrives as maid-of-all-work, marries and has a son (her soldier husband dies in WW1 and she returns as Lizzie Peacock and stays until Brangwyn's death)

1905 Designs British Room at Venice Biennale. Takes summer school to Nieuport

1906 Etching 'Santa Maria della Salute' awarded Grand Prix at the Milan Exhibition. Designs for interiors of Palazzo Rezzonico, Venice (unexecuted) Takes summer school to Bruges. Paints 'Venetian Funeral' (oils). Elected corresponding member of Society of Illustrators USA. Member of Asociación de Artistas Españoles

1907 Designs British room at Venice Biennale. 30 etchings awarded a special diploma at Barcelona International Exhibition. Paints 'Blake's Return after the Capture of the Plate Ships' for Lloyds Registry of Shipping company boardroom. Travels to Montreuil and has an extended stay in Venice

1908 'The Return of the Messengers from the Promised Land' exhibited at RA. 'The Rajah's Birthday' bought by RH Kitson and presented to Leeds City Art Gallery. Commissioned to paint 11 panels for Lloyds Registry of Shipping, the central one measuring 8x22 ft (completed 1912 and installed 1914). Commissioned by RH Kitson to make mosaic mural for the apse and chancel steps of St Aidan's Church, Leeds (completed in 1916). Enlarges the studio adjoining Temple Lodge. Probable holidays with Alfred East in his house in St Ives, Cornwall and to Bruges where Lucy breaks her ankle

1909 Commissioned to paint murals for the Canadian Grand Trunk Railway Offices, London (completed 1910). Travelled to Taormina, Sicily, to design interiors for Kitson's villa, Casa Cuseni, is emotionally affected by the recent earthquake at Messina

1910 One-man shows in Rome and at the Gross-Berliner Kunsthausstellung. Awarded Austrian state medal for Art. Travels again to Casa Cuseni to paint murals using fresco. His paintings of the ruins of Messina shown at Fine Art Society. Travels with Lucy to Paris to Paris where she has a fit

1911 Commissioned to paint murals for Cuyahoga County Court House, Ohio (completed 1915). Designs some of the street decorations for coronation of George V. Made Chevalier of the Order of the Crown, Italy. Royal visit from Crown Prince of Sweden. Travels with Lucy to Spain and the Lot, France

1912 Exhibition of etchings at Galerie Durand-Ruel in Paris. Commissioned to paint murals for Christ's Hospital school chapel, Horsham (completed 1923). Designs stained-glass windows for St Mary's, Bucklebury, Berkshire. Awarded a gold medal at Berlin Salon. AT True assists until 1914. Breaks rib in January. Travels with Lucy to Paris. Later in year suffers from rheumatism and depression

1913 Designs British Room at Ghent Exhibition using murals for Lloyds. Paints 'Master and Wardens of the Carpenters Company embarking on the Company's Barge to attend the King and Queen coming from Hampton Court to Whitehall' for Carpenters Company. Corresponding member of Prussian Royal Academy and President of the Royal Society of British Artists

1914 Designs murals for the Panama-Pacific International Exposition. San Francisco. Poster–'Britain's Call to Arms' commissioned by Frank Pick. Exhibition of etchings at New York Public Library. Gift of works to the Albertina Gallery in Vienna. Assistant JA Murphy

1915 Commission for murals in Missouri state capital, Jefferson City (completed in 1925) Poster–Kitchener's appeal. Gift of a complete set of his etchings to the Musée du Luxembourg, Paris

1916 Designs billiard room at Horton House, Northampton for Captain Winterbottom. 'The Poulterer's Shop', exhibited at RA, is purchased for the RA by the Chantrey Bequest. Exploratory operation for suspected cancer

1917 Designs a nativity window for St Mary's Church, Bucklebury. Designs exterior mural in mosaic for church (unknown) in Battersea. President of the Senefelder Club, London. Commander of the Italian Order of St Maurice and St Lazarus, in return makes gift of complete collection of his etchings. Member of the Royal Watercolour Society. Designs three lithographs for the American Navy. Brangwyn exhausted. He and Lucy escape bombardment in Hammersmith and rent a cottage at Coombe Wood on the South Downs at Ditchling

1918 Commission for lunette for Manitoba Legislative Building, Winnipeg (completed 1921). Paintings exhibited at Brooklyn Museum. Elected to the Institute of France. Designs Kyoraku Museum of Sheer Pleasure and Brangwyn Museum, Tokyo for Kijoro Matsukata (unexecuted). Poster–'Put Strength into the Final Blow', commissioned by the National War Savings Committee. Buys The Jointure in the village of Ditchling, Sussex, to which Gill, Pepler and Johnston have already moved

1919 Awarded Commander and Cross of the Order of Leopold I, Belgium. Becomes full Royal Academician. Designs Peace Pageant decorations in London. Poster–'The Ruins of War' for Canadian War Memorial Fund

1920 Enlarges The Jointure. Assistant Frank Alford until 1921

1921 Designs stained-glass window for the United Reformed Church, Northampton. Designs mosaic dome for Selfridges (unexecuted). Associate of the Royal Watercolour Society

1922 Stations of the Cross for Father Ryan's leper mission in South Africa. President of the Society of Graphic Artists. Assistant Laurence Bradshaw until 1924

1923 Gift of plates, etchings and lithographs to Albertina, Vienna

1924 Stations of the Cross for Arras cathedral (uncompleted). Exhibition of prints at the Fine Art Society, London. Large one-man exhibition at Queen's Gate opened in May by the prime minister, Ramsay MacDonald. Paints backdrop for Pageant of Empire, Wembley, London. Commissioned to paint British Empire Panels for the House of Lords, funded by Lord Iveagh (completed in 1933). Lucy dies 2 December of bronchial pneumonia

1925 Exhibition of Brangwyn's etchings at Whitechapel Art Gallery. One-man exhibition at the Vose Galleries, Boston, USA. 30 watercolours and collection of etchings donated to Cardiff. Kenneth Center assists until 1956. British Empire Panels commissioned

1926 Empire panels

1927 Empire panels. Lord Iveagh, his patron, dies. Designs stained-glass window for St Winifred's, Manaton, Devon

1928 Empire panels. Brangwyn travels to Venice. Presents Netherlands with gift of over 250 etchings and lithographs. Assistant Dean Cornwell employed intermittently until 1930

1929 Empire panels

1930 Empire panels, temporarily installed in House of Lords, are rejected. Brangwyn's designs for Pollard's exhibition in Oxford Street include whole interiors including furniture, carpets, ceramics, glass, lamps, textiles, even ashtrays. Designed in the 1900s they are seen as typifying Art Deco. Commissioned to paint huge mural for Rockefeller Center, New York (completed 1931). Designs three dining rooms for the SS *Empress of Britain* (completed 1931 but sunk 1941). Designs Egyptian setting for Chelsea Arts Ball

1931 Empire panels, work continues but with no destination. Presents Birmingham with 45 drawings. Designs stained-glass window for St Patrick's Cathedral in Dublin. 'Charity' in memory of Lord Iveagh

1932 Receives Albert Medal from Royal Society of Arts for services to decorative and commercial art. Suffers severe attack of sciatica

1933 The British Empire panels are exhibited at the Ideal Home Exhibition London. One-man exhibition at Ferens Art Gallery, Hull, and Wolverhampton Art Gallery. Designs wooden facia for the Rowley Gallery, London

1934 Stations of the Cross printed on sycamore wood. Designs for murals at the Guildhall, Hull (unexecuted). Exhibition by Brangwyn and Albert de Belleroche at Worthing Art Gallery. The British Empire panels are installed in the Swansea Guildhall. Designs Christmas cover of *Radio Times*

1935 Designs lunette for Odhams Press, London (completed 1936). Exhibition of etchings and lithographs given to Brighton Museum and Art Gallery. Proposes gift of works to preserve Morris's birthplace, the Water House, at Walthamstow (opened in 1950). Gives up the lease of Temple Lodge in Hammersmith

1936 The Brangwyn Museum opens in Bruges. Made Citoyen d'Honneur (for the third time) and Grand Officer of the Order of Leopold II, Belgium

1937 'Stations of the Cross' and 'The Last Supper' (oils) for Marist College, Middlesborough (completed 1945). Elected President of the Society of Graphic Arts. Designs stained-glass window for St Andrew and St Peter, Elvedon, Suffolk

1938 Designs crucifixion window and ten lancets for St André's monastery near Bruges. Converts the coach house at The Jointure as a garden studio and adjoining cottage. Gives up lease of Temple Lodge

1939 Exhibits in mixed exhibition, 'Painters of the Sea', at the Palais des Beaux Arts, Brussels

1940 Completes 'Stations of the Cross' with Belleroche. Buys Dover's Court in Chipping Campden, Gloucestershire

1941 Knighted but declines to attend ceremony. Starts drawings for a life of St Francis (unpublished). Visits Chipping Campden, thenceforth he never leaves The Jointure

1946 Designs 'The Wine Press' and 'The Last Supper' tapestries for the Dovecot Studios, Edinburgh (completed 1947), 'The Last Supper' and 'Transfiguration' for St Joseph's, Stokesley, North Yorkshire

1948 Produces 33 etchings for the Book of Job

1949 Brangwyn presents self-portrait to the Uffizi Gallery, Florence (49 years after the idea was suggested)

1950 The William Morris Gallery opened by the prime minister, Clement Attlee

1951 One-man show at Worthing Art Gallery opened by Sir Gerald Kelly, President of the Royal Academy

1952 First-ever retrospective of a living artist at the Royal Academy

1954 Exhibition of work in the Usher Gallery, Lincoln. Sold Dover's Court

1956 Brangwyn dies on 11 June at The Jointure of senile arteriosclerosis. Buried beside Lucy at St Mary's cemetery, Kensal Green, London. Brangwyn left £39,162 before tax and had given away over £100,000 in gifts of his and other artists' works. (1956 valuation)

I am indebted to Dr Libby Horner for additional information

BIBLIOGRAPHY

DE BELLEROCHE, William, *Brangwyn Talks*, Chapman & Hall, 1944

DE BELLEROCHE, William, *Brangwyn's Pilgrimage*, Chapman & Hall, 1948

BRANGWYN, Rodney, *Brangwyn*, William Kimber, 1978

BIRCH, Mrs Lionel, *Stanhope & Elizabeth Forbes*, Cassell, 1906

FURST, Herbert, *The Decorative Art of Frank Brangwyn*, Bodley Head, 1924

FRANKLYN GOULD, Veronica, *The Last Great Victorian*, Yale University Press, (Paul Mellon Centre for Studies in British Art) 2004

GALLOWAY, Vincent, *The Oils and Murals of Sir Frank Brangwyn*, F Lewis, 1962

HOFFMAN, Werner, *Gustav Klimt*, Studio Vista, 1972

HOLLIDAY, Peter, *Edward Johnston, Master Calligrapher*, Oak Knoll Press and the British Library, 2007

MACCARTHY, Fiona, *Eric Gill, A Lover's Quest for Art and God*, EP Dutton 1989

MACER-WRIGHT, Philip, *Brangwyn, A Study of Genius at Close Quarters*, Hutchinson 1940

NAYLOR, Gillian, *Art Nouveau 1890 to 1914*, Edited by Paul Greenhalgh, V&A Publications, 2000

PEPLER, Father Conrad, 'Ditchling, a community of craftsmen', *Dublin Review*, vol 233 No 482, no date

SALAMAN, Malcolm C, *Modern Masters of Etching*, London, no date

SHAW SPARROW, Walter, with Frank Brangwyn, *A Book of Bridges*, Bodley Head, 1920

SIMPSON, Joseph, Art in the Business Place, from the *Weekly Dispatch*, 15 April 1923

TIMMERS, Margaret, and WALTON, Ruth, *The Power of the Poster*, V&A exhibition catalogue, 2000

VALLENCE, Aylmer, *The Life and Work of William Morris*, (1897) reprinted Studio Editions, 1995

WERTENBAKER, Lael, *The World of Picasso*, Time-Life Books, New York, 1967

References

Acknowledgments
1   Walter Shaw Sparrow, *A Book of Bridges*, Bodley Head 1920

Introduction
1   Joseph Simpson, 'Art in the business place' *Weekly Dispatch* 1923
1   Vincent Galloway
2   Rodney Brangwyn
3   Rodney Brangwyn

The Gothic Revival
1   Philip Macer-Wright
2   Philip Macer-Wright
3   William de Belleroche

The Arts and Crafts Movement
1   Herbert Furst
2   William de Belleroche

The Newlyn School
1   Rodney Brangwyn
2   Rodney Brangwyn

Colourist
1   quoted by Herbert Furst
2   Philip Macer-Wright
3   Rodney Brangwyn

Art Nouveau
1   Gillian Naylor
2   Aylmer Vallence
3   Gillian Naylor
4   Gillian Naylor
5   Werner Hoffman

Decorator
1   Herbert Furst

Muralist
1   *Of Decorative Painting and Design in the Arts and Crafts*, essays edited by William Morris, 1893

2	Veronica Franklyn Gould
3	Veronica Franklyn Gould
4	Veronica Franklyn Gould
5	Veronica Franklyn Gould
6	William de Belleroche *Pilgrimage*
7	Rodney Brangwyn
8	Rodney Brangwyn

WORKS ON PAPER

1	Ruskin, *Letters to the Workmen and Labourers of Great Britain*, 1872, Margaret Timmers
2	Malcolm Salaman
3	Rodney Brangwyn
4	Rodney Brangwyn
5	Ruth Walton
6	4 April 1918, *The Letters of Arnold Bennett*, vol 3, OUP, 1970
7	see Johnston *Writing and Illuminating and Lettering* p251
8	Lael Wertenbaker

DITCHLING ARTIST-CRAFTSMAN

1	Philip Macer-Wright
2	Rodney Brangwyn
3	Philip Macer-Wright
4	Fiona MacCarthy
5	Fiona Macarthy
6	Fiona McCarthy
7	Fiona McCarthy
8	Conrad Pepler, 'Ditchling, a Community of Craftsmen' *Dublin Review*, no date
9	Rodney Brangwyn
10	Malcolm Yorke
11	Malcolm Yorke
12	Malcolm Yorke
11	Peter Holliday
14	Conrad Pepler
15	Herbert Furst
16	Malcolm Yorke
17	Peter Holliday

ARCHITECT

1	Herbert Furst
2	Rodney Brangwyn
3	private collection

4   private collection
5   letter from Fiona Rossington, Rowley's descendant, private collection
6   Simpson (see above)
7   Rodney Brangwyn
8   Rodney Brangwyn

THE BRITISH EMPIRE PANELS

1   Herbert Furst
2   Rodney Brangwyn
3   Rodney Brangwyn
4   Philip Macer-Wright

APPLIED ARTS

1   Mackmurdo quoted in Furst

THE ROCKEFELLER CENTER

1   Rodney Brangwyn
2   Rodney Brangwyn

MUSEUMS

1   Philip Macer-Wright
2   William de Belleroche *Pilgrimage*
3   Hilaire Belloc, 8 Sept 1935, private collection

RETROSPECTIVE

1   letter from FB to Philip Macer-Wright
2   Rodney Brangwyn
3   Rodney Brangwyn
4   Rodney Brangwyn
5   private collection
6   Rodney Brangwyn
7   Philip Macer-Wright
8   Rodney Brangwyn
9   Lael Wertenbaker
10   private collection

ISABELLA BIRD

Judith Jordan

ISBN: 151472703X
ISBN 13: 9781514727034

TABLE OF CONTENTS

INTRODUCTION

When Isabella Bird was sixty-four in 1895, she had the most frightening experience in all her years of travel. It was the only time that she recognized danger. "I felt the position serious," she wrote. She was two thousand miles into the interior of China. Antiforeign feeling against the "barbarians," as the Chinese called Caucasian invaders, was rampant. Hoping to neutralize hostility, Bird traveled in an open chair and wore Chinese dress. It was impossible, of course, to conceal all signs of racial differences. "What ugly eyes and straight eyebrows!," "Why is her hair like wool?," and "What nasty big feet she has!" were frequent comments. As she was carried through the city gates of Liang-Shen Hsien, "Men began to pour into the roadway from every quarter, hooting...and yelling. The crowd became dense and noisy...I recognized many cries of 'Foreign Devil!' and 'Child-Eater!'...the narrow street became almost impassable; my chair was struck repeatedly with sticks; mud and unsavory missiles were thrown with excellent aim; a well-dressed man, bolder or more cowardly than the rest, hit me a smart whack across the chest...others from behind hit me across the shoulders; the howling was infernal...There was nothing for it but to sit up stolidly, and not to appear hurt, frightened or annoyed, though I was all three."

Bird gained entry to an inn and was thrust into a shed. The innkeeper barred the street door, but it was stormed by a mob of fifteen hundred to two thousand who broke it down and poured in. "There was then a riot…The men had armed themselves with pieces of the doorway, and were hammering at the door…of my room, surging against it to break it down."

The upper door began to yield and was about to cave in when soldiers arrived. A sudden silence ensued, a rush of many feet, and the yard was clear. The soldiers remained the night. Bird concluded, "No one who had heard the howling of any angry Chinese mob can ever forget it." Next morning, a new pole fixed to her chair, Bird resumed her journey.

As the *Spectator* editorialized after her death, Bird "had never been deterred from any undertaking by its discomforts or dangers…" Isabella Bird acknowledged fear—on horseback alone in the dark with the howling of nearby wolves, clinging to a narrow precipice with a two-thousand-foot drop, threading her way over a bridge in imminent danger of collapse into rushing snow-cold waters—but with true courage, she gave fear no attention and continued on her way.

Bird, in fact, preferred her adventures spiked with peril. Picture her in Malaya perched on the lid of a basket, holding aloft a much-used umbrella. Her basket was attached by rattan to another basket, upon which sat a Malayan lad. Both baskets straddled the sides of an elephant. A scantily clad driver sat cross-legged on the elephant's head. The awkward rolling gait of the elephant caused the panniers to pitch and toss. Since Bird was heavier than the Malayan lad, she was always sliding downward and trying to wriggle herself up.

"This mode of riding," she wrote, "is not comfortable," but the "fearful joy" of the ride continued.

The driver bounced off, and the pachyderm, left to its own desires, turned into the jungle, began tearing up trees, and then went into a mudhole where he sucked up the water and squirted it over himself and his riders, soaking Bird's clothes. He then seemingly stood on his head by stiffening his proboscis and leaning upon it. Bird had had enough of this beast. She gave him a lusty whack with her umbrella, he let out a mighty roar, the Malayan lad jumped off, and Bird pitched down, clinging to the rattan. Finally, after the elephant gave himself an extravagant mud bath, order was restored. The majestic beast rolled on, down a steep bank, and into a broad river. Shortly, the elephant was entirely submerged, only the end of his trunk, far ahead, showed above the water line.

Bird wrote to her sister Hennie, "Of course we were sitting in the water, but it was nearly as warm as the air, and so we went for some distance up the clear, shining river, with the tropic sun blazing down upon it, with everything that could rejoice the eye upon its shores, with little beaches of golden sand, and above the forest the mountains with varying shades of indigo coloring." Bird concluded with, "There could have been nothing left to wish for if you had been there."

Fording a river in Tibet proved a less benign experience. She was on the back of a yak, which she described as a "mountain in motion," but switched to a horse to cross a river swollen with the spring runoff of melted snow. This was hazardous business. "The Tibetan servants knelt on the banks and prayed for safety…the interpreter, white-lipped with terror, wore dark goggles so as not to see the booming surge; everyone dashed quantities of ice-cold water over their faces 'to prevent giddiness'; girths were tightened, loads hoisted higher, and with shouts of encouragement the whole caravan plunged in." Soon the guides were up to their armpits in the roiling waters. The swollen stream had undercut the far bank, which projected in a shelf. The lead horse made it, and the man gave encouraging shouts to Miss Bird. In a desperate effort, her horse jumped for the bank, but fell short, and rolled over backward with Bird under him. Strong arms extricated her, but the force of the water knocked her down again. The horse was drowned, but she was lifted and dragged to shore, suffering severe bruises and a broken rib.

Who was this woman?

Isabella Bird was a Victorian traveler who journeyed alone to virtually inaccessible parts of the world, places then almost unknown to the English public. White women were equally unknown to the native populations, and often Isabella Bird, the first white woman they had seen, incited intense curiosity.

Isabella Bird's story is all the more exceptional, for neither Victorian patriarchal society nor her family encouraged her to pursue her interests. On the contrary, the weight of their tacit opposition was a burden she carried all her life.

The dates of Isabella Bird's birth, 1831, and death, 1904, securely bracketing the Victorian era, meant that she suffered the impediments that gender imposed on English women. The middle-class and upper-middle-class Victorian woman was expected to devote herself to her family, expected to spend her life in social duties that were, other than the nurturing of children, trivial. For women of energy, ambition, and intelligence, the Victorian age was a stifling corset.

Added to the oppression of this society, with its highly polarized sexual roles, Isabella endured the burdens of her family's elevated Evangelical principles. These Evangelical principles, with an emphasis upon practical Christian philanthropy, self-denial, and zealous proselytizing, were intensely felt. Bird's father and mother were well educated, high-minded, and of uncompromising idealism. "Good causes" were the staple of the day—not surprising in a family whose prominent cousin was William Wilberforce, liberator, humanitarian, and Christian gentleman, and whose relatives were an impressive assembly of bishops, missionaries, clergymen, members of Parliament, Oxford and Cambridge dons, and clerical wives.

Throughout her life, Isabella was faithful in her charitable deeds and in her earnest discourse to her childhood home and its Victorian, Evangelical dictates. Given these pressures, the extent of her liberation from the Victorian norms for women is astonishing. Victorian women traveled, but usually as dependents upon a husband, to the far-flung outposts of the empire or to tourist shrines or health spas. Bird traveled alone, and she eschewed the well-beaten path. Isabella Bird's uniqueness was precisely that she overcame the pressures to be submissive, self-effacing, and content with marriage, children, and a sedentary life. These strictures were particularly confining for Isabella, for she had a desire for adventure, plus the fearlessness and curiosity usually associated with the male.

That she had an operation for the removal of a spinal tumor when she was young and, years later, had additional surgery on her back make her achievements even more remarkable. Back pain was only one of her ailments, which, paradoxically, aided her escape from conventional life. Her precarious health, in fact, gave her the rationalization she needed to travel. Nineteenth-century physicians frequently prescribed travel for well-to-do patients as a remedy for what they could not cure. Isabella was never able to accept her unusual nature and the freedom that it required. She was deeply conflicted between her unacknowledged anger at being so repressed—her severe depression was a symptom of this anger—and guilt that she could not be pleased with a life devoted to service as her family expected. But the release she felt away from British society was an indication that only in such circumstances could she reconcile the anger and the guilt in her personality. Significantly, Isabella found that when she travelled on great adventures, her nervous symptoms, so common to Victorian women—depression, insomnia, backaches, headaches—disappeared. Indeed, in her middle and later years, Isabella was capable of incredible physical exertion and hardship.

Whenever Isabella Bird traveled, she wrote to her sister, Hennie, letters of extraordinary detail, written with such frequency that one wonders she had time for anything else. Her ink and papers were always with her, and no sooner was she settled than out they came. She wrote with wonderful freshness and observation, doing her best to describe fully everything that happened to her. In putting words to paper, she was exercising a control over the flux of her life. She was discovering in writing, as other women have, the need to make a narrative of her life. Virginia Woolf said that nothing was real until she wrote it down. The avidity, the tenaciousness of Bird's writing suggests that she, too, was making her life "real."

At the completion of each trip, using her journal and letters as a basis, Bird published a book. Her books sold well and eventually earned her a nationwide reputation as a traveler. Although Isabella Bird was a pioneer in the writing of travel books, she did not go to exotic places in search of material; she went as a traveler. She traveled for "recreation and interest solely." She was not a romantic and did not seek the picturesque. In an age when the English felt it a pity that not everyone was English and Christian, she was sincerely interested in people as they were, neither charmed nor shocked. Her books were, at least in the beginning, a by-product. "Travelers," she wrote her sister, "are privileged to do the most improper things with perfect propriety." Her purpose, which she never acknowledged, was adventure. Adventure was the elixir of her life. Unconventional travel liberated her; she was able to ride like a cowboy, to sleep under the stars, to wear loose garments that she insisted were feminine, and, most welcome, to avoid English society.

In the choice between comforts of civilization versus a horse and a tent, the former held no appeal whatsoever. She deplored modern river steamers that "dissipate the romance of travel by their white enamel, mirrors, gilding and electric light." Astride a horse was her favorite means of transport, particularly at a wild gallop, but she employed yak, elephant, pony, mule, scow, junk, and sampan to transverse rivers, deserts, plains, and mountains, and she slept in tent, stable, hut, caravanserai, shanty, or hovel. She delighted in staying with peasants, with remote tribes, in those areas that were "no regions for tourists" with the "savage freedom of the wilds" where she could be "blessedly bereft of the fatiguing and chattering society of the English."

In Hawaii, Isabella Bird wrote, "My eyes seek the dome-like curve of Mauna Loa...for it is as yet an unfinished mountain. It has...a pit of unresting fire on its side; it throbs, rumbles, and palpitates; it has sent forth floods of fire over all this part of Hawaii and at any moment it may be crowned with a lonely light, showing that its tremendous forces are again in activity." That the mountain was "unfinished" and that she was in its proximity excited her. "It is most interesting to be in a region of such splendid possibilities."

Isabella Bird, despite all obstacles, was able to release the "tremendous forces" within her to become the woman she was capable of being, to realize her "splendid possibilities." Certainly the path she bushwhacked of traveling by the most primitive means in remote places—Hawaii, the Rocky Mountains, northern Japan, Malaya, Persia, Korea, Tibet—of staying in native huts away from hotels and resorts, was one that had no female precedent. For a woman brought up as she had been, to make these rugged excursions, traveling in the wake neither of husband nor of the Union Jack, driven only by a love of adventure, was in itself remarkable. Isabella Bird wrote nine popular travel books and was the first woman elected to the Royal Geographical Society. This historical fiction explores and celebrates her achievements in overcoming the limitations that Victorian society placed upon her, and that she made the choices that expressed her basic nature, which enabled her to "write her own script."

CHAPTER 1

ISABELLA'S PARENTS, EDWARD AND DORA

The flames of Evangelical zeal leaped high in Dora Lawson. She was the daughter of Isabella and the Evangelical Reverend Marmaduke Lawson of Boroughbridge, Yorkshire. For many years Dora rented, from her own small allowance, a room in the village to conduct Sunday school. Teaching her five classes, from lisping little ones to young women ready for service, was her favorite occupation. Dora had not yet called herself a spinster, but at age twenty-seven, she was settling into that role when her friendship with the new curate, Edward Bird, ripened into affection.

Edward Bird had Evangelical fervor the equal of Dora's. His belief in Christianity was a massive oak that gave shelter and status to his life. He had been graduated, as had his four brothers, from Magdalene College, Cambridge, then studied law and was called to the bar at Lincoln's Inn. He joined the East India Company as a barrister of the Supreme Court in Calcutta, where he had sailed with his wife, Emma, in 1825. Emma died of cholera, and their son, Edward, died three years later. Broken in health and spirit, he returned to England, where the acorn of his belief germinated, and his conviction took root that "Without *me* ye can do nothing." Thirty-eight years old, he took Holy Orders. His first curacy was in Boroughbridge, Yorkshire, where he set himself to make up for his wasted years, to gather in souls for Christ, to achieve in the years that remained to him a lifetime's work in God's vineyard.

One late afternoon Dora Lawson told the other ladies to go home, that she would finish cleaning up the rectory. The ladies had been experimenting with making rag paper to use on the inside covers of the hymnals. The sheets were arrayed on the deal table in the kitchen to dry overnight. Inspecting them, Dora decided that the papers colored with mustard seed and heads of grain were the most successful.

The Reverend Bird, standing in the doorway, startled her. "What is the busy-as-a-bee lady doing today?" he asked.

Dora explained the project and asked which papers he favored. He pointed to the rich tones that onionskin had produced. "I like the contrast between the worn leather bindings and the glowing color of the endpapers. You can't tell a book by its cover," he laughed. Dora nodded in assent, and the Reverend Bird continued, "I feel like a threadbare old volume myself."

"Oh no, Reverend Bird, not at all. How can you say that?"

"Yes, a distinctly down-at-heels number, but what remains of my life, I dedicate to the Lord."

"Praise be to God."

"Yes, Miss Lawson." Reverend Bird drew a deep breath and looked resolute. "I believe the good Lord has directed me to you."

The Reverend Bird looked distinctly uncomfortable. He shoved his fists into his vestment pockets.

"If you would be so kind…" he began. "That is," he continued as he started to pace around the kitchen, "that is, I am hoping that you would consider becoming my partner."

Dora's heart lurched. Too full to say anything else, she repeated, "Your partner?"

"That is…" Reverend Bird felt now that he could stay the course so he plunged right in. "Will you enter the holy state of matrimony with me?"

Dora's pale cheeks lost color. The Reverend Bird went on.

"I am aware this must be a shock to you. But I have been observing you for the two years I've been in Boroughbridge. You are tireless in your service, exactly the helpmate I require. My admiration for you has ripened into affection. I ask you please to disregard the outer wrappings and heed only my pure intentions."

Still floundering, Dora managed to whisper, "Reverend Bird!"

"You're thinking of your obligations to your father. I have already secured his permission to seek your hand in marriage. I assured him, and I assure you, he would have a home with us and be welcome at our table."

Dora's head was in a whirl. She had not been thinking about her father but was questioning what she had just heard. Had dear Edward actually proposed marriage?

Reverend Bird clasped his hands together. "This is difficult, but I am honor bound to tell you that I have been married and that I had a son."

Dora lifted her eyebrows in surprise.

"Yes, I lost them both to cholera in the subcontinent."

When Dora murmured a sympathetic, "Oh," he continued.

"I was young and rash. I had not accepted Christ's offer of salvation. I now want to devote all of my energy to the Lord's work to make up for my squandered youth. If you can envision yourself as my partner in that labor, I humbly offer you a role at my side. May I hope, dear Miss Lawson?"

Dora stammered, "I am honored." She was flooded with a tempest within: sorrow for Edward's loss, pleasure that he had confided this personal history to her, pain that he had already had a wife and a child, and joy at his proposal, and yes, if she were honest with herself, disappointment. She feared the first pressings of his heart lay buried in India with his dead wife and son—but she daydreamed about his telling her that he was swept off his feet. Dora sighed and chided herself, *Those thoughts are unworthy. Edward is a fine man. No one is more fervent than he in his service to the church. That will suffice for me. Our union will be purely spiritual.* She pictured Edward, a loyal husband, and she, a devoted wife, both of them working side by side in the house of many mansions.

"I would be honored to be your wife," she murmured.

After accepting Edward's proposal, Dora had allayed her fears of union with a man by telling herself that Edward, after all, was in his midthirties; she would be spared "that" aspect of marriage, whatever "that" was. Furthermore, Edward had been married and had even fathered a son, so presumably he knew about such things, and she trusted he had outgrown them.

The wedding night was a shock and revealed an aspect of marriage that continued to be an onerous duty. Fortunately, Edward's needs were infrequent. Dora was not aware that she was caught between what Edward regarded as his old sinful life and his new righteousness.

Although Dora knew this slovenly business had something to do with how babies were born, she had only the vaguest idea of what transpired in the nuptial bed. No one had told her anything. Her exceedingly dour and reserved mother had been dead for many years; six years ago, her sister, Barbara, had been expelled from the house for her refusal to attend church. No, she was not prepared. Not for the pain, not for the blood, not for the mess. But as Edward had told her, the first time was the worst. She knew that as a wife she had to endure, so meekly she submitted. Since it had to do with begetting children, the yoke was easier to bear. Perhaps she would give birth to a boy.

On October 15, 1831, a year after their marriage, Dora and Edward rejoiced at the birth of Isabella Lucy, named after her two grandmothers. The tiny dark-eyed infant bundled in a shawl, cradled in Edward's arm, became a familiar neighborhood sight.

"The little one making calls with you, Rector?" one of Edward's communicants asked as Edward rode around his parish on his horse with Isabella in front of him.

"Yes. Dr. Marshall said to keep her out of doors as much as possible."

"She's right little and pale. "She looks like a bird," the church member guffawed.

Isabella, although frail and sickly, survived her first birthday. Her face was often white with fatigue, for Dora firmly believed in the precept "Never sleep the sun up; prayer should dawn with the day." Isabella was not too young to be taught this soul-redeeming habit. Consequently, although Dora spent many nights on her knees at Isabella's cot in prayers and supplications, she aroused Isabella before sunrise to join her in morning thanksgiving.

Although Dora yearned to hold Isabella close to her bosom, she schooled herself not to succumb to this temptation. Her duty, above all, was to drill obedience into Isabella. If she were lax, or too soft, Isabella might become headstrong and willful. The Lord demanded that His servants obey Him. Edward expected his child to be devoted to God's will. Dora had no choice.

Propping Isabella in a chair, Dora arrayed on the table in front of her a favorite book, a ball of bright yarn, a silver mug, a furry bear. When Isabella's little hand reached for the bear, Dora rapped the knuckles sharply.

"Not until I give you permission," she said. Isabella cried and looked at her, bewildered. Dora longed to hug her but did not, for she was fearful that Isabella's precarious health had made her overindulgent. Dora repeated the exercise until Isabella heeded her before reaching for an object.

This rapping of the knuckles was Dora's sole raising of her hand. She examined herself minutely on this issue, for her own mother had freely employed the switch. Dora questioned if she were remiss, for the Bible said, "He that spareth his rod hateth his son; but he that loveth him, chasteneth him betimes." But Dora could not compel herself to switch her child.

Dora's next confinement was rewarded with a boy, named Edward after his father. *Now, at last,* Dora thought when she saw Edward's radiant face peering at his son, *I've found favor. I'm on par with the sainted Emma.* But after a flickering three days, God called the infant to His own.

"The baby's soul," Dora told Isabella, "belongs with the angels."

Her breasts still leaking milk, her womb still oozing blood, Dora let her embroidery hoops fall into her lap. In her hands was a pillow sham whose half-finished floral wreath, white on white, she had put aside months ago to make the binders, the gertrudes, the hemmed nappies, and the matinee jackets that now had no use. Dora's quiet tears were more eloquent than sobs, for she habitually kept her feelings to herself.

"Edward, sometimes," Dora faltered, "sometimes I find His cross too heavy to bear." She was raking over her ledger of behavior, the commissions, the omissions, how she had failed to serve, how she deserved this punishment.

"Yes, the mills of God grind slowly, yet they grind exceedingly small," Edward concurred.

Dora, raw with loss, laid her hand on his, wanting to find solace in his arms, wishing to soften her grief against his shirtfront. She knew that Edward felt that the Lord was punishing him for his earlier worldly desires of making his fortune.

In a gesture unusual for him, Edward covered Dora's hand with his own. "We must learn to lay up our treasure in heaven," he said. "The Lord giveth, and the Lord taketh away. Blessed be the name of the Lord, through Jesus Christ, our only Mediator and Redeemer."

A few days later, when Edward was calling on a parishioner, Dora needed to confirm a quotation and went into his study. She stopped to straighten the articles on his desk, and as she was putting away a penknife, she found at the back of the drawer a small velvet-wrapped object. There in her hand was a miniature of a girl whom she knew immediately was Emma. The artist had painted her in profile, her pink cheek etched with a dimple, and her blond curls secured with a pink ribbon on the top of her head. One tendril of hair escaped and curled on the nape of her neck. Her shoulder was bare, and she looked young and vulnerable.

The lump in her throat was so large that Dora had trouble breathing. Why had Edward never shown her this picture? Why did he keep it in his top drawer? Did he sit here every day and look at her? Dora thought, *I was second best to my father, finding favor only when my sister, Barbara, was out of the household, and I am second best to my husband.* The fierce heat of jealousy blazed within her, jealousy of the dead Emma. *Emma was accepted. She found favor just as she was. But I have to be even more compliant,* Dora seethed, *even more devout just to be tolerated. Try as I do to be exemplary in every way, I can never measure up.* Her throat ached with unshed tears as she wrapped up the miniature and placed it back in the drawer.

She resolved to say nothing to Edward until she had smothered the jealous fiend and could talk about the portrait in a matter-of-fact voice. For several weeks she was more withdrawn than usual and spent even more time at her devotions, repeating again and again, "Teach me to accept Thy will."

When she could trust herself to speak, she told Edward that she had seen Emma's picture. "Why do you keep it in your desk?" she asked.

"I look at it occasionally, Dora, to remind me of my worldly ways."

"Your worldly ways?" Dora echoed.

"Yes, in those days I thought only of following a path of commerce and industry. I never thought of salvation, only of self-gratification." Edward remembered setting out for India with his bride at his side, a slip of a girl, barely eighteen. The wind blowing back Emma's bonnet, they had stood on the deck of the Indiaman *Felicity,* laughing with joy. Adventure, the thrill of sailing to a distant shore, the challenge of making his fortune, his sensuous delight in Emma were on his mind. His only concern was to pile up wealth here on Earth as his father had done. "God punished me by taking away my wife and son."

Dora didn't know what to say, and Edward continued.

"Now that I know that Christ is my Redeemer, I see the wickedness of my former ways. God has rewarded me with you."

Dora felt consoled. She knew Edward was sincere; dissembling was not in his character. But in a curious way that she could not understand, she also felt bereft. Edward, like her father, was attracted to her only because of her piety. She must become even more devout.

"Would you like to display her picture on your desk or bureau?" she asked, knowing she would not like that but unable to prevent herself from asking.

"No," Edward answered curtly.

Dora was relieved, and at the same time, she surmised that Edward did not want Emma's picture sullied, did not want her exposed to the gaze of ordinary people like herself.

"No," Edward continued, "that way of life came to an abrupt end. Christ, in his mercy, has shown me the way to salvation."

And I, Dora vowed, *must stamp out any tendency to laxness in myself or in my daughter. I must be more rigorous in discipline. My tendency to make excuses, to make allowances, to overlook must be curbed.*

Dora gave birth to Hennie when Isabella was three years old. Hennie, an infant with an angelic disposition, crowned with a halo of golden curls, adored her older sister. She looked up at Isabella with her wide blue eyes and wiggled with pleasure when her big sister peered at her over the edge of the cradle.

Being the wife of the rector, and the mother of the rector's children, compounded Dora's charge. In the face of her children's misbehavior, what would the neighbors and parishioners say? She would be judged a failure unless her daughters displayed model deportment. Her mother had also been the wife of a rector, and she had schooled her three children to be ever mindful of their role. No wonder her mother's face had so often been tense and nervous.

Hennie was compliant, but Isabella! In her, Dora saw noxious weeds to be uprooted: she was willful; she never sat still; she interrupted with blunt or outrageous comments. Only yesterday, when a petitioner came soliciting aid, she had stood in front of him and in incisive tones demanded, "Sir Malpas de Grey Tatton Egerton, did you tell my father my sister was so pretty because you wanted his vote?" She asked impertinent questions. She even told lies. She had to be curbed again and again and be told, "That is God's will."

Dora's profound fear was that Isabella would be like her own older sister, Barbara. Dora referred to Barbara as "you-know-who," for her name was not allowed to be spoken, not even in whispers, for she had declared that she no longer believed, ceasing to attend her father's services. She was unmoved by every persuasion to convince her of the truth of salvation. Dora was thankful that their mother had gone to her rest prior to Barbara's defection and that Mama, at least, had been spared that grief. The son pleaded on Barbara's behalf, but he could not placate his father, who read Barbara out of the family.

No, Dora could not permit herself to be lenient. She must be severe. Under Dora's tutelage, any idea that life was to enjoy was as foreign to Isabella and Hennie as an exotic bird of paradise in their northern English garden.

As soon as she could toddle, Hennie became Isabella's golden shadow, even doing her lessons with Isabella. Papa explained, "Women must be taught to be good wives and good mothers, for a man cannot be a good man without a good mother." Dora was patient in teaching ciphering, drawing, needlework, history, scriptures, but the responsibility of teaching the girls to be model Christians, of leading them to salvation, was awesome, and Dora was not patient; she was harsh.

Edward Bird was a man driven almost entirely by the passionate spirit that animated him in harvesting souls for the glory of God. That zeal far exceeded his stamina, for his feeble constitution could not sustain his work. After two years he was compelled to admit that he could not continue such arduous labors. His cousin Reverend Bird Sumner, bishop of Chester, interceded and presented him with the quiet living of Tattenhall in Cheshire.

Isabella was a few months old when her father accepted the curacy in Tattenhall. There his labors were crowned with joy, for he brought many to Christ. Not only did he fill the church, but he also met with petitioners at all hours who sought his spiritual guidance.

CHAPTER 2

DAY OF ATONEMENT

Isabella's most unsparing punishment took place on a Monday. The transgression itself had happened Sunday, but the Lord's Day could not be sullied, so the response to Isabella's offense was postponed. Mama and Papa's grieved faces that Sunday were a prelude to the punishment.

To Isabella, Sunday's routine was of unvarying monotony. Sick or well, winter or summer, her mother, Dora Bird, got up in the chill predawn to have more time for morning devotions; she roused her girls early so that they, too, would not develop habits of sloth. As Dora said, "Never sleep the sun up; prayer should dawn with the day."

Night terrors assaulted Isabella. It was often early morning before she was in a deep sleep, but lying abed was not permitted. In recognition of the holy day, the girls were rooted out of bed even earlier. The breakfast prayer was long, and before the dishes were cleared, Ellen and Bridget, the maids, joined the family for a lengthy exposition and earnest prayers. If it was not raining heavily, Isabella and her sister, Hennie, were allowed to walk in the garden on the gravel path, but they had to observe strict silence. Miss Ryan, their neighbor, promenaded in front of her house.

The girls were permitted to bow gravely and to say good morning. Isabella could not resist telling Miss Ryan that she had on a beautiful lavender gown, Isabella's favorite color. Miss Ryan dimpled with pleasure and acknowledged in her light voice that, thank you, she thought it was pretty, too, but the sleeves, she confessed, were set so low that she couldn't raise her arms, and she lifted them to demonstrate. The offending sleeves were inserted low off the shoulder in a series of pleats and then ballooned to the elbow to be caught at the wrist in long, tight cuffs. The skirt was pleated at the waist and descended only to the ankle, where the hem was edged in lace. Her poke bonnet was lavender silk; on the inside white lace circled her auburn curls. Dark-purple ribbons trimmed the bonnet and were loosely tied under her chin. Miss Ryan did not carry a Bible, but a silk parasol edged with tassels. She lingered a moment before her brother, Mr. Dennis Ryan, crossed the lane and took her arm.

The girls were then directed to their room to predispose their minds for the service. Shortly before eleven, as the bells began to peal, Isabella's father, the Rector Edward Bird, in his black robes, led the family, also dressed in black, carrying their Bibles and hymnals, the short distance to the church. Isabella liked the procession: being part of a greater whole, having a role to play, and being the cynosure of the congregation. Above all she liked the tolling of the five deep bells and the knowledge that only when her father, in his surplice and stole, took his place would the service begin.

Service lasted until one o'clock, when the procession reversed and the family returned home to a dinner that had been prepared the day before. Papa, in a protracted grace, entreated God to bless the cold roast, with its congealed juices. Unless the girls spoke about God's gifts, they were to be silent during the meal.

After dinner Papa and Mama retreated to separate rooms to lie down. Isabella and Hennie, still dressed in their hot and sober black, could not play with their dolls or even with the Noah's ark.

Isabella could not read her beloved books, nor could Hennie draw. They were forbidden to go to the garden; they were too old to nap.

Every Sunday Isabella was ordered to read aloud to Hennie a book of edifying sermons, *Line Upon Line: Here a Little, There a Little*, full of admonitions to those who had not closed with God's offer of redemption, nor taken up the cross in baptism, for God was a jealous God, and one was either a child of God or a child of wrath. An hour later Mama walked them to Sunday school, where she taught the older girls. Isabella and Hennie attended the infant class, after which they came home to tea.

Back to church again for evening service, where Father preached once more, then home again for family prayers. Sunday services kept the girls up later than their usual bedtime, and after praying, "If I should die before I wake, I pray the Lord my soul to take," Isabella fell into bed, exhausted with the bleak tedium of the day.

When Uncle Seymour, the bishop of Chester, came to officiate in his scarlet habit, embroidered cope, and tall miter, carrying his staff and attended by his chaplains, Isabella's heart swelled with pride. Isabella said she was going to be a bishop when she grew up. This was repeated in the family as childish naiveté, for, of course, only men were clergy; only men took part in the church procession or sang in the choir.

Isabella enjoyed the hymns, for she could change her position from sitting to standing. She belted out each protracted syllable.

My faith looks up to thee
Thou Lamb of Calvary,
Saviour divine!
Now hear me while I pray,
Take all my guilt away,
O let me from this day
Be wholly thine.

Prayers and responses followed, then readings from the Old Testament and readings from the New Testament. Finally the congregation settled into an agreeable repose—Papa did not insist, as some Evangelicals did, that the congregation remain on their feet—to listen in a semidoze to the hour-long cadences of his sermon.

Isabella's mind kept roaming. Other than the ancient stained-glass windows, whose blue, scarlet, green, yellow, and purple saints gave Isabella welcome diversion, the church offered little to distract the worshipers—no altar cloth, no reredos, no carved choir, only a simple lectern. The rector who had had the living before Papa had installed, amid much contention, four stone shields carved with the Evangelists' symbols: the winged man of Saint Matthew, the lion of Saint Mark, the ox of Saint Luke, and the eagle of Saint John. Isabella's eyes traced each incised bas-relief. Miss Ryan came to her mind, trailing an aura of the forbidden. Miss Ryan lived just across the lane, but that byway might have been the flames of purgatory, for Miss Ryan belonged to that Scarlet Woman, the Church of Rome. Isabella longed to see the Scarlet Woman, and she watched the Ryans' front door assiduously in hopes that she would emerge.

Isabella thought of the ants she had seen a few days ago. Their waists were tiny, just like Miss Ryan's. Noticing an ant hole near the sundial, Isabella had flung herself flat on the ground, heedless of pinafore and petticoats, to watch an ant labor with a crumb. She scrutinized the shiny black bodies with their six legs, each bent at the knee, coming and going from the tiny hole. She was curious: were the ones that disappeared into the hole the very ones that reappeared? She put her chin level with the ground in an effort to distinguish one ant from another. Then a shadow fell upon her, and the toe of a neat black high-laced boot nudged her.

"What are you doing?" Mama asked.

Isabella responded gravely, "I am helping this ant get her crumb into storage."

"Helping?" Mama challenged.

"It's a big load. The crumb keeps slipping to one side. She asked me to help," Isabella explained, certain that this appeal to charity was admissible. Catching sight of Mama's horrified face, Isabella insisted, "She really did. She had the funniest scratchy voice."

Mama pinched Isabella's shoulder between her thumb and forefinger and marched her into the kitchen, where she seized a bar of the dreadful lye soap and washed out Isabella's mouth. "Telling lies is an abomination to the Lord."

Lye was a familiar taste, for Mama found many occasions to wash out Isabella's mouth. Lies were the most serious of Isabella's transgressions, but the list included taking the name of the Lord in vain, muttering angry words, and making rude remarks. But Isabella was learning to swallow her anger, for the laundry soap had a terrible bite and left her mouth puckered for hours.

During services, the family sat in the rector's pew at right angles to the lectern. Isabella had been trained to look only at her father, not at the congregation. She tried again to listen to Papa. He was representing the Day of Judgment and asking each one if he, if she, were prepared to rise in a cloud of glory to meet the Lord, if they had closed with God's offer of redemption, if they were dwellers in the tents of the righteous. This was familiar terrain. At that moment, her eyes focused in the prescribed direction, a tiny mouse crept to the foot of the lectern. To Isabella's delight, the mouse sat quietly for some minutes with only his whiskers quivering, imbibing Papa's sermon. He then skittered to the sidewall, whereupon Isabella committed her terrible sin. She darted from the pew to see where the mouse had gone. Papa, launched in his peroration, did not pause, but Mama, her cheeks pink with embarrassment, swooped after her and pulled her back to her seat.

On Monday Mrs. Bird aired her outrage. "To think that you actually got out of the pew and walked in front of the lectern!" she gasped. "How, tell me, how could you do that?" Genuine astonishment threaded her voice. "Whatever possessed you?" This was a rhetorical question, as Mrs. Bird knew well what possessed Isabella. It was Satan.

"I do listen, Mama. I can tell you every word. It was that…"

"That what?" Mrs. Bird interposed.

"That the dearest mouse came creeping out. He wanted to hear the sermon, too," Isabella finished in a flush of inspiration.

Mrs. Bird was even more perturbed. This guileful remark was clearly falsehood. "God hates prevaricators, Isabella. You must try to act like Hennie," Mama enjoined. "You don't see her disobedient. I fear you don't heed the word of God. If you were truly attentive, the Devil would not beguile you. And think: it is your own papa who is giving the sermon. Most little girls would risk the sin of pride if their father were the rector. But you, you actually walked right out of your pew in the middle of the sermon! Do you know how humiliating it is that the rector's own daughter, that very daughter whom he prays over so earnestly, listens not to him but to the Devil? You cannot hope to join the righteous if these transgressions continue. Hennie is younger, but she acts the way God wishes her to act."

Mrs. Bird's way in discourse was to embroider, to loop back, to repeat, to make verbal circles. "Your punishment is to sit in the entrance hall. I have placed a chair there in front of the coatrack. I have lettered a sign for you to wear: 'Don't speak to me. I have offended the Lord.' Anyone who comes in to see your father will know of your disgrace. You are not to move from this chair; you are to stay there until I give you permission to leave. It grieves me to do this, but it grieves me more that you entertain Satan." Mrs. Bird's forehead was pinched and her lips thinned, her habitual mien when she chastised Isabella.

Isabella knew protest was futile. She might have objected strenuously if she had realized what a grueling punishment it would prove to be. Mama led her to the entryway, sat her brusquely in the horsehair chair, and hung the placard around her neck.

"Now, mind you," she warned, "you are not to say a word. If you talk at all, your punishment will be extended." Mrs. Bird withdrew, drawing together the parlor doors.

The clock, its tick, its tock, mesmerized Isabella, just as it had a year earlier when she had earned the first halfpenny in her life. Uncle Lawson had bet her that she could not sit still for five minutes. Isabella won the wager, but those five minutes, looking at that inane sun painted on the dial, watching that minute hand drag from eleven to twelve, had been intolerable. Although Papa was pleased that she could control herself, he compelled her to return the coin, and he admonished his brother-in-law for introducing an innocent child to the sin of gambling.

Isabella could see only the brass disk of the grandfather clock, up the stairs on the landing, as it ticked back and forth, back and forth. After a while, Hennie came and sat on the lowest step close to her. Hennie did not say a word. Mama was always extolling Hennie as an example of what she, Isabella, should be.

Hennie was not phlegmatic, but she had none of Isabella's quicksilver quality. For her it was no hardship to sit quietly. She dearly loved to work on her cross-stitch sampler, a task that was irksome for Isabella. She dearly loved to help Mama with the morning chores and would trot happily at Mama's heels. But Hennie also dearly loved her sister. She loved her energy, the things that she said, the stories that she told, and she never once echoed Mama's rebukes or set herself up in a prim or superior way.

The result was that Isabella loved Hennie more than anyone. In the very core of her soul, she learned to wish that she were like her sister and to distrust herself.

Hennie sat, her hands folded in her pinafore, not saying a word but bringing comfort to Isabella. It troubled Hennie that her sister was so often punished. She felt sorry for Isabella, and she learned from Isabella's predicament never to question what Mama did, to lie low and never make waves. She learned to quell her natural curiosity and not to come to Isabella's defense.

Mama discovered her sitting there. "Hennie, I'm surprised at you! Aren't you ashamed?" Mama exclaimed as she dragged her away.

"Mama, Hennie didn't say a word. She was as quiet as…" Isabella paused, unable to think how quiet Hennie was. For the first time that day, tears gathered in Isabella's eyes. A quick burst of inspiration allowed her to finish, "A flower."

"Be that as it may. She has no right to interfere with my discipline."

Mrs. Snapitt, a member of the parish, lifted the knocker. Isabella, seeing her through the glass pane of the door, got up to let her in, when Ellen brushed past her and said, "I'm sorry, miss. Mrs. Bird's orders," and went to the door. Mrs. Snapitt read the sign, nodded her head in approval, and swept past, clutching her skirt as if Isabella might contaminate it.

At length Isabella heard the noon dinner being prepared and the table set. That was her chore, and she yearned to do it. She felt comforted thinking that deliverance was near. But no, an almost-silent meal—Isabella could only occasionally hear muffled voices from the dining room—passed without her. Mama came and brought a dry crust and a glass of water.

"You may be excused for five minutes, Isabella, to attend to nature, to wash your hands, and then you may eat this bread of affliction. Let us pray that after today you will learn not to listen to the devil but will bear the cross of Christ."

The afternoon crawled. Isabella's legs were too short to reach the floor unless she stood. Tucking her legs under her was intolerable, for even through her skirts the horsehair pricked. She was in agony to move but feared to defy her mother.

Dr. Bell, another parishioner, came to see her father, and he growled good-naturedly, "Here now, don't look so woebegone." He rummaged in his pocket and brought forth a lemon drop sticky with lint. Isabella would not have risked accepting it, but he placed it right on her tongue. "Not a word now," he cautioned looking at the sign and winking at her. The lemon drop melted on her tongue.

After Dr. Bell left, Isabella expected Papa to rescue her. She felt protected by her father, who only punished her at Mama's insistence. Often when Papa went on his calls, Isabella accompanied him, a habit formed in infancy when a doctor, concerned about her small size, ordered as much outdoor air as could be managed. Papa rode Autumn, a tall, gentle mare, and Isabella sat sidesaddle on a pillow in front, Papa's arm securing her, her fingers twisted in Autumn's black mane. Here began her love for Papa, and her love for horses and for nature.

As Autumn plodded along, Papa pointed out the testimonies of the Lord's goodness: the first anemone of spring, its scarlet vivid against the drab earth; the tremulous snowflower; the yellow crocus that bloomed even if its feet were sprinkled with snow; the round dirty-white eggs, spotted with dark, bloody blotches, of the stone curlew, lying without any nest on the bare ground in the field—the moment its young were hatched they ran, led by their dam, to skulk among the stones of some flinty field where their feathers blended exactly—the green shaggy flowers of the oak, five or six threads that emerged from a bud, or the little red knots that swelled and turned green, then brown, and become acorns; the powdered black and orange and white colors of the butterfly, with its snail horns; a hawk trembling its wings, hanging quite still for a moment in the deep blue; the dark rings on the grass that Papa extolled as "God's wonders" and Bridget called "fairy rings" in which mushrooms and toadstools grew. Papa drew her attention to the fields—in grass, or crops, or fallow—to the farmhouses, their dairies and press houses, telling her the uses of all, whether a waterwheel was undershot or overshot, how each gate was hung, about animals seen and parishioners met. Every day Papa named the wayside and meadow flowers, for flowers were, above all, God's bounty. Papa then questioned her minutely on what they had seen.

But not today. Today she heard Papa moving in his study, but he did not appear. The disappointment was unbearable. The long afternoon continued, broken only by the ticking of the clock. Isabella felt a shriek rising within her, which she smothered with difficulty. Rage possessed her. Her body became rigid, and her fists clenched. She turned her lips inward and bit them until the blood welled with the strain to contain her wrath.

Pain chewed her back: an insistent pain, like the gnawing of a tooth. She tried to ignore it, but it drilled into her. Suddenly she saw the image of a snake. It was the devil claiming her for his own. Yes, it was the Devil. His fangs fastened into her back; his venom poured into her body.

Isabella screamed, "Make him let go! Make him let go!" She fell off the chair and crumpled onto the floor, one hand clutching her back. "Make him let go! Make him let go!"

It took many weeks for her to recover from the outward effects of this Day of Atonement. Her unusual docility convinced Mrs. Bird that those nine hours had produced the effect she desired. But Isabella did not learn what her mother had intended. What she did learn was to be cautious of what she told her mother. With devastating consequences she learned to distrust herself. Her pleasure in herself leaked like a slowly oozing hemorrhage and was replaced with the bile of self-loathing.

CHAPTER 3
TATTENHALL

Tattenhall was seven miles from Chester, but the road was paved for less than half that distance with a smooth stone track for wagon and carriage wheels, and small stones turned on end for horses. It was dairy country with flat pastures as well as swelling ridges. The land bunched up to the west, a gentle domestic terrain with its hawthorn hedgerows, its herds of red-and-white Ayrshire short-horns grazing on grasses and clover, and its plots of vegetables and berry bushes tilled in the tenacious clay.

For many centuries Tattenhall had been particularly distinguished for its manufacture of Cheshire cheese. Most of the farmhouses had their own dairy, often a separate thatched building dug several feet into the clay to ensure temperate coolness even in August. The dairymaid was usually a big, strapping woman who could scour the huge vats and lift the ninety-pound wheels of cheese. The making of cheese and whey butter were the principal sources of income for the farmers, and therefore, on the large farms, the head dairymaid was highly regarded, because the superiority of the cheese depended upon her skill. She could produce quality cheese even on a farm of poor herbage. There were no exact rules. Some of the best dairymaids claimed to have secrets, but it was no secret that the cheese dairy was a place of hard work dependent upon extreme cleanliness, close observation, and flawless judgment.

Due to the nature of the work, the making of the cheese and whey butter had to be performed on the Sabbath, just like any other day. To Edward Bird's crusading spirit, such labors were a desecration, a manifest breach of divine law.

"Remember the Sabbath, and keep it holy," Edward Bird countered. This conflict, broached when Edward Bird first arrived in Tattenhall, marked his tenure for the eight years he lived there.

Isabella remained a fragile child. A doctor suggested she be kept out of doors as much as possible. This medical prescription was the explanation for a familiar sight: the tiny child in a smocked frock, bundled in a shawl, buttressed by her father's arm as he rode around his parish on his horse. Her intense dark eyes missed nothing in their swift glances. Her face, however, was often white with fatigue, and she would complain, "I very tired."

Dora's primary anxiety was less for Isabella's physical well-being than for her soul. Isabella's unusual intelligence was not a source of pleasure to Dora, but of concern. She had before her the example of her own brilliant sister, Barbara. Barbara was never mentioned, not even in whispers, for she had declared that she no longer believed and had ceased to attend services. Like Mary Ann Evans (George Eliot), Barbara was unmoved by every argument to convince her of the truth of the Gospels. Dora's father lived to see both his sons, Marmaduke and Andrew, graduates of Cambridge and both members of the House of Commons, honorable and useful men. Yet Barbara persisted in her rebellion, and Dora found solace that her mother had gone to her rest prior to Barbara's defection and had been spared that grief. Dora feared that Isabella lived in peril, for a clever child stood on the edge of damnation. Isabella must be brought to God, to confess her sins, to throw herself upon God's mercy, to ask Jesus to intercede for her.

Dora's conduct, character, psyche, and soul were forged upon the anvil of the Evangelical view of the world and its perils. The central doctrine of the Evangelicals was a conviction of the totally depraved nature of man. Conversion to escape eternal damnation was the only thing that mattered.

Damnation was a vivid and immediate concept. Examination and soul-searching dominated life. "I wish God would give me something to do for Him" was their most sincere prayer. They were philanthropic, and missionaries extraordinaire. They founded Sunday schools, ragged schools, vice societies, and went around the world to found missions. Among their achievements were the abolition of slavery and the slave trade, the reform of the penal code, and an infusion into all of society ideals of responsible government. These concerns stamped them with seriousness, and "serious" was used as a synonym for Evangelical. By the time Isabella was five, Evangelical precepts were deeply internalized within her.

But Isabella, unlike her mother, never lost her sense of fun, nor her rock-bottom enjoyment of life. The spring of 1836 had been cold and damp. The past week had been rainy, sometimes in stinging gusts, occasionally in dense downpours, often in a fine drizzle, but at no time was Isabella allowed out. Despite the cold, spring made her ubiquitous assault: boughs were pregnant with bud, and branches that last week were bare were now trimmed with pale green. The damp chill did not discourage the primroses. Dora Bird had carefully uprooted primroses from neighboring pastures and had directed the gardener to plant bulb after bulb in a large circular bed, and there they were, exultant, a gold-and-crimson frenzy. Isabella saw them from her bedroom window, a brave declaration, sometimes flattened by the wind, then upright in joyous color. Isabella yearned to go out and visit them, but all week she had been kept in with a cough, a fever, and even today, Sunday, Mama decided that she was not well enough to attend services.

The sun was out, the world was rejoicing, but the ground was still wet, and Isabella was still sickly.

Mama wrapped her in an afghan and bid her stay in bed until after church. Isabella had fantasized of visiting those primroses, to count them, to peer closely at them, to congratulate them, to dance by their side. She waited until she knew the service was well started. Ellen was busy in the lower regions—she would not stir up here or in the drawing room—and Bridget, with whose soul Rev. and Mrs. Bird were wrestling to rescue from Popish idolatry, was required to attend both morning and evening services. Isabella poked two inquisitive feet over the edge of the bed and, without putting on her shoes, pattered down stairs.

The doors of the drawing room opened directly onto the lawn, and Isabella darted across the grass, cold and wet and startlingly delicious under her feet, to the flowers. Round and round she danced, rejoicing in them, touching them, kissing them, filling her whole being with the joy of them, and only when she was sated with pleasure did she run upstairs back to bed. She did not tell her mother, nor even Hennie, and her escapade was never discovered. For a while the memory of those flowers, of the gold and the scarlet, was a treasure, which now and again she recalled with mild delirium, and then, gradually, the incident was forgotten.

Or she thought it was forgotten; she had been only five. Twenty-two years later, on a trip to the Hudson Bay Territory among the wild Indians," she was standing on a little pier waiting for the gangway to be lowered from a steamer she was about to board. She was jostled off the jetty into the deep water between pier and steamer.

The water closed over her, and she experienced that phenomenon of sudden recall, of vivid illuminations of one's life, but here flashed only one scene: her disobedience that day when she had danced with the primroses. A tall red Indian leaped into the water and seized her, saving her life, but not before that stab of memory on what she had felt was the Day of Judgment.

CHAPTER 4

TAPLOW HILL

E very summer Isabella and Hennie were sent to their paternal grandparents' homestead, Taplow Hill. The first few years, their parents came with them, but one summer Papa was too ill to travel, and the girls, accompanied by Ellen and the coachman, were allowed to visit by themselves. That summer established a custom: Papa and Mama remained a few weeks, and then the girls stayed without them under the tutelage of Aunt Rebecca. During their visit uncles, aunts, and cousins arrived, for Grandmother and Grandfather had ten children, and one widowed daughter, with her children, still lived at Taplow Hill. Two of the married daughters, Elizabeth and Lucy, made annual summer visits with their husbands and children, and many of the others paid summer visits as well.

Life at Taplow Hill was much more prodigal than in the rectory at Tattenhall. There were cousins to play with. Merttins and Hannah, with their mother, Margaret, lived there all the time. Margaret was the widow of Grandmother and Grandfather's youngest child, George, who died in India of fever. Other cousins, sometimes as many as ten, came for extended visits.

The manor house, its built-for-the-ages Elizabethan center flanked by large wings extending on each side, was constructed of the golden stone native to the Cotswolds. On the first floor were a large gallery, a drawing room, a family parlor, Grandfather's office, a library, a dining room, a staff dining room where the troop of fourteen grandchildren ate when they were all present, pantries, a sprawling kitchen, a cooling room, and a broad square staircase leading to the bedrooms above and to the third-floor bedrooms, schoolroom, sewing room, and nursery.

Taplow Hill was a dwelling that employed many of the villagers to maintain its upper-middle-class comfort: Betty, who supervised the housekeeping and the service at table; fat Nora, the cook with a harelip; the upstairs maids, Madge and Sarah; the sculleries, Polly and Nan; short-tempered Mary Dee and her daughter, who washed and starched and ironed; and Mrs. Mallop, who came to sew for weeks at a time. In addition, visiting families brought their personal maids and coachmen. Outside there were the gardeners, and a stableboy, a carpenter, dairymaids, and scores of laborers.

The spacious wing on the south side of the house had been added when Grandmother and Grandfather were married in 1780. The rooms were then decorated in the latest taste and had not been altered. Pediments with classical moldings and details surmounted windows and doors. An elaborate cornice topped the walls in all three rooms, but the drawing room walls were covered with white-and-blue-figured damask that matched the upholstery and the draperies that hung in loops and folds. The walls in the other two rooms were wood paneled. The drawing room rug had been specially woven in light tones of blue with an overall pattern of flowers and a flowered border. In the drawing room were arched niches, with a marble bust of a frowning Roman senator, a robed Grecian slave, an Eros, and a winged Mercury.

The drawing room opened into the parlor, and these doors were almost never closed. It was possible to sit in the drawing room and to look down the length of that room, with its two fireplaces and its seven windows, through the spacious parlor, to the library with its rich leather-bound volumes. Although the library was the smallest room of the south wing, it had three tall windows to the west and two windows that faced south, as well as a fireplace, and floor-to-ceiling glass-fronted bookcases of golden oak, between which were carved pilasters.

The morning properly began in the parlor with family prayers. All the servants, outdoor as well as indoor, attended and sat in straight ranks to hear Grandfather read in his vibrant voice the lessons and a prayer for the day out of Thornton's *Family Prayers*. The prayer finished, Grandfather gave a courtly bow to the men and maids as they filed past him with courtesies and salutes. The day ended here with the family and only the indoor servants grouped around the piano singing "The Pilgrim Fathers," "The Curfew Bell," or "The Captive Knight," then a familiar hymn and a prayer in which all would join.

The damask, the draperies, the upholstery were faded, but the soft colors added to the delicate ambiance. Furniture with tapered, fluted legs, a console table of satinwood, a ladies' secretary, work-tables, and side chairs with oval backs and with frames carved with floral wreaths graced all three rooms, as well as mirrors, decorated clocks, candelabras, and Wedgwood china. The rooms breathed an air of powdered wigs, embroidered satin waistcoats, and violins and cellos, an air at complete variance with its present earnest inhabitants. Only Grandfather, with his twinkling eyes, his dimple deep in his chin, his boutonniere, his pleasure in the things of this world, bridged the gap between that bygone age and the Bird family in the 1830s.

Taplow Hill was a working farm, its center a busy courtyard. Drawing ale, chopping wood, plucking chickens, shelling peas, slopping hogs, scouring pots, and churning butter were accomplished here. Speckled hens and cats—calico, striped, black, white, and motley—and short-tailed sheepdogs that took no notice of the children had free range. The stables opened onto the courtyard.

Grandfather kept twelve heavy workhorses in addition to Trumpet, a horse he rode himself, and Buttons and Bows, who despite their names bowled along smartly with Royal and Crystal, pulling the four-horse chaise. There was a huge cow barn with its stanchions, a chicken house, a kennel for the hounds, a sheepfold and crib, a granary, beehives, a smokehouse, a cheese dairy, a carpenter's shop, and a washhouse.

There was an extensive kitchen garden, and a trellis hung with green and purple grapes, and a walled flower garden with larkspur, tiers of geraniums, borders of alyssum and verbena, beds of the damask pink-and-white English rose and the small moss rose that Grandfather wore in his lapel, and stands of lavender and cornflowers.

There were tools and equipment, bridles and harnesses for the horses, rollers to break the soil, harrows, plows, carts with high, heavy wheels, wagons, scythes, nets for capturing birds, and poles for fishing. Mr. Adam, the carpenter, worked in his shop, repairing benches and stools, building a dovecote, fixing the tools. There were long red raspberries or round green gooseberries to pick, mushrooms to gather, fish to catch, a stream to explore, in which Isabella and Hennie splashed with bare feet.

Often the day brought an itinerant laborer: a chair mender to repair rush bottoms; a tinker with bellows to solder kettles; a knife grinder with his wheel; a peddler with pots and pans, ribbons and buttons, lace and caps; or a passing caravan of Gypsies.

There was Flag, Grandfather's collie. He would submit to Isabella's and Hennie's embraces, for he was a courteous dog, but his heart belonged to his master. Even while the girls' fingers were entwined in his thick white scruff, his brown eyes followed every move that Grandfather made. When Grandfather was away, Flag resigned himself to await his return, and then Flag trotted to meet him, his tail, uncharacteristic of a collie, upraised, which was why he had been given his name. He was a joyous but dignified gentleman, but once in a while, only when Grandfather was absent, as he was lying in the courtyard with his long nose on his paws, he watched the hens as they pecked and scratched, or a cat as it promenaded past, and the "old Adam" would seize him, and he would make a sudden start to enjoy watching the chickens scooting and squawking. A cat, who had not hastened her steps but who had nonetheless jumped nimbly onto a wagon, turned from her perch and gave him a look of disdain. Flag grinned foolishly at his own mischief and settled down again for Grandfather's return. Hennie often squatted next to him, thumb and forefinger softly folding and unfolding his velvet ears.

There was a long table set with a cornucopia of food: grilled trout, leg of roasted mutton, covered bowls of peas, asparagus, new potatoes, jellies, puddings, currant tarts, gooseberry tarts—all from the farm. Grandfather never suggested, as Papa sometimes did, that if the pudding was Isabella's favorite, custard studded with berry, that she practice self-denial and refuse to eat it.

And when the long, fruitful day was over, there was the library. Before bedtime at Tattenhall, Isabella and Hennie were taught to review the day's lessons. Instead of the normal flow of conversation, they systematically questioned one another. In this way they memorized pages of French vocabulary, Milton, and, of course, the Bible.

At Grandfather's they relaxed this practice. Isabella had discovered fiction, and it was almost impossible to wrest her away from a book she had started, and Hennie had made a discovery: a large, beautiful atlas with page after page of maps showing the "animal kingdoms" and "provinces" with vertical diagrams to illustrate animal distribution by height. Hennie was enamored with the droll marginal illustrations: lions, one-horned rhinoceroses, elephants, and birds in the Oriental regions; a unicorn in India; elephants, camels, lions, ostriches, monkeys, rhinoceroses, dragons, and croc-odiles in Africa; reindeer, elk, and bears in the Arctic; opossums, macaws, llamas, snakes, and alligators in South America; deer, beavers, rabbits, turkeys, and domesticated goats, cows, pigs, and horses in New England.

Hennie softly turned the pages during the long English twi-light, chuckling to herself, examining in detail the features of the land, the flora, and the fauna, and turning to Isabella every now and then to show her a drawing. Isabella, who had been picking books from the shelves at random, came across the words of an obscure poet that delighted Hennie:

> On a round ball
> A workeman that hath copies by, can lay
> An Europe, Afrique and an Asia
> And quickly make that, which was nothing, all.

"Grandfather, are we permitted to select any book?" Isabella's voice rang with disbelief.

"Certainly, child. I don't own books that would corrupt a young mind. Read any book you want. Remember, however, that I do not tolerate volumes taken from this room. You are to read them here. I do not want to find my writer friends scattered about the house."

At home, books were shelved in Papa's study, where the girls were not allowed to enter. They were certainly not permitted to take any book that caught their fancy. Moral fables, edifying tracts of Maria Edgeworth, bound sermons, history, and the Bible formed Isabella's reading material. Mrs. Bird took care that no work of fiction came into Isabella's hands. Mrs. Bird disapproved of fiction, since by definition it was not true, and nothing of this nature must inflame Isabella's mind. Grandfather did not share this attitude.

After family prayers one morning, Grandfather said to Isabella, "Let me have good reports of you today, and I'll have something to show you tonight."

"Show it to me now, Grandfather, and I shall surely be good," Isabella immediately countered.

"No, my dear," Grandfather laughed, his dark eyebrows, which at rest formed perfect half circles, lifted into the middle of his forehead. "I shall ask your aunts."

Isabella vowed that she would be well behaved. Her problem was her sharp tongue. Her diminutive aunts, of whom she was a trifle wary, especially of Aunt Rebecca, admonished her about her quick retorts and about what they called her combativeness, particularly with her cousin Merttins. Merttins was her age and much larger, but Isabella thought that she was entitled to do anything that he could. She was, in fact, a much more skilled equestrian than he was, and she was much more daring, galloping her horse, jumping from heights, climbing out on limbs, feats that frightened him.

Merttins lorded over his sister, Hannah, and tried to lord over Isabella and Hennie, but Isabella would not tolerate it. But when Isabella was reading in the crotch of an apple tree or was watching activities in the courtyard, Merttins would find Hennie alone, and then he could not forbear. She was such a pretty, gentle thing, with no more backbone than a basin of jelly.

"Hennie, Hennie, no bigger than a penny," he taunted, and Hennie looked at him with her large blue eyes and said not a word, but if Isabella came upon them, she rushed to her sister's defense.

"Better be small and nimble than big and awkward like you. And besides," she added, "your mind's just a spongy rubber ball." Today Isabella kept watch over her tongue.

The day sped past, as did all the Taplow Hill days—except Sunday. Sunday's ritual here was much as it was at home, with the addition that the aunts insisted that everyone stand during the entire service. This was wearisome to all the cousins, but to Isabella it was torture. Standing aggravated the pain in her back, a pain that gradually increased until she had surgery for a spinal tumor when she was eighteen. A girl with less curiosity and drive than Isabella would have spent her youth languishing on a sofa.

After dinner, Grandfather summoned Isabella into the library. "These have just come from my book dealers. You might sample one of them." He gestured to eight volumes richly bound in dark-red leather. He opened the bookcase and eased a volume from the shelf, with a beautiful golden thistle spread lavishly across the cover, on which *Waverley Novels* was boldly lettered in gold, the *W* superimposed upon another thistle.

"Ah," Isabella involuntarily gasped, her hands reaching out for the precious book. Of all the cousins, none read with Isabella's passion. *Waverley* smelled of leather and ink, it had gilt edges, and the paper was smooth and creamy. The frontispiece had a drawing of towered castles, armored knights, shields, proud horses with arched necks and uplifted knees, and two noble black-and-white collies. Each chapter began and ended with an engraving. Almost every page had its embellishments of a medieval artifact or curiosity. Isabella studied the pictures, particularly an officer of the Black Watch, with a bonnet covered with plumes, wearing a purse and a kilt, his plaid across his shoulder, but skipped the numerous prefaces and the lengthy introduction. Not until page fifty-four did she come to "Chapter the First." Her attention then became riveted as she discovered Bradwardine Manor, with its topiary of rampant bears, and unearthed literature and history with the sweet-tempered Rose, and then the excitement of a visit to a Highland robber.

"Isabella! You heard the bell." Ellen was not asking a question but making an accusation. Ellen did not read, and her limits of concentration were stretched by turning a heel when knitting. She had no patience with her young charge's stubbornness, for that is what she called it, stubbornness. A few times a week, if Ellen did not go and fetch her, Isabella might miss evening prayers entirely. "Isabella," Ellen's strident tones repeated. "You heard the bell."

Isabella returned the book to the shelf as if she were placing there her own limb and followed Ellen into the parlor. Grandfather looked at her kindly, but his son-in-law, the Reverend Marmaduke Thompson, who was conducting the evening service, scowled at her.

"Dearly beloved brethren, the scripture moveth us, in sundry places, to acknowledge and confess our manifold sins and wickedness…"

The phrases rolled over Isabella, but not one word penetrated. She dumbly recited the response, kneeling with the others, "O Lord, have mercy upon us, miserable offenders. Spare thou those, O God, who confess their faults. Restore thou those who are penitent according to thy promises declared unto mankind in Christ Jesus our Lord," but her lips could have been mouthing kidney beans for all the sense the words yielded. Isabella was in the Highlands. The moon had risen as she and Edward and their guide with the battle-ax, Evan Dhu, were rowed across the lake ringed with peaks. The oars dipped in cadence into the molten silver as two stalwart mountaineers chanted a Gaelic song.

"Yon's ta cove." Evan Dhu pointed to a small flicker of light.

The Reverend Thompson read the second lesson. "But if our gospel be hid, it is hid to them that are lost…them which believe not, lest the light of the glorious gospel of Christ, who is the image of God…For we preach not ourselves, but Christ Jesus the Lord; and ourselves your servants for Jesus's sake."

Isabella heard not a word; her skiff was passing the point of rock on which fire blazed. As she quietly drifted into a cavern, four or five shelves of rock descended to the water, forming natural steps. Behind them she heard the fire hiss as it was quenched with water. In the dark she felt herself lifted from the boat and carried into the recesses of the cave. A sharp turn, and there before her eyes was the hideout of the Highland robber Donald Bane Lane and his wild warrior band. Five or six stout warriors dressed in kilts were enfolded in ample plaids. Pistols hung from their goat-skin purses, and broadswords dangled by their sides. A cauldron bubbled over the charcoal fire and emitted a strong savory smell. Flames and pine torches illuminated the large cavern. Carcasses of a sheep and two cows hung by their heels in one recess.

Then, "Isabella, you're not listening!" hissed the ubiquitous Ellen, and Donald Bane Lane was gone.

That night Isabella could not fall asleep. Outside, the land was in thrall to the full moon. She must continue reading *Waverley* and meet Donald Bane Lane. Surely he looked like Uncle George. She had seen a miniature of Uncle George painted when Napoleon was defeated at Waterloo, and Uncle George had been only fourteen. The miniature was mounted in an oval of pearls. The young man's face did not look grave, which was most surprising, but looked as if he had just smelled perfume of roses, for a gentle delight suffused his features. He was wearing a teal-colored frock coat, and a frill of white lace was at his throat. His hair hung in thick golden waves with a lock that curled on his shoulder. Isabella had been shown this treasure when she was a little girl, and the miniature quite captured her heart. She was confident that Donald Bane Lane looked like Uncle George. She could not possibly wait until morning. She knew she could not take the book from the library, but Grandfather had not said she must remain in her room.

Without a candle Isabella found her way down the broad, moon-light-streaked stairs, across the wide hall, through the parlor, and into the quiet library. She located the matches and lit the tapers of the candelabra. The darkness of the room jumped at her, but her eyes adjusted, and she found *Waverley* where it projected from the shelf. She spread it open on the table in front of the candles. The Highland robber came forward into the red glare of the cavern fires: "The profession that he followed—the wilderness in which he dwelt—the wild warrior forms that surrounded him, were all calculated to inspire terror...Waverley prepared himself to meet a stern, gigantic, ferocious man...Donald Bane Lane was the very reverse of all these. He was thin in person and low in stature, with light, sandy-colored hair, and small pale features...he appeared...a diminutive and insignificant figure."

That could not be. Isabella reread the offending passage, "sandy-colored hair, and small pale features...a diminutive and insignificant figure," again. She sat with her chin on her hand, her eyes abstracted, her dark hair in waves over her forehead. At that moment, a candle in his hand, Grandfather approached her. So intent was Isabella upon her own thoughts, she was unaware that it was late at night.

"Grandfather," she lamented, "Donald Bane Lane doesn't look the way he should look."

"How should he look?" To Grandfather's credit he did not immediately tell Isabella to go to bed. He was fond of this grandchild of his, the only one for whom reading was a necessity, and who, like himself, responded deeply to all of life and nature.

"I thought," Isabella said shyly, "that he might look like Uncle George."

"Yes," Grandfather echoed, his memory summoning not the boy George of the miniature, but the young man who had set sail for India and whom he was never to see again. He and Lucy had made the long trip with George to Liverpool in the chaise; he was glad that they had.

"He should be big and brave looking with bright-yellow hair."

"What does this paragon do?" Grandfather asked, for he had not read *Waverley*.

"He's head of a robber band."

"And you believe he should look like a hero?" Grandfather questioned.

"I'm not sure." Isabella was puzzled. "He's a robber, and that's bad, but I'm not certain he's a villain."

"It sounds as if Scott has created a complex character. I'll have to read it. You know, Isabella, you cannot always rely upon how a person looks. Sometimes men who appear to be virtuous are scoundrels, and sometimes ordinary-looking men are noble and generous."

Isabella listened gravely to this intelligence and commented, "That Reverend Ewart who was just here, he's not a very promising-looking man, is he? And I suppose he is good."

"Come, child, enough of these questions. We'll go to bed." Taking her by one hand and holding the candle with the other, Grandfather led her upstairs. At the door to her room, he kissed her on the forehead. "You can read *Waverley* tomorrow," he said.

CHAPTER 5
EMMA

Back home at Tattenhall, the girls memorized a vast sheaf of religious and sentimental poetry. Isabella enjoyed this part of lessons, but she did not like drawing or sewing, for which she had little aptitude. Isabella had been taught to examine her soul every evening, to question if she had done God's will, to balance the ledger. Had she been bad? What good deeds had she done? Had she found favor in God's sight? And she often wondered, but did not say aloud, was she lovable?

Papa entrusted to Mama the task of educating the girls, for the higher curricula—Greek, Latin, mathematics, rhetoric, logic, history—were not necessary for women. Mama was patient in teaching them simple rhetoric, ciphering, drawing, needlework, and scriptures. But the responsibility of teaching them to be model Christians, to lead them to salvation, was awesome. Her teaching was based upon an Evangelical handbook, *A Practical View of the Prevailing Religious System of Professed Christians in the Higher and Middle Classes in this Country Contrasted with Real Christianity* by William Wilberforce. His book was addressed to her as a woman, for he wrote, "Women in their roles of mothers and governesses could best influence the next generation. A man cannot be a good man without a good mother." Mama was fond of quoting him.

Mr. Wilberforce, Mama explained, opposed staying late in bed. He said that scarcely anything else was equally injurious, that he had seen many instances where from lying in bed late, private prayers had been neglected. Mama boasted that Mr. Wilberforce was related to them through two branches of the family, not only Papa's but through her family also. Mr. Wilberforce was the generating spirit and moral reformer, Mama told them, who had succeeded in getting Parliament to abolish slavery.

Isabella's interest waned; she had heard about Mr. Wilberforce so many times. She imagined that he looked like one of Grandfather's sheep, with a sausage of white hair curled over each ear and, like the sheep, always bleating.

One overcast morning Hennie was holding a piece of chalk as Mama was talking, and Isabella told her, "Don't hold the chalk that way, Hennie. Do it this way."

"You're not to give orders, Isabella," Mama said, irritated by her lack of attention.

"But, Mama, we give orders to Jesus."

"Whatever do you mean?"

"Why, that prayer that we start lessons with, isn't that an order, 'Hear me, holy Jesus?'" Isabella was referring to the couplets she and Hennie repeated daily:

Jesus, from Thy throne on high,
Look on me with loving eye,
Hear me, Holy Jesus.

Be Thou with me every day,
When I learn and when I pray,
Hear me, Holy Jesus.

"Isabella, you are deliberately being perverse."

"But it is an order. We're telling Jesus what to do."

"Isabella, I will not have it. 'Fairest and best adorned is she whose clothing is humility.'" Mama repeated one of her favorite saws. "You are to stand in the corner with your back to us until you are contrite." Mama conducted her to the corner.

That evening while Dora plied her needle and Edward was reading the *Edinburgh Review*, Dora said, "Edward, I fear for Isabella, that she lives in peril. Whatever will become of her? She's the granddaughter of a minister, the daughter of a minister, but she is willful. A clever child stands on the very brink of damnation." Dora had the ever-present specter of her sister, Barbara, on her mind.

Edward, closing the periodical over his finger, answered, "Isabella is clever, but she is a young child, Dora. She will be brought to God. She will learn to confess her sins. Surely your fears are premature?"

Dora looked up from her embroidery silks and confessed, "I see in her some of the same characteristics as in you-know-who."

"Isabella has the blessing, Dora, of your example."

"My parents were exemplary. Remember you-know-who had the wisdom of their instruction."

"The difference is that your sainted mother died when your sister was still a child, and your father had no thought that such a transgression could happen. It sprang upon him when he was unaware. We have the benefit of knowing what to look out for."

"True, that is an advantage." Dora picked up her hoops again. "We must see that Isabella throws herself upon God's mercy and asks Jesus to intercede for her."

Edward and Dora believed in the underlying premise of Evangelicalism: that mankind, by his nature, was utterly depraved. Salvation in order to escape eternal damnation—damnation was a vivid and immediate concept—was the only thing that mattered.

"You are right. We must be ever vigilant," Edward agreed as his eyes sought the paragraph where he had been interrupted.

The next morning the door to Papa's study was open. This was unusual, and Isabella could not resist. She and Hennie were allowed there only by invitation, but she had finished volume one of an English history book, and Papa was to be gone all day. Surely Papa would not object to her taking volume two? Isabella, at seven years old, could not remember not knowing how to read, and she avidly pursued anything she could get her hands on: moral fables, the edifying religious tracts of Maria Edgeworth, the Bible, and her favorite, history. However, she was not allowed to read fiction, for fiction by definition was false; nothing of that nature must defile her mind or corrupt her virtue.

Isabella opened the glass door of the bookcase, replaced volume one, and found next to it volume two. As she turned to leave, her eyes fell on Papa's desk and an unfamiliar black-bound book. What was Papa reading? She picked it up and was surprised that it was full of Papa's tidy handwriting. Opening it at random, she read:

Twelve years since Emma breathed her last. Now in a different clime, under different skies, I toil only to please you, O Lord. In Dora I have a helpmeet above reproach, a devoted wife, a laborer with me in your house. Today making my calls in this gentle English countryside, I saw not these hedgerows, but the gaudy colors and the thronged lanes of Calcutta. My heart was there with Emma on that colonnaded scented veranda where we lived those first happy months, and with my wide-eyed son when he learned to walk clinging to my fingers. I confess, O Lord, I questioned your ways. Let Christ forgive me, I am a miserable sinner, unworthy to wear your mantle. I struggle daily to subdue my carnal nature.

Tears stood in Isabella's eyes. The handwriting blurred. What did it mean? Who was Emma? Who was the "wide-eyed" son? Were Emma and the son Papa's "real" family? What was "carnal nature"? Isabella's mouth became dry, and she struggled to get her breath. She heard footsteps in the hall. Hastily she replaced the diary on Papa's desk and scurried from the study.

In her bedroom, she opened the history book, but all she saw was Papa's handwriting. She knew Papa had been in India as a barrister for the East India Company. She was even proud that he had worked there for the Supreme Court because it sounded important. But a son? Did Papa care for Emma and his son more than he cared for her? Papa had not mentioned her or Hennie in the diary. Did Papa—even her thoughts stumbled over the word—love her?

She couldn't ask Papa about it, for that would involve telling him that she had been in his study, that she had read something she knew was not meant for her eyes. Papa "a miserable sinner"! What did he mean? She was afraid she would burst, but Mama's constant reiteration that Isabella should think before she spoke cautioned her. She must not reveal what she had read.

Nonetheless she could not prevent herself from asking, although she was careful to be oblique. "Papa," she asked at dinner, "tell me about your life."

"What do you want to know?"

"About India."

"That was before I took Holy Orders. In that sense I was blind and could not see."

"Tell me about it." Isabella had to bite her lips to prevent them from saying "Emma" instead of "it."

"Like my brother, and like Grandfather, I was graduated from Magdalene College, Cambridge. Then I studied law and was called to the bar at Lincoln's Inn."

"But what about India?" Isabella insisted. She daydreamed about India, part of the British Empire, colored pink on the globe, full of little brown people and of trees covered with vines. She vowed that one day she, like Papa, would cross the ocean to India.

"As you know, I was a barrister there, but India was only preparation." Papa dismissed India. "When I came back to England, my conviction took root that without Christ, we are nothing. I was already twenty-eight. I hope now to achieve, in the time that remains, a lifetime's work to make up for my wasted years."

"Papa," Isabella began, but Mama interrupted.

"That's quite enough, Isabella. It's time to remember that children should be seen, not heard."

Isabella subsided, but there was a secret here, and Mama knew it. Mama was saying, "Papa's first curacy was in Boroughbridge, Yorkshire, where we met and where you were born, Isabella."

"Was I born there?" Hennie asked.

"No. Papa was given the curacy in Maidenhead, and that is where you were born. Papa's efforts there were crowned with joy, for he brought many souls to Christ."

"Why did we move from Maidenhead to here?" Hennie asked.

Isabella knew that she was not going to find out about India and Emma and the son from Mama and Papa, and she concentrated on keeping her mouth shut.

"Papa's constitution could not sustain his fervor. Not only had he to fill the church, but his spiritual guidance was sought by parishioners at all hours. The efforts were too much for him."

"Is Papa's constitution all right now?" Hennie asked, wondering where Papa kept his constitution.

"Yes, this quiet Tattenhall parish is just what Papa needs." Dora silently thanked the bishop who had sent Edward to this parish. "Papa is a rector now, and he has made converts here as well," Mama said.

Isabella found herself looking at Papa and wondering why she had never heard about Emma and a son. Several times she was on the verge of asking and caught herself just in time. She resolved to ask Grandfather. They were leaving for Taplow Hill the next day; otherwise she could not have contained herself and would have blurted out the fearful questions.

The following day at Taplow Hill, as soon as she had Grandfather alone, she spilled forth. "Grandfather," she asked, "who is Emma?"

"Emma?" Grandfather countered. "What have you heard about her?"

"I haven't heard anything, but I was reading this book on Papa's desk that he had written, and he wrote about her and Calcutta." It was easier to tell Grandfather what she had done than to confess to her parents.

The old man placed his hand on his granddaughter's head. *Bless the child's honesty,* he thought. He saw in Isabella the same intelligence and curiosity, the same keen enthusiasm that he had seen in her father, the son who had followed in his footsteps at Cambridge, at Lincoln's Inn, and who had sailed, as he had done, to India to seek his fortune—with such tragic results.

"Emma was your father's first wife," Grandfather said. "They went to India, and they had a son, but she, like so many, died of cholera. Two years later the little boy, who was also named Edward, succumbed to the fever."

"Poor Papa," Isabella cried.

"Yes, poor Papa. He came back to England, his health broken, his spirit, too." Grandfather paused as he remembered his son, pale and dejected, his fire quenched, and now so rigid and doctrinaire. He chose his next words carefully, for Edward, after all, trusted his child to him. Thinking of that charge, he said, "Then Evangelicalism gave renewed purpose to his life."

As he spoke he recalled a long visit Edward had made to Taplow Hill after he had been converted, how insistent Edward had been that he, his father, and Lucy, his mother, become Evangelical. When Lucy acceded to their son's pressure that Evangelicalism was the sole path to salvation, Edward had then brought all his energies to bear on him. He remembered how irritated Edward's constant proselytizing had made him. The recollection made him stiff-backed even now.

Edward had said, "Father, your soul will not be saved unless you give it to the Lord."

He had answered, "I am willing to bow to Lucy's wishes, to have an Evangelical household, to attend Evangelical services, even to have my other children convert, but I will not fall on my knees and declare myself a miserable sinner!" His hands had tightened on the knob of his walking stick. "I am thankful that you are happy again, but respect my beliefs. The Apostles' Creed and the Eucharist satisfy me. I don't need to rake over my soul every day."

Since then, although Evangelicalism had inundated all branches of his family, Grandfather remained adamant that the fervors of piety, the zeal of apostolic charity, the enthusiasm of self-renunciation were not for him. His less emotional, less guilt-ridden religion pleased him. He and Edward came to an understanding: Edward would cease trying to convert him, but if Edward were ever to have children, he would not criticize Evangelicalism in their presence.

"Wasn't your Papa fortunate in finding your mama and in having you and Hennie?" Grandfather said, giving Isabella a pat.

Isabella began to feel comforted.

"Your father is a man"—as Grandfather said it, he wished it were not a fact—"driven almost entirely by his dedication to harvest souls for the glory of God."

"Yes," Isabella echoed, knowing this to be true and yet unable to reconcile this Evangelical zeal with the passion hidden behind the words in Papa's diary. "Yes," she repeated. But she wondered if Papa truly loved her.

CHAPTER 6
REMEMBER THE SABBATH

E dward Bird was an active member of the Society for the Reformation of Manners, which was dedicated to the reform of the lower orders, that is, the cessation of drunkenness, and particularly the enforcement of the fourth commandment against Sabbath breaking. The rector's zeal that had attracted souls in Maidenhead alienated souls here. The issue was the sanctification of the Sabbath.

To Edward Bird the fourth commandment, "Thou shall remember the Sabbath and keep it holy," was given by the mouth of God and written by his finger on Sinai. It was, as were all the commandments, a perpetual obligation, an expression of divine will regarding right and wrong. Man was to enjoy the Sabbath as a holy day until the end of the world.

In recognition of the Sabbath, farmers were willing not to work in the open fields, but, they argued, cows must be milked, whey pressed, and cheeses cured. With reluctance, Reverend Bird conceded that cows must be milked, but that concession made him all the more zealous in his opposition to what he saw as unnecessary work in the dairies and presses, work which to him was a manifest breach of divine law. The observance of the Sabbath was the law of the living God. In his heated championship of the Sabbath, the rector, standing in the pulpit, pointed his finger at offending farmers and dairymaids and accused them of violating the law of the living God. His protests against Sunday labor, against serving Mammon drove the convicted farmers from a church where they could find no comfort.

To Dora Bird all the commandments weighed heavily, but the third commandment, "Thou shalt not take the name of the Lord in vain," she enforced with ardor. When Isabella, imitating a farm-hand, said, "Goddamn it," Mama washed out her mouth to remove every trace of the offensive words. Mama was truly affronted, and Isabella never again allowed any blasphemy to escape her lips. Dora's vigilance was not only against misusing the name of the Lord, but she also exercised untiring vigilance on how the girls spoke, for taboos surrounding language were legion. Isabella and Hennie were not allowed to utter words like "chemise," "drawers," "knickers," "breeches," "chicken thigh," certainly not "breast" or "bitch," and they were not given names for parts of the body nor for bodily functions, an omission that contributed to a lifetime embarrassment of the daily and the natural. As little girls they were taught to void before they left home, for in public there were neither the words nor the facilities for their needs. As they got old-er, menstruation, intercourse, even childbearing were mentioned only in veiled references: a pregnant woman was "confined." These taboos deprived women, for there was no language to discuss their primary experiences.

"Thou shalt keep the commandments of the Lord, thy God," roared Papa one Sunday morning from the pulpit, "to walk in his ways and to fear him."

With this introduction Isabella surmised that Papa's sermon would be another about his favorite commandment: the one that prohibited work on Sunday.

Papa's efforts to observe Sunday's sanctity were unceasing. In his daily rounds, Papa buttonholed any rate-paying man he encountered to sign a petition to enforce the fourth commandment, to make working on Sunday illegal.

Many of the men refused, saying, "Reverend Bird, I'd like to oblige you, but I make my living selling cheese, and that cheese must be made seven days a week."

Papa persevered, not accepting no for an answer, but advising the man to think it over more carefully. After all, it was a question of the man's immortal soul. What was more important than his salvation?

Isabella was often embarrassed by the farmer's discomfort that Papa evidently failed to see. Isabella wanted to ask Papa to drop the petition, but, of course, she didn't have the effrontery.

Yes, Papa was quoting the relevant passages from Deuteronomy: "Keep the Sabbath day to sanctify it, as the lord thy God hath commanded thee."

Isabella silently recited the rest of the verses; she had heard them so often she knew them by heart. *Six days thou shalt labor, and do all thy work, but the seventh day is the Sabbath of the lord thy God; in it thou shalt not do any work.*

Mama, who usually sat still as a statue, was restless, and her cheeks burned with color. Twice she twisted around to look at the congregation. Isabella knew that Mama was worried about church attendance; Papa's relentless petition effort had reduced attendance by half. But Papa said that eventually the farmers would acknowledge he was right, and return, and Dora had "the most perfect and implicit faith in the superiority of her husband's judgment, and the most absolute obedience to his desires."

Of course Papa is right, Isabella repeated to herself, but weren't the dairymen and women right too? What if attendance continued to dwindle? Would Papa have to move to yet another parish? She turned around to find out who was in church and who was missing. The worshipers did seem restless, and Nellie, the big, strapping dairymaid on Squire Albright's farm, had a peculiar look on her face. Was Nellie thinking about her sin of working on Sunday?

In admiring Nellie, Isabella mirrored the respect of the neighborhood, for head dairymaids were highly regarded. Nellie not only scoured the big vats and lifted the ninety-pound wheels of cheese, she also knew the proper heat for setting the milk, decided the quantity of rennet, the amount of salt, the degree of color, and the length of time for curing the cheese.

"The commandments declared by God himself are an expression of His divine will regarding right and wrong. The keeping of the commandments is the very foundation of national prosperity," Papa thundered. The congregation shifted uneasily in the pews as they received this broadside.

Isabella admired Papa's voice. It sounded so deep and important that she wished more people could see him. The chancel was elevated one step above the nave. Isabella had once asked him, "Papa, don't you think that people want to see where the voice is coming from?"

"Raising the pulpit to a greater height is a modern craze, and I think it vulgar. Church is not theater; it is not necessary that I be exhibited."

Building to his climax, Papa pointed his finger, trembling with earnestness, at one after another of the farmers and dairymaids in the pews. "When you desecrate the Sabbath, you are violating the law of the living God. If you work on Sunday, you are committing a grievous sin. The sanctification of the Sabbath is your Christian duty and your privilege." Each parishioner turned red, and not one met Papa's gaze until he pointed to Joshua Wheelwright.

Mr. Wheelwright, a prosperous farmer who cultivated many acres of pasture for his herds of dairy cows, returned Papa's gaze. To everyone's surprise he rose and strode down the aisle toward the exit, his cheeks blotched with fury, his heavy heels reverberating on the stone floor. The church was hushed.

"Remember the Sabbath, and keep it holy," Papa called after the retreating farmer.

Mr. Wheelwright spun around. "Bees make honey on Sunday. Cows must be milked. Cheese must be made," he countered, spitting out the words as if his tongue were blistered.

The congregation sucked in its breath in sheer astonishment, and Isabella, tense with alarm, startled at Mama's sharp intake of air as Mr. Wheelwright actually marched down the aisle and left church, slamming the door.

Behind her, Isabella heard whispers and the rustling of skirts. Her own heart pounded, and she noted that Mama had folded her lips until they disappeared. Papa, quaking with righteousness, continued the service until the final benediction exactly as if Mr. Wheelwright had not stomped out.

After the service, Papa walked with long, purposeful strides down the aisle, as he always did, and stood in the doorway to greet his parishioners one by one. Mama and the girls hung back as always, expecting the exiting parishioners to shake Papa's hand. Not today. Most of them scurried past, their eyes averted, ignoring his outstretched hand. Papa continued to stand in the doorway, not saying a word, nor did anyone speak to him. Shame crimsoned Isabella's face.

In single file the family walked home. Finally when they were seated around the table with its cold Sunday roast, Isabella exploded. "I think those people were just dreadful. I felt so sorry for you, Papa. It's not fair; you were only telling them what the Bible says."

"Remember, Isabella," Papa admonished her "on Sunday we speak at table only to praise Him."

Isabella was hot and rebellious, but she had to swallow her anger. Didn't Papa know that Mr. Wheelwright and the congregation had rebuffed him?

Papa conducted Evensong to an almost-absent congregation. The family was seated again at the table when Papa finally voiced his own complaint. "I don't understand these farmers and their dairymaids. Scripture is clear: 'Remember the Sabbath, and keep it holy.' Like all the commandments, it is a perpetual obligation. Yet these farmers persist in desecrating His day!"

"Papa," Isabella interrupted, "how did you feel when Mr. Wheelwright got up and walked out?"

"In the middle of the sermon," Hennie added, her eyes grave with the affront.

"We don't have to concern ourselves with Mr. Wheelwright. 'God works in mysterious ways his wonders to perform.' In time, Mr. Wheelwright will see the error of his conduct."

"But, Papa, didn't you want to stop him?" Isabella persisted. "Has anyone ever done that before? Just stood up and walked out?"

Papa sighed. "My task is to preach the word of God, to offer salvation, to bring the Way to those who are lost or heavily burdened. I, too, must trust God. We don't know the drama in Mr. Wheelwright's soul, but we can be assured that he will suffer."

"Do you think he will be burned at the stake?" Isabella asked, her sympathy rushing to Mr. Wheelwright's defense.

"Isabella, don't be ridiculous," Mama interposed.

But to Isabella, who knew the stories of the Christian saints and martyrs, it was no trouble at all to cast Mr. Wheelwright in that role.

Dora turned to Edward. "I thought you had gotten the congregation to agree not to work in the open fields, nor to allow their laborers to work."

"Yes, in recognition of the Sabbath, they've made that concession. But they continue to milk the cows, to press the whey, to cure the cheese."

Papa was right, but Isabella pictured the cows with their bulging udders.

"I have conceded," Papa continued as if he were reading her mind, "that cows must be milked, but that makes me even more zealous to oppose any other work performed on Sunday. I will not condone the unnecessary labor in the dairies and presses, a manifest breach of divine law. The Sabbatarians, and I'm proud to be one of them, go so far as to prohibit the poor from using bake-houses to cook hot meals on Sunday."

"Papa," Hennie asked, "who are Sabbatarians?"

"Sabbatarians are people who appeal to Parliament to declare Sunday a holy day and to enact strict observance of the Sabbath. By passing a law, Sunday work would be illegal."

Even the young Isabella knew that the farmers had to cool the milk, particularly in this hot weather. That was why the dairy houses were dug several feet into the clay, to ensure coolness, and that was why the cheese-making process had to begin. She wanted to ask Papa what the farmers should do. If the cows had to be milked, which they did, then didn't it follow that the milk must be cared for? She opened her mouth, then thought better of it. Papa did not like to have his wisdom questioned.

Papa continued his harangue as if he were arguing with Mr. Wheelwright. "I am aware that Cheshire cheese and whey butter are the farmers' principal income, but that does not excuse their breaking the commandments."

"Yes," Dora concurred, "the early patriarchs kept herds. They must have been aware of milking and making cheese. And yet scripture clearly prohibits Sunday labor."

Papa and Mama were right, that was what scripture said, but how had Abraham managed? Isabella was not surprised that the farmers had stayed home from Evensong, but she couldn't say that to Papa. With Papa's zeal against Sunday labor, the farmers could find no comfort at Saint Albans, and attendance continued to decline. Each week Papa declared that his parishioners would return, but they did not.

In bed one evening, Isabella thought Mr. Wheelwright was right: bees did make honey on Sunday, and it didn't matter what old Abraham had done. She felt disloyal even thinking this.

Isabella was wide-awake. Listening to Hennie's quiet breathing, she felt jealous of her sister, who fell asleep so easily and who never did anything sinful. And just then she recalled a guilty secret that at this very moment she was concealing from Mama. It had started a few months ago, when two packages had arrived from the mysterious Aunt Barbara.

"Who is Aunt Barbara?" Hennie had asked.

"Aunt Barbara is my sister," Mama explained tersely. "She has been away, but in a recent letter she wrote that she is returning and wanted to send you girls something special to make up for all these years."

Packages of any kind were rare, and these boxes were large, identical in size, and wrapped in paper sealed with tape.

"What are they?" Hennie wondered.

"You must open them and find out," Mama said, a trifle nervous, for Barbara had renounced God. Who knew what she might send the girls?

Under Mama's supervision the girls carefully loosened the tape, which Mama then wound into a ball. Below the wrapping the boxes were covered with silver paper that they were instructed to remove without tearing. When the girls lifted the covers off the boxes, whatever was within was hidden with pink tissue paper. Isabella tore aside the tissue paper. Hennie sat back for a moment to gaze in wonder. Then she, too, lifted the paper.

"Look, Hennie," Isabella said, "a doll, with blue eyes and blond hair, just like you."

"And mine," Hennie said, taking her doll gently into her arms, "has brown eyes and brown hair, just like you."

Both dolls' hair was parted in the center. They had ribbons around their heads, and their lips and wax cheeks were touched with a delicate blush. Hennie's doll looked a bit startled, as if she had just been awakened; Isabella's looked more complacent.

Mama wailed, "How could she be so extravagant?"

Isabella had never seen a real girl wear such an elaborate dress, a creamy white taffeta with an embroidered bodice, puffed sleeves, a blue sash circling the waist, and blue ribbon bows around the scalloped hem.

"I love my doll's pink dress," Hennie said, running her finger on the doll's pale-pink gown. Her doll's ribbons were dark rose.

The girls closely examined the dolls: the hair, each strand of which was set into the head, the eyelashes framing the glittering eyes, the exquisitely made clothes.

Isabella lifted her doll's skirt. "Look at these petticoats, Hennie," she exclaimed. Hennie drew back her own doll's skirt. "Did you ever see such tiny tucks? A knit petticoat and pantalets tied with a ribbon and a lace frill."

"Mine has dear little pink shoes and white stockings."

"And mine has blue shoes."

"Oh, I love her!" Hennie cried and hugged her to her chest. "I love her! I'm going to call her Louise." The girls had started French lessons; these dolls looked so exotic, so different from the plain stuff of their acquaintance, that a French name seemed appropriate.

Isabella, for once, followed Hennie's lead and said, "I'll call mine Adele."

"These dolls are not for every day," Mama announced firmly. "They are to be played with only on rare occasions. I shall put them away." Mama moved to gather up the dolls.

"Oh, Mama, couldn't we keep her on the bureau? I promise not to touch but just to look at her," Hennie implored, clasping Louise close to her chest.

"No, indeed not. I don't want your mind on such frippery. I don't know whatever possessed your aunt Barbara." Mama was adamant. She took the doll from Hennie's arms.

Mama rewrapped the dolls in their tissue paper nests and carried the boxes to her room. Hennie, who was always so docile, followed her.

"Oh please, Mama, could we please keep them in our bedroom for just one night?"

"You see? Such frivolity has already had a pernicious influence. No, you will write to Aunt Barbara to thank her for thinking of you, but the dolls shall remain in their boxes in my closet."

Isabella was impressed with the dolls and with the novelty of being given such an expensive gift, but she thought with longing of Merttins's gift last summer, a heavy bow with a quiver of six arrows that he never allowed her to touch.

She added, however, her plea to Hennie's until Mama snapped, "If you don't stop this minute, this very minute, you will not be allowed to see the dolls again."

Tears rolled down Hennie's cheeks. "Mama, I'll be so good. Only let me hold Louise every night. Please, Mama." Hennie in tears induced Mama to relent.

"Once or twice a week, if you have behaved yourselves and have been dutiful little girls, I'll allow you to hold the dolls."

Each time Hennie cradled Louise was a special occasion, and each time Louise had to be buried again in her tissue paper mound caused a pang of sorrow. Isabella, however, found Adele boring. Adele closed her eyes, but she never opened her mouth. She always had the same slightly stupid expression.

One winter afternoon when they had been allowed to play with the dolls, Isabella got an idea. She got out her workbasket and, finding a scrap of material, basted together a rough pair of trousers. Unbuttoning the tiny buttons, off came Adele's dress, off came the two sheer petticoats, the knitted petticoat, and the pantalets to expose a dull muslin-covered body to which the wax arms and legs were attached. Isabella looked between Adele's legs to see how that was handled. Nothing. Isabella stuffed Adele's legs into the makeshift trousers. For a shirt, Isabella tucked a length of material around her arms. Then she took her scissors and lifted up the blond hair.

"What are you doing?" Hennie gasped.

"Cutting her hair."

"You can't do that!" Hennie was aghast. "You'll ruin her!"

"But she needs to have short hair," Isabella insisted.

"What will Mama say? Why don't you make a cap and pin up her hair?"

Thinking of Mama's reaction, Isabella demurred. The solution was not easy to effect. At length, Adele's offending hair was bunched into a knot on her head and hidden by a band. It didn't quite do, but at least the hair was out of sight. Then Isabella took a Noah's ark, transformed it into a sailing vessel, and forced Adele to walk the plank. Adele was too large for the boat, but Isabella enjoyed enacting the swaggering pirate captain and ordering that fainthearted cabin boy Allen to walk to his watery grave.

Whenever Mama gave permission to the girls to play with the dolls, Isabella improved Adele's male wardrobe. The dainty lace and ribbon-trimmed dress and undergarments were removed. In their place Adele wore trousers, a shirt, and a cap with a visor that Isabella thought redeemed her bland expression. Adele was pressed aboard a pirate ship; she walked the plank. She went on tiger safaris in India and rode elephants in Africa. While Isabella made up adventures for Adele, Hennie sat, her blue eyes on Isabella, Louise in her arms, listening in wonder. The more restricted Isabella felt, the more extravagant were Adele's escapades. She mounted wild stallions. She scaled mountains. She rode rapids and crossed flooded torrents. She balanced on ice floes. She even devised a slingshot and deposed the pirate king.

Isabella was ever fearful that when Adele was dressed as a boy and she was relating one of Adele's exploits that Mama might walk in. How could she explain Adele's transformation into Allen? The thought of Mama discovering Adele's life as a boy struck terror into her heart. Like the Sunday dairy workers and other abominable sinners and liars, Isabella would find herself in that lake that burned with fire and brimstone.

Isabella sat up in bed, lit the candle, and scratched away in her journal, listing her sins. Remaking Adele into a boy, reading Papa's journal, going outside on the Sabbath were enough to convince her that she was a wicked child. Reading this catalog made her stomach writhe, and now her back ached. To relieve the pain, she arched while digging both hands deep into her spine.

She picked up her pen, dipped it in ink, and in her journal drew a curlicue under her list and added, "God, forgive me." She sat pensively, the point of the pen touching her chin.

As she was about to blot the page and put it aside, she remembered Mr. Wheelwright stomping out of church, and the people not shaking Papa's hand. "What if nobody comes to Papa's church? What if nobody speaks to Papa?" She wrote the shameful thoughts in her journal. "What will happen to us?" She blew out the candle and huddled under her quilt.

CHAPTER 7

THE COMING OF THE
RAILROAD

Isabella never tired of watching the narrow boats with their gaily painted roses, castles, and stenciled landscapes. Pulled by mules whose only purpose in life was putting one foot in front of the other, they plied the Chester Canal. Isabella usually waved at the man standing at the tiller, who often waved back. She surmised that his wife and children were aboard those boats sporting lace curtains and potted plants. Isabella envied those children. They saw something new every day, they could dangle their feet in the water, and she was sure that they didn't have to sew fine seams and wear starched petticoats.

People began to worry that if railroads continued to web the country, canal boats would soon be out of business. Talk invariably turned to the railway and the loss of canal jobs. Most locals were opposed to the railway, and all had intense feelings on the subject.

"How can the railway carry the loads that the canal boats haul?" At the stile to Mr. Griscomb's property, Isabella listened again to

Papa's argument with Mr. Griscomb, the barrister. "Consider the bulk: coal, limestone, casks of cider, salt, bales of wool, and finished goods, pottery, cheese, boxes, and cases of all kinds. How is that to be loaded into a railway carriage?"

"One engine can pull several carriages and thereby carry the contents of many narrow boats. Stands to reason, Rector," Mr. Griscomb elaborated. "By canal, goods take three weeks to go from Manchester to Liverpool. By train I can go from Manchester to Liverpool, and cross the Atlantic to Boston in three weeks."

"I grant you," Papa countered, "the railway has the edge when it comes to speed."

"Do you know what that speed means?" Mr. Griscomb rejoined. "Consider our shire, dairy country, right? Farmers will be able to place their cheeses right on the train, and within a few hours, they will be in Birmingham, Liverpool, or even London. Entirely new markets."

Papa repeated what he knew. "The canals are the veins of this country, carrying the lifeblood of its commerce and wealth."

"Now they are, yes, but canals will be replaced by the railway. Mark my word: this Shropshire Union Canal, its packets and narrow boats, will be a thing of the past, like the longbow and arrow."

On a nearby chair, Isabella wanted to protest, but she knew better, for if she were not quiet and unobtrusive, Papa would not allow her to accompany him on parish calls.

Sure enough, surveyors soon appeared, followed quickly by excavators who dug cuttings through hills, creating twenty-foot embankments, built a wide tunnel twenty-four feet high, and erected an arched bridge crossing the river Dee. In digging the tunnel, two Roman coins, one Augustinian, and one of the Vespasian era, as well as several skulls and the remains of a Roman camp, were unearthed.

Papa read aloud the *Chester Chronicle* article about these findings and then directed the girls to the globe to show them where

Rome was located. With his finger on the spot labeled "Rome," he told them about the Roman legions that had occupied most of Europe and Great Britain, and that the very name "Chester" was Latin, signifying "place" or "station." The Romans had left remains of their presence in streets and walls and baths and these coins that the railway had unearthed. To Isabella these people didn't have meaning; they were too heavily shrouded in the mists of time.

Hennie wondered, "Do you think those Romans liked being so far from home?"

"They probably did," Isabella volunteered, "just as I'd like to see distant places." But it was hard to think of Chester as a distant place.

A few months later when Papa opened the *Chester Chronicle,* he pointed to an advertisement. The North Staffordshire Railway was looking for personnel: porters, police, brakemen, switchmen, crossing guards, signalmen, ticket collectors, and engineers. Isabella thought Mr. Griscomb was right. The railway was hiring far more men than worked the barges and stagecoaches combined. The advertisement stated that applicants must be "sober, honest, and with a steady character" and that "testimonials of a respectful disposition are favored if signed by the rector." Candidates must be "clean in their persons and clothes, shaved, with their shoes brushed." Papa was petitioned to sign several: one for a discharged soldier, one for a man who had been in gentleman's service, and two for agricultural laborers. All four were hired, and to Papa's surprise, the former dairy laborer, who could neither read nor write, was given training as an engine driver.

One day, Papa brought home a line drawing of an engine with two wheels, with smoke emerging like a banner from a tall funnel-shaped chimney, followed by a car filled with coal, on which a man stood, and by a carriage with three compartments with people sitting in them. In large Gothic print under the drawing, it said:

The North Staffordshire Railway

NOTICE IS HEREBY GIVEN,
that on and after Wednesday next, the 17th of June, the portion of the railway between Chester and the station in Crewe will be open for the conveyance of passengers, parcels, carriages, and horses. Until further notice there will be only two trains each way per day, viz: from Chester Station 9 a.m. and 1 p.m. from Crewe 11 a.m. and 3 p.m.

No trains will run on Sundays at present.
The fares between Chester and Crewe: First Class, 4 shillings; Second class, 2 shillings 6 pence.
Gentlemen's Carriages and horses must be at the stations at least a quarter of an hour before the time of departure of the trains.
An inaugural train will run from Chester to Crewe at 9 a.m. Tuesday, June 16th, 1840.

Papa showed them the announcement. "I am going to take your mother and you girls to the inauguration ceremonies next Tuesday. It is not every day that a railway opens." Papa had struggled with himself, but his sense of history—and curiosity—had triumphed over his fears that he was self-indulgent.

For Isabella seeing the railway was almost beyond imagination. She reread the broadside until she had memorized it. She studied the drawing. She asked, "What was the man doing standing in the coal? How could gentlemen's carriages and horses fit into that car?" She thought Tuesday would never arrive.

After breakfast early Tuesday morning, Trojan and Shag were hitched to the carriage headed for Chester. Along the road were cottages that, with their brown thatch roofs, their whitewashed walls, and their timber uprights, looked appealing, but Isabella had been inside when Papa made his calls, and she knew that inside they were dark and wretched. They had clay floors lower than the road or the surrounding land, and those floors were often wet, and always damp. The roofs and walls made with interlaced twigs were old and leaky and full of vermin.

"Papa," Isabella had questioned, "can't they put floors in those cottages?"

"Yes, I suppose they could. But you know, Isabella, it's none of our business."

Today with Shag and Trojan trotting briskly along, with the dew still sparkling on the pastures, with the sweet sun shining, the cottages looked beautiful. Isabella watched for a noble beech with dark-copper leaves in a park-like pasture that was almost half-way. From Chester came a handsome carriage and four, the near wheeler and the leader ridden by postilions in bright-yellow livery, and within, an old gentleman in a velvet cap. They passed farmers with their carts and wagons going to Chester, and other carriages and chaises. Soon they reached the crest of a sharp hill, and they were almost there. Down below was a rich valley bound by billowy hills, and in its midst was a walled town with smoke, chimneys, and steeples, dominated by the square brown tower of the cathedral.

They passed the public bath and washhouse, a hospital for the poor, and near it, a house of correction and a gloomy-looking workhouse. They passed "the Roodee," a treeless meadow with a racecourse around it, on which boys in blue-skirted coats and breeches and stockings played. Papa hitched the carriage near the blackened old ramparts, whose battlements were broken down in one place by a cannon aimed by Oliver Cromwell. Papa explained that they weren't going into Chester; the station had been built in a meadow, a short distance outside Chester, and passengers were conveyed from the station to the center of town in a new railway omnibus, the *British Queen.*

Isabella liked Chester: crossing the canal, with its long, narrow boats laden with coal; going through the monumental arched stone gate built by the Romans; and walking along the top of its wall, which had a five-foot-wide path with a stone balustrade on one side and an iron railing on the other. One tower in the wall had a rude carving of a phoenix and under it an old tablet that was engraved "On this tower stood Charles the First, and saw his army defeated." She enjoyed walking the crooked paved streets with their narrow, steep-gabled houses—many with their second stories frowning over the sidewalks, supported by stone posts, creating shadowy arcades—and the thatched houses with cozy dormers. She delighted in the many inns and taverns, The Crown and Castle, The Pied Bull, The Green Dragon, and the new market building with its iron roof, from which, on a hot day, the pigeons fled. Papa pointed out a house whose beam was inscribed "God's Providence is mine Inheritance—1652," and he explained that the family residing in it was the only one in the city that entirely escaped the great plague of that year.

Today, however, they were not entering the town, but were joining the throng of well-dressed spectators gathering near the station. The sun was bright, the bells of the churches were pealing, and at the station, the horns and kettledrums of the Fifth Dragoon Guards in their snug blue uniforms played martial airs. Railway policemen paraded on the station platform in tight-waisted navy-blue uniforms and tall beaver hats, keeping the press of people away from the chocolate-colored carriages until time to board. A man in knee breeches and red stockings was striking a donkey with a stout stick across his long, expressive ears.

"Oh, Papa, make him stop!"

Papa spoke to the man, "Why do you abuse that poor creature?"

The disgruntled man snapped, "What have I done unto thee? You just mind your own affairs, and I'll mind mine." With that he lifted down a stool and one of the cans of milk slung on each side of the donkey and poured a foaming cup. "One pence a cup, fresh this morning," he offered.

Isabella saw a dashing young man in a red-coated military uniform with a scarlet cap riding a sorrel mare, whose quivering shoulder he patted; and a sooty-faced boy with a Kilmarnock bonnet, carrying two pewter mugs; and a tall Welsh girl balancing a tub on her head, her glossy hair half covered by a white cap, wearing a short striped petticoat and hobnailed shoes.

Then the most amazing event: Papa extracted from his wallet four paper squares printed with numbers. They were, he said, tickets. They were going on the train. Passengers were admitted to the trains by numbered tickets corresponding to numbered seats. Each of the coaches carried the company's coat of arms on its center panels, as well as the Union Jack hoisted upon the roof. The train, consisting of two first- and two second-class carriages, was headed by the locomotive *Rob Roy*, whose name was lettered on its side. *Rob Roy* had two five-foot-six-inch driving wheels—just Papa's height—on each side of the boiler. The engine driver was standing on the footplate, and he waved as they went past him.

The ticket collector examined their bits of paper and pointed. "Second car down."

The band started playing "God Save the Queen." Queen Victoria, Isabella remembered, had been on the throne only three years; what had they played before that? The carriages were crammed to capacity, and people were standing in the corridors, all flocking to ride a train for the very first time in their lives. Papa and Mama and the girls found their seats in a compartment where four seats were already taken by a young couple and two elderly men. The padded seats were covered with light-brown fabric and were clearly numbered in the rack above them. Hennie sat next to the window, and Isabella sat opposite her. Isabella thought she would burst. She looked through the window at the thousands cheering.

The train gave a great shudder, then a neighing like a huge metal horse expelling its breath, a bell clanged, a whistle shrieked, and they started to move. Papa looked at his watch, 9:10 a.m. Isabella could see the astonished gazes of the people as the train moved. The train rolled along in the most beautiful manner possible. *Click, click, click* went the rails; the whistle hooted; *click, click, click*, faster and faster.

Chester quickly receded. Dark smoke and sparks pelted the windows. In the corridor one of the ladies screamed as the landscape flew past. A uniformed trainman came through the carriage and told them that the train was maintaining an excellent pace, thirty miles per hour. Isabella could see farmers standing still in their fields, and women in front of their cottages, their hands twisted in their aprons, and children with their mouths agape.

The train made three stops on the journey, one to take on water, and at 10:50 pulled into Crewe, which, like Chester, had a single platform for trains in both directions. At Crewe everyone got off, and the train lurched forward to a turntable. The station was hung with evergreens, the crowds were even larger than in Chester, and the Fourth Royal Irish Dragoon Guards played a thumping march. In a few minutes, there was the *Rob Roy* and the carriages coming toward them.

Isabella felt very special, indeed, that she and Hennie and Mama and Papa were among the privileged ones who had tickets. Five minutes later the train was setting out on its return run. They maintained the same breakneck speed on the journey. At one point there was a jolt, but the train did not halt. Only later did Isabella learn that a sheep had been killed. She was glad that she hadn't known that at the time, for nothing had marred this perfect day. At length, the train, in gallant style, pulled into Chester at 12:27. Their tickets did not entitle them to partake of a cold collation with meats, jellies, confections, and fruits, but Mama had brought bread and cheese and pickled onion, and they could listen to more music played by the band, to the speeches and toasts while eating their repast.

On the way home, Isabella was impatient with the slow *clop, clop, clop* of the horses.

Mama leaned back against the cushions and gave a great sigh. "Oh, it's a relief to be going home. I'm thankful to have Trojan and Shag."

"Mama"—Isabella actually felt betrayed—"how can you say that?"

"The train may be very well in its place, but it's not for civilized people," Mama stated emphatically. "The noise and the dirt! No, I'll happily stay at home or take the stagecoach anytime."

CHAPTER 8
THE "HEATHEN"

Lessons continued at Taplow Hill during the summers. Aunt Rebecca taught the four cousins, Merttins and Hannah, Isabella and Hennie. Isabella enjoyed classes with her cousins and often knew the answers when her older cousins did not. She knew she had a better mind than Merttins, but she also knew that unlike her male cousins, she could not go to Cambridge because she was female. The thought that Merttins would automatically go to Cambridge, while she would not, left her fuming.

Isabella also envied Merttins and Hannah for living at Taplow Hill all the time. She knew she *should* feel sorry for them because their papa had died, but she could not reconcile their father, George of the miniature, with the slow, rotund Merttins in front of her.

Isabella envied Merttins and Hannah in another way. Their mother, Margaret, often had her arms about them. She kissed them on the forehead or hugged them. Ill at ease, Isabella stood at one side observing them, unable to identify what she was feeling. She could not remember one instance of being held or kissed by her mother or father. Nor had she ever seen her own parents embrace.

Standing next to a globe that was almost as tall as she was, Aunt Rebecca taught geography. The children traced latitude and longitude and the line of the equator. Peering through her round glasses, Aunt Rebecca pointed out the subcontinent of India and the location of Calcutta, where "Brother Robert and his dear wife and children and sister Mary labored."

Isabella looked at a pink mass on the globe labeled "Asia" and compared it to the tiny irregular island of Great Britain. In her mind's eye, she saw the perpendicular cliffs of the Chinese teapot; she saw range after range of mountain peaks; she saw waterfalls and torrents, forests of dense pine, and yellow people with upturned eyes.

"Who lives there, Aunt Rebecca?" she asked.

"The heathen," Aunt Rebecca replied, as if biting off pieces of thread. "The heathen."

One morning after prayers, Grandfather read aloud a letter from Aunt Mary, sent from India, where she worked as a missionary. The letter, on thin paper, written horizontally and vertically across the page, was full of pathetic stories of poverty, heathen spiritual barrenness, and of the need for greater missionary endeavors. The fervor of Protestant guilt was made explicit early. Isabella and her cousins were often told how fortunate they were compared with the unwanted babies in the streets of Calcutta. Grandfather cleared his throat and began.

For self-devoted zeal, none can surpass our missionaries. In one instance, the wife of an officer found that the newly arrived missionaries, practicing self-denial, ate no meat. Determined to care for them, the officer's wife sent them poultry ready for table from her own farmyard, which obliged them to eat it.

"I'm not convinced," Grandfather interposed, looking over his glasses, "that not eating meat helps to convert natives." He took up the letter again.

It will give you some idea of the depravity of the natives to mention that we passed today a pretty little girl, singing at the top of her voice. Robert told me that the words of the song were so utterly detestable and vile, that only the worst man in London would sing them and then only if he were intoxicated.

Yesterday Robert visited a Hindu who is to be hanged today for the murder of his wife. She was unfaithful, and in reprisal he cut her throat. The magistrate found him perfectly callous and unmoved. The guilty man said, "God put it into my heart to kill my wife, so that if there is anything wrong in it, it is not my fault; what does it signify if I am hanged tomorrow or not. I must die someday." Thus that wretched Hindu left this life in Satan's hands.

Nothing can equal the abominations of the Hindu deities and modes of worship. The verses taught to children are such as cannot be repeated. Think what must be the state of a nation, when children are systematically trained in wickedness, and their acts of worship consist of crimes. Mrs. Janvier was saying the other day, that although the abolition of Sati was good for women, still the condition of a Hindu widow is often so lamentable as to make death preferable.

"What is Sati?" Isabella interrupted.

"A Hindu widow is expected to jump onto her husband's funeral pyre."

"They burn the dead? And the wife is expected to burn herself?"

"Yes, immolate herself. Her sacrifice is a symbol of wifely excellence and devotion. If she doesn't throw herself onto the flames, her family is disgraced." Grandfather continued reading:

At the orphanage, Miss Laing conducts morning and evening worship, and one of the missionaries preaches to them on the Sabbath. Miss Laing told me that the average expense of each child, exclusive of house-rent (which is quite high in Calcutta) and of the teachers' salaries, is three rupees, or six shillings a month. How many could subscribe this sum, and thus rescue an orphan from wild beasts, or from men who are even worse.

In starting her orphanage Miss Laing said she had anticipated many trials, but had never thought of having to attend the deathbeds of the children under her care. In five years she has lost three. One, an infant, who could just repeat a little hymn, and say a little prayer; the other gave good hopes of her salvation; but the most touching, yet comfortable death of all was that of a child who was given the name of Isabella. Miss Laing took the poor little thing, who was then about five years old, and brought to her from the street. From the day she was admitted she was a truthful, quiet, intelligent child, who learned with great facility.

When she was suffering from an attack of dysentery, Miss Laing one day said to her as she was passing through the room, "Isabella! Do you know that you are a sinner?"

Isabella burst into tears and answered, "Oh, yes, I am a great sinner. I pray to Jesus to take away my sins."

Miss Laing was astonished at the emotion so unusual in a native. Some time after Miss Laing found her on her bed; Isabella Green seized the hand of her kind instructress and said, "Oh I love you so much, for you have led me to Jesus."

From that time all her expressions were full of hope. She longed to depart and be with Jesus. No person entered the room without Isabella exhorting them in the most solemn manner to flee to Christ for salvation. Miss Laing never left her, but read the numberless passages of scripture she asked for until, without a sigh, her happy spirit fled with all the confidence, joy, and faith of a saint to be forever with the Lord.

May the account of this glorious deathbed and the vision of that New Jerusalem, when I trust all those dearest to us will see the reality and will "walk with the Lamb in white" sustain you. Yours in Christ, Mary.

That unknown Isabella, whose death the aunts spoke of as "beautiful," and the Hindu women immolating themselves usurped Isabella's imagination. Taplow Hill, Tattenhall, those were realities; New Jerusalem and the Lamb in white were too vague to have form or shape.

A few weeks later, Grandfather's collie, Flag, breathed his last. He died as he had lived: waiting for Grandfather. Both girls were choked with grief, for Flag had been part of Taplow Hill for as long as they could remember. In comforting them, Aunt Catherine used the same word, "beautiful," about his death and explained that Flag had not suffered.

"Will Jesus find room for Flag in heaven?" Hennie asked.

"Yes," Aunt Catherine assured her, "Flag will be there, wagging his tail in joy."

Hennie found solace in the picture of Flag in the marble corridors of eternity wagging his tail, but Isabella was doubtful. Isabella did not want to upset Hennie, but she needed to puzzle it out.

"Aunt Catherine," she asked, "is Flag like a baby?"

"No," Aunt Catherine answered, not sure what Isabella's question meant. "No, Flag is not like a baby."

Isabella's doubts were affirmed. An infant can be baptized, she had been taught; in fact, an infant needed baptism to ensure salvation. But every child of her age, of Hennie's age, must bear personal responsibility to seek for herself the way of salvation. Salvation could not be given to children as it could to an infant. If Flag was not like a baby who could be baptized without that personal responsibility, under what clause could he enter eternal bliss? Isabella was not sure how old that Isabella was, but it sounded as if she were six or seven.

"Are children in India allowed to be baptized younger than we are in England?" she asked.

Grandfather looked at her sharply, but Aunt Rebecca answered that the position of missionaries in a school or in charge of an orphanage was different than that of a parent, that the missionaries stood in place of the parents.

"The missionaries take responsibility for the children?" Isabella asked. "Why can't ministers here take that responsibility?"

"Children here have knowledge of the Gospel," Aunt Rebecca answered, but Isabella was not satisfied. How could a baby, and even Flag, have salvation, but she and Hennie could not unless they declared themselves for Christ?

Aunt Rebecca's patience seemed at an end, but Grandfather shot her a smile that stayed her tongue.

"A fine question," said Grandfather as Rebecca squirmed. "As fine question indeed. Now then, dessert must be on its way."

CHAPTER 9
HORSEMANSHIP AND CHESS

Isabella wondered if she had heard correctly. Had Grandfather actually said that each of his four grandchildren could have a horse if they would care for it? Isabella's eyes widened and her mouth dropped in sheer bliss.

Merttins and Hannah had first call. Isabella crossed her fingers. She desperately wanted Buttons, a roguish three-year-old. To her relief Merttins chose Royal, and Hannah wanted Crystal. Buttons was hers, and a staid mare named Bows was Hennie's. Isabella mumbled a hasty "excuse me," pushed back her chair, and vaulted down to the stable to talk to Buttons, curry his coat, comb his black mane, and select one of the sidesaddles that the aunts had used when they were girls.

Marlowe the coachman undertook to school the children. Isabella wished he were not so particular; every detail had to be precisely as he instructed. She learned to muck out the straw each day and pile it in a tidy heap, to put four inches of fresh straw into the stall, to curry Buttons's sleek bay coat, to examine his hooves for pebbles and his molars for decay, to feed and water him, to bridle and to saddle him, and to tell from his behavior what his mood was. If his eyes were large and confident and relaxed, Buttons was ready to be saddled. If, however, his eyes were squinting and he was swiveling his ears and swishing his black tail, Isabella learned to move slowly, to humor him, to talk to him gently. She particularly liked to run her fingers against the short, stiff hairs on his forehead, then stroke and smooth them into place.

A few weeks later, Grandfather, mounted on Trumpet, saw Isabella stamping her foot and scowling. Royal, Crystal, Buttons, and Bows were at the far end of the pasture.

"Is Buttons being fractious?" Grandfather asked.

"I can't get him to come."

"He wants to stay with his friends, enjoying his freedom. Is that it?"

"I have a carrot for him, but he pays no mind."

Grandfather swung down from Trumpet, putting the reins over the horse's head. "Let's see what can be done. We can't have Buttons dictating when he's going to work and when he isn't."

"Should we put all four horses in the stable, then let the others out, and keep Buttons?"

"No, that's not the solution. He'll just learn resistant behavior. You need to follow Buttons. When he starts to move away, you move too. This is not a large pasture. Whatever direction he goes, you follow. You must allow plenty of time. Don't be in a hurry. Eventually, you'll catch him. Then bridle him, walk him a few steps, and release him."

"You mean let him go? Why?"

"You've rewarded him for his compliance. You made him do what you wanted him to do, but he gets to do what he wants to do, stay free in the pasture."

Grandfather moved toward Buttons, who immediately came to him as if to disprove Isabella.

"Grandfather, he wouldn't come for me," she wailed. When she had tried to ambush Buttons, Marlowe had spoken sharply to her. He wasn't going to allow Buttons "to be spooked."

"What you need to do, Isabella, is to be persistent. Take care not to chase or ambush him. Just quietly tag after him. Eventually, Buttons is going to stop and look at you. He is going to ask you what you are doing. Stand still. Come to a complete stop. When he moves off again, resume walking in his direction. Do this until he allows you to approach and catch him. Then give him a reward, your carrot, kind words, a pat."

"If I follow him around, will he come when I call?"

"Always follow this routine, and I guarantee you will be rewarded. Allow plenty of time. Teach Buttons how persistent you can be. And do not lose your patience. Buttons will understand that you don't intend to quit. Don't frighten him; just outlast him. Catch him a few times without riding him. Think of it as a visit. You've come to the pasture to greet him. You'll see. He will come when you ask him to."

Buttons was a strong-willed horse, and Isabella became impatient. Each time, however, she followed Grandfather's instructions well, trailing Buttons around the pasture until she was able to put his halter on him. Almost a dozen "visits" took place before Buttons came to her when she called. But the day came when he did.

One July morning, Kathleen, one of Grandfather's housekeepers, came into Isabella's room to draw the heavy drapes, and to lay out clean drawers, stockings, and pinafores. Isabella was stretching luxuriously, her toes exploring the perimeters of her four-poster bed, not like home, where she always had to be roused. Here she woke up without being called. Here Isabella never suffered the recurrent nightmare that plagued her at home: Satan seizing her by the ankles, turning her upside down, and stuffing her into a large, airless bag.

Isabella saw the small mound of Hennie in the other bed and smiled when she noticed the linen covers of the huge pillows frothing with crocheted lace. Grandmother's creations. Her hands always fluttered with her crochet hook. All the linens—sheets, pillow

covers, pillow shams, summer spreads, canopies, tablecloths, nap-
kins, doilies, dish towels, curtains, antimacassars—every inch spoke
of Grandmother's industry, crocheting kilometer after kilometer,
and she was still in production. Did anything remain untrimmed?
Here, as at home, every piece of furniture was covered with heavy
material that reached to the floor. Every window was obscured by
curtains, velvet drapes, and ample valances. Small items, teapots,
needle cases, pincushions, picture frames were disguised by bulky
covers or encrusted with seed pearls or fake flowers. Isabella wondered if anything was permitted to be what it was. Then she remembered drawings of medieval times, and she was thankful that
horses were not caparisoned now as they had been then.

Isabella bounced out of bed, hurried to the windows, reeled
them open, and sat herself in front of them to submit without
complaint to Kathleen's ministrations with brush and comb, for
Grandfather insisted that his grandchildren be well-groomed: no
crooked collars or flyaway hair, no matter how early. Isabella never
failed to present herself at sunup looking spic-and-span for a pre-
breakfast ride with Grandfather. She loved Grandfather, and she
loved horses. Merttins hated to get up. Hennie and Hannah liked
their mounts well enough but could wait to ride until later in the
day.

Sparrows twittered and chirped, larks caroled, and far off a
blackbird rehearsed his two-note repertoire. Farther from the
house, a magnificent beech worked its gnarled toes into the soil.
White sheep, each with its nose to the ground, spotted a nearby
field like a green-and-white still life. Hawthorn hedges, heavy with
bloom, outlined the erratically shaped fields like embroidery stitching crazy quilt pieces together. The undulating swellings of land,
punctuated here and there with a single oak or laurel, stretched to
the purple of the Malvern Hills.

As Kathleen started to redo one curl, Isabella complained,
"Oh, Kathleen, don't fuss. It's fine. I need to go." Kathleen secured

the heavy chestnut-brown tresses with tortoise combs, and away Isabella dashed.

"Pretty as a picture," Grandfather said as he nodded good morning.

"This riding costume was Auntie Catherine's when she was a girl," Isabella explained. The blue velvet skirt and tight waist made Isabella feel grown-up, as did the matching bowler with a curling white feather and chin strap.

Trumpet was saddled and whinnying his impatience in the courtyard, but Isabella closed her eyes and took a deep breath through her nose, the better to savor the horse smell. Buttons was impatient to be out and stepped sideways, shifting his weight. Isabella adjusted his blanket and then gave him a sharp rap on his barrel side.

The sun was just chinning himself over the earth's edge as Trumpet and Buttons were picking up their feet with the lovely arched-ankle movement that Isabella admired, the courtyard gravel crunching underneath. They were headed for the upper pasture encircled by a wagon trail where the horses could stretch out in a lively gallop. A frightened rabbit bounded out of the grass darkened with the long shadows of the elms.

Isabella touched Buttons's neck, and he responded by quickening his pace. Sidesaddle, she thought, was truly awkward. She couldn't use her knees to control the horse but had to depend solely on her hands as Grandfather had taught her. She wished she were a boy and could wear trousers and ride astride. Trumpet lengthened his stride, and both horses began to gallop. A gallop was the best possible gait. It was smooth and effortless with a cool breeze refreshing the face. Then, the best part, Isabella felt herself meld with Buttons until she and the horse were one ribbon of movement. A black walnut tree, a crumbling chimney, Mrs. Foster's kitchen garden, landmarks that had been distant, flew past. Twice around the pasture and then Grandfather reined in Trumpet, and

Isabella pulled steadily on Buttons's reins, both horses trembling with exertion.

The gallop had caused a tortoise comb to fall out, and Isabella's hair was tumbling about her face. When Grandfather questioned her, she said, "It doesn't matter, Grandfather."

"It's no trouble. We'll retrace our steps." Sure enough, there it was only a short distance back. Grandfather dismounted, retrieved it, and with a courtly gesture handed it to Isabella.

A quiet walk to a nearby copse cooled the horses and riders. Then came the walk back to the stable. Seeing the sun arise and the world fresh with dew, with birdsong, with the beauty of being, with Grandfather at her side and a powerful horse under her, Isabella felt God's presence enter her soul. She'd have no trouble being good if the world were always like this. They returned to the house for breakfast.

Isabella preferred to keep the odor of horses on her hands, but this was strictly forbidden. Grandfather required that her hands be washed before re-entering the house.

As she and Hennie were leaving the breakfast room, Grandmother Bird, putting a restraining hand on Isabella's arm, asked her daughter Catherine, "Would you please introduce this child to me?"

Didn't Grandmother know her? She had been coming to Taplow Hill for as long as she could remember. Auntie Catherine presented her, but a few moments later, Grandmother again asked to be introduced. Auntie Catherine told Isabella she must overlook Grandmother's periods of forgetfulness.

What would it be like, Isabella wondered, to forget someone you saw every day? Was poor Grandmother's world always full of strangers? Not to recognize Hennie! Isabella made a vow that from then on, she would always smile at Grandmother and stand next to her when they gathered around the piano to sing hymns. Now she understood why all her aunts consulted Grandfather about household matters.

After a busy morning picking raspberries for Nora and helping Auntie Catherine arrange cascades of flowers, it was time for dinner. Isabella was grateful to have been graduated from the nursery and permitted to sit at the dining room table. No matter how engrossing the conversation that swirled around her, she was allowed neither to question nor to comment unless she was directly addressed.

The family had decided opinions about every issue, and Isabella often closely followed the impassioned discourse: Catholic Emancipation, temperance, atonement and the baffling question of the Unitarians, the Chartist movement, penal reform, and overseas missions. Guests, often from missions in China, India, or West Africa, told stories—of a man who had jumped overboard thinking he was in Eden, of natives who lived in grass huts, of Hindu widows who had flung themselves into flames.

The Reverend Robert Ewart, a gentleman thin as a nail who was raising funds for a school in India, told of a dust storm in the middle of the afternoon. "Suddenly it was so dark I could not see the bottle of ink in front of me. I went groping about as if at midnight. The dog ran against me without seeing me, and I only found my wife by her voice, as it was impossible to see one's own hand. It lasted about two hours. I told the children, their ayah, and the Mohammedan bearer, and the Hindu bearer, that thus would the Day of Judgment come, suddenly as a thief in the night, and that on that dreadful day, idolaters would have no friend, that Christ Jesus was the only saviour of men."

The aunts were questioning if they should continue their practice of not using sugar in their tea, a practice they had begun as a sacred protest against slave-grown products. Slavery had been abolished in the British colonies several years earlier—the lifelong endeavor of their cousin William Wilberforce—but in agriculture, those former slaves were still apprenticed to their masters. Aunt Catherine suggested that since the apprenticeship would automatically cease in 1840, their sacrifice was no longer necessary. Aunt Rebecca and Aunt Margaret demurred. The apprentices were almost slaves and were still in bondage. They were confident that the dear departed William and Henrietta would agree. The aunts had just overruled Catherine and had agreed that the ladies of the family would continue to drink their tea unsweetened "in sympathy with those who were heavily laden." They bid one another not to mourn their sugarless tea but to be cheerful and willing about the sacrifice.

At that moment Isabella asked, "May I have sugar, please?" The aunts greeted Isabella's request with shocked reproof, but she had not heard a word.

Isabella had been having a conversation with the stout mandarin on the side of the Derby teapot. She was too polite to ask him if all the Chinese were built as he was, like an overturned top, but she did ask if those vertical cliffs really were that steep in China. His hands were hidden in his kimono sleeves, but he nodded his head in assent, causing his shoelace mustache and his fringe of bang to bob.

He had just invited her for tea, and Isabella, who did not like the bitter unsweetened brew, asked, "May I have sugar, please?"

Grandfather put two or three lumps into his own cup, then handed the jolly fat basin to her along with the little silver tongs she so dearly loved to use.

The Bird family had a decisive cast of mind, not comfortable with nuance, not given to compromise. All were adamant about their own revelations of the truth, but Edward Bird and Aunt Henrietta, while she lived, carried their opinions to a martyr's pitch. When either Papa or Aunt Henrietta was convinced that he or she was right, no persuasion on Earth would alter that conviction. Just as Papa believed that Sunday was the Lord's Day, that any work on that day was a defilement, so Aunt Henrietta had decided beliefs about infant baptism.

Aunt Rebecca argued that she thought the children ought to be required to stand throughout the Sunday service, and Isabella had to bite her tongue to prevent herself from speaking. She had been thankful this summer that she had not been compelled to stand, for standing aggravated the pain in her back.

"It troubles me, Catherine," said Aunt Rebecca. "You know Henrietta would insist on the children standing. She would charge them to endure and to be happy in service for the Lord."

"You are right. She would."

Rebecca, sensing a weakness, rushed in. "She would never tolerate Christians who slumped. We need to remind ourselves that, as Christians, we are soldiers who battle with evil. Keeping our spines erect as warriors of the Lord is our Christian duty."

Isabella liked this reason for a straight back, being a warrior of the Lord. Still, she could have a straight back when she was sitting down.

"Of course, I want to endorse whatever Henrietta approved, but in this instance, I think standing is too much of a hardship. It is enough that children sit up straight and not make this sacrifice."

"Henrietta suffered for her beliefs, and we in the family should honor her and them," Aunt Rebecca answered decisively.

Isabella knew that she ought to be willing to behave as Aunt Henrietta decreed, for she had gone, as everyone knew, to her reward this past winter, but she hoped that Auntie Catherine's opinion would prevail. What Isabella wanted to know was, how had Aunt Henrietta suffered? She saw flames licking at Aunt Henrietta as they had licked at Latimer, Ridley, and Cranmer, who had been burned at the stake for their Protestant beliefs.

Isabella remembered Aunt Henrietta beckoning her and saying, "Allow me to show you this pearl without price." Aunt Henrietta led her to the reading stand upon which rested an open Bible, which she lifted from the stand—almost as tall as she was—and carefully placed it on the table. Reverently she turned the black leather cover and pointed to the blank sheet before the title page.

Although Isabella could read the copper script that was written there, Aunt Henrietta proudly read aloud the inscription. "To my beloved cousins at Taplow Hill, yours devotedly in Christ, William Wilberforce." Isabella could see the little pointing finger and hear the high-pitched voice. "Bear in mind, Isabella that this great man is your cousin. We must all strive to follow in his footsteps."

Isabella looked at the curled serifs of the script and then turned to the title page, which announced that this Holy Bible contained the Old and New Testaments, and was translated from the original tongues, and was diligently compared and revised with former translations.

Henrietta's small hand rested lovingly on the book. "I trust you will esteem this book above all others."

What had tiny Aunt Henrietta done?

"What did she do?" Isabella whispered.

"Infant baptism," Auntie Catherine answered cryptically. Isabella did not know what she meant, nor would Aunt Rebecca, nor even the aunts' sister-in-law Aunt Margaret satisfy her curiosity. It was only later when she was again at home that Papa explained.

Aunt Henrietta had been engaged to a clergyman. The engagement was announced, the date set, the banns read, when Henrietta discovered that she and her intended did not share the same doctrine about infant baptism. Aunt Henrietta had assumed, of course, that her husband-to-be knew that baptism was essential to remove any taint from the infant soul, for were we not, after all, born in original sin? The Reverend Arthur Renshaw, it became apparent, did not think that the baptismal sacrament was for that purpose. He thought infants were created by God without blemish, and that baptism was solely a ritual consecration into the Christian community. The engagement floundered on this dissention. Despite the public humiliation, Aunt Henrietta broke off the engagement rather than modify her stance. Her show of conviction rent her in two as if she had hacked a chasm within that she was not able to bridge, for immediately she dwindled. Her nervous tremors and headaches became daily ordeals. When she succumbed to pneumonia that winter, the family held that her death had been a sacrifice to her beliefs.

Henrietta was a martyr like Henry Prime, a friend who had served in India, for whom no offering, even life itself, was too extreme to give. Henrietta would have made an admirable missionary, her sisters affirmed. If Isabella wanted to see China or India or any faraway place, she wondered, would she have to become a missionary?

That evening, Grandfather brought out, from its special drawer under the rosewood table with its inlaid board, the chess set to teach his grandson John to play. Isabella put aside her book. Marmaduke and Merttins preferred to prance around on their broomstick hobbyhorses, brandishing wooden sabers, but Isabella was entranced with the chessmen that Grandfather had bought many years ago in India.

Half of the pieces were a creamy ivory, and the other half were ivory stained red. They all lived in little pockets in a velvet-lined box. The pieces that Grandfather called "knights" Isabella liked the best. They were on charging horses, and those he called "bishops" were fat elephants with detailed tusks and tails, and those who rode in howdahs on the backs of elephants were the "kings" and "queens." The "pawns," or mahouts, elephant keepers and drivers, were on one knee, carrying a stick that leaned against a shoulder.

Grandfather advised John to think of the pawns as foot soldiers, with one significant difference: they were the only pieces that, if they negotiated the entire length of the treacherous board, could be exchanged for any other piece—except a king.

"You mean, Grandfather, that they can be redeemed?" Isabella asked, thinking of all the sermons she had heard exhorting the

congregation to be soldiers of the Lord and they would be rewarded with salvation.

"Just so."

"Does Papa play chess?"

"Yes, I taught him myself." Grandfather sensed that Isabella was
worried since Papa disapproved of so many games. "I am sure that
Papa will not object to your watching or even playing, for chess is
not a game of chance. It is completely skill and artistry."

It intrigued Isabella that the pieces had assigned roles. The
player could determine where each piece went but could not alter
how each one moved. *Something like that sermon last week when the
preacher said that we must all occupy the stations where God had placed us,
and that whatever that position was, that was our destiny.* Isabella doubt-
ed that message, however, when she remembered how a pawn, if he
lived a good life, could be transformed into a knight or a bishop.

Isabella's hand reached out and picked up one of the horses.
Grandfather spoke sharply, "You are invited to watch, Isabella, but
you must not touch." He was dismayed to see tears form in her
eyes, and he added, "Girls don't play chess, but if you don't touch,
you may look."

Isabella, a slight child, perched like a chess piece herself on
Grandfather's knee, and Grandfather continued, "I was telling
John that once you touch a piece, you are obliged to move it."

"What if I want to move something else? Or I change my mind?"
John asked.

"It is a hard rule. If you touch a piece, you must move it."

There is no going back, Isabella thought.

"Furthermore, if you touch several pieces, your opponent has
the right to choose which one he wants you to move."

Isabella was learning that even a game was hedged with rules,
but at least in chess she could see where she was going, and the opponent was out in the open and not lurking in so many forbidden
activities.

"Every move has to be thought out before I begin?" John looked troubled. Isabella understood that once a move was started, it could not be stopped.

"Exactly. Learn to play patiently, and don't touch a piece until you are sure you want to move it."

There was that word again. Patience. Mama said that Isabella had no patience, and Papa was always saying, "Possess your soul with patience." Hennie certainly had patience; it must be something you were born with. But she had learned to be patient with Buttons. She laughed at herself. She must be patient to learn patience.

"Once you take your hand off a piece," Grandfather continued, "the move is complete and cannot be retracted. There is only one exception. You may realign your pieces without penalty. You must, however, say beforehand, '*J'adoube*,' or 'I adjust.'"

Isabella followed the game closely, not speaking, not moving until Grandfather said, "Checkmate." And he demonstrated how John's king was not able to move in any direction without being captured. Grandfather took the box and carefully replaced each piece into its little pocket. He tipped Isabella to the floor, stood, and announced, "Evening service."

Auntie Catherine sounded a gong for evening prayers with the family, and the indoor maids gathered around the piano. Grandfather did not question them, like Papa did, about what they had done that day for the glory of God. Papa petitioned God to shield Isabella from Satan and from nightly visitations from Satan's invisible demons, but Grandfather did not mention the devil. At Taplow Hill, Isabella barely had time to arrange her pillow before sleep embraced her.

CHAPTER 10

GRANDFATHER'S FUNERAL

One April morning when the elixir of spring suffused the air, and as the porridge cooled, Papa intoned a particularly long grace that concluded with "O grant, most merciful Father, for the sake of Christ Jesus Our Lord that we may hereafter live a godly, righteous, and sober life to the glory of thy holy name." He cleared his throat and then explained, "In order that the rest of my life be pure and holy so that at the last I may come to eternal joy, I have decided to accept the call at Saint Thomas."

Isabella's breath stopped. When Papa prefaced his remarks with statements about salvation, she knew that he was broaching an important subject. "Saint Thomas, Papa?"

"Yes, I have been beseeching the good Lord to show me the path to hasten his kingdom, and in his wisdom and heavenly benediction, he led me to Saint Thomas."

Isabella asked, "Papa, where is Saint Thomas?"

Hennie chimed in, "Is Saint Thomas in Chester?"

"Saint Thomas is in Birmingham, a three-day journey from here."

"Birmingham?" Hennie wondered, rolling the unfamiliar name over her tongue.

"Birmingham is a large city with factories and workshops, a manufacturing city, quite different from Tattenhall," Papa said.

"Will we still go to Taplow Hill and visit Grandfather?" Isabella wanted to know.

"Yes, that won't change."

"When are we moving to Saint Thomas?"

"As soon as we can get ready."

"Papa, are we moving because so few people come to church?" Isabella, for the first time, voiced her fear. She had been anxious. The pews were almost empty. Only the men and women known as "Bird's saints," whom Papa had brought to Christ, attended regularly. What would happen if no one came? Papa's crusade against Sunday labor had drained the church of the dairy farmers, maids, and hands who found no comfort at Saint Albans.

On the question of the Sabbath, Papa knew he was right. The commandments ordained a day of rest, and that was the end of it.

Wouldn't God accept some kind of farm work? Isabella silently sympathized with the dairy workers. When she accompanied Papa on his calls, they would inevitably meet one of the dairy farmers. Whereas formerly there had been a pleasant exchange, now the farmer either brusquely touched his hand to his hat without speaking or stared straight ahead and rode on. Isabella felt miserable. Didn't Papa care? She had learned to keep her thoughts hidden. Like Adele's masculine clothes, Isabella's traitorous sympathies were hidden.

"Not at all," Papa declared. "Saint Thomas itself is in a state of neglect. It seats more than two thousand souls, but only a few hundred worship and they attend erratically. Without question I am charged to bring the living Christ and the glory of salvation to the multitudes in the city." Indeed, when Papa heard that the pulpit at Saint Thomas's in Birmingham was vacant, his overzealous conscience prodded him. He should be doing more for Christ. The Tattenhall living paid £180 annually, which made it an attractive parish, whereas Saint Thomas in Birmingham paid only sixty pounds. With his independent income, supplemented by the monies he received through Dora's inheritance, they could practice frugality and forgo that additional salary. Papa convinced himself that duty—and no Lorelei was more persuasive—summoned him to leave the pleasant pastures of Tattenhall and move to Birmingham.

Birmingham, like bees in clover, buzzed in Isabella's mind with questions. "Will we live in a rectory? Do we know anyone there? Will Hennie and I go to a school? Will we take Shag and Trojan?"

But Papa, concluding the discussion, rose from his chair, saying, "No more questions. You'll know in good time."

The familiar routine was disrupted as the cellar, the attic, and the carriage house were ransacked. Closets were emptied, drawers opened, cupboards stripped, carpets rolled. Both Papa and Mama supervised Ellen and Bridget in packing trunks of clothes, hampers of linens, crates of books, boxes of kitchen equipment, and barrels of tools.

The bureaus and chairs in Isabella and Hennie's bedroom had been hauled to the downstairs passageway to expedite loading the wagons the next morning; the room already looked forsaken. Their dark-print dresses lay neatly over the footboard, and the carpetbags Mama had given each of them gaped wide with the clothes and personal items she had selected for the three-day trip to Birmingham. Tonight was their last night in Tattenhall.

Hennie was sniffing with her effort not to cry.

"Isabella, can you get asleep?" she whispered.

"No, I'm too excited."

"I wish Papa had never heard of Birmingham." The words emerged from Hennie's mouth like popcorn popping.

Isabella put her arm around Hennie, and that loving gesture released the floodgate of Hennie's tears. Her sobs surprised Isabella. Hennie was always so compliant. Isabella didn't know what to say to comfort her sister. What stimulated her—the totally new scene, a big city, different people—was precisely what frightened Hennie.

"You'll see, Hennie. You'll find things to enjoy. There might even be a garden. Or maybe there's a bay window and we could contrive a greenhouse. You'll like it, Hennie. Truly you will."

But Hennie only mourned, "I can't take my pets. Think of how Pug will miss me. He won't know where I've gone." Mama didn't allow her to have pets, but Hennie had befriended a neighbor's terrier. She always managed to find some small creature who needed care. At present she had a box turtle whose shell was cracked, as well as a baby bird that had fallen from its nest. "And my roses." Hennie was an assiduous gardener, planting, weeding, watering, mulching, who talked to each bud and encouraged it to bloom. "I can't bear to leave them."

Isabella, remembering how Aunt Margaret drew Merttins and Hannah to her and patted them gently on the back, wiggled closer to Hennie and stroked her shoulder. She felt awkward, but she couldn't bear Hennie's tears. "You can grow other roses, Hennie, and you'll find other dogs to befriend."

Isabella was silent for a few minutes. Then she added, "Besides, Hennie, you'll still have me, and I'll still have you. We'll always be together."

"You're strong and brave, Isabella, and I'm not. I need you."

"And I need you, Hennie. For one thing, you'll have to remind me not to mention Tattenhall."

Isabella was referring to Mama's dictate made while Mama was folding their woolen garments to place in a trunk and directing the girls to put items for immediate use in the carpetbags. "I need to have a talk with you," Mama had said. She stopped folding and straightened up. "I want you girls to understand," she had said, "that Papa, in accepting this call, is undertaking to carry a heavy yoke. We must ease Papa's burden in every way we can. Christ carried the cross for us, and now Papa is carrying Christ's words of salvation to the multitudes."

Isabella, who had never looked at Papa in this light, was silent with the wonder of Papa being Christ's messenger.

Hennie asked the practical question. "Mama, what can we do to make it easier for Papa?"

"One of the important things that you can do is never to compare Saint Thomas with Saint Albans. I don't want to hear you say, 'At Saint Albans we used to do it that way' or 'Papa, don't you wish we were in Tattenhall?' Saint Thomas in Birmingham is where God has led him, and it is our Christian duty to help him in whatever way we can."

The girls understood only that speaking about Tattenhall was forbidden, and they nodded their heads in assent.

Isabella comforted herself that within a month they would be at Taplow Hill with Grandfather. Remembering Mama's cautions and her own habit of talking without thinking, Isabella snuggled closer to her sister and repeated, "We'll always have each other."

The next morning, an overcast day in early May, the boxes, trunks, crates, bags, and barrels were corded and labeled, and the wagons were at the gate, when Papa received a letter delivered by the new penny post.

He broke the seal, unfolded the single sheet, and scanned it. "Father…" he began. "Father," he repeated in a rough voice, "has gone to his reward."

Isabella felt herself cleave in two. What! Grandfather gone to his reward? No, it wasn't possible. Taplow Hill without Grandfather? No.

Tears flooded her eyes, and Papa gently rebuked her, "Grandfather has earned his rest."

Dora rose and stood by him, one hand on his shoulder. "Edward, isn't it a merciful act of God that we are still at home, and not on the road, where this letter would not have reached us?"

"I don't understand," Hennie questioned. "What's happened to Grandfather?"

"Grandfather's dead." Isabella said the word that the others were avoiding.

"Yes," Papa said, "he has ascended in glory."

"Papa, will Grandfather go to heaven?" Isabella stammered. She was learning to keep her doubts about faith, her resentment at Mama and Papa's constant flow of commands, to herself. Icicles of terror took over her stomach anytime she thought that Mama or Papa might discover her heresy, but she couldn't help it. The path they trod and demanded she follow was too narrow. Grandfather ate sugar; he stopped to listen to the song of a lark; he allowed her to read fiction. She would model herself on him.

"The true worshiper," Papa expounded, "shall worship the Father in spirit and in truth. Scripture tells us that whoever drinks of that living water shall have everlasting life."

Isabella knew that "living water" was Christ himself. That Grandfather was on such close terms with Christ was a revelation.

"But, how…" Isabella started and then bit her tongue, cautioning herself to keep her doubts private. How could Grandfather ascend in glory when he was not one of the chosen? When he had not accepted salvation? The thought of Grandfather, hat in hand, hovering around the pearly gates, seeking entry was too much. Of course the good Lord would accept him. Grandfather was the best person on Earth. But he wasn't on Earth anymore. He was dead.

That death was final, like a room with a massive door slammed shut, locked and bolted, from which no one could escape, Isabella had learned this past winter when the family had made an unexpected trip to Taplow Hill to attend services for Grandmother. On the way she had been ashamed that she did not have an appropriate response to Grandmother's death. She ought to have been comforted that Grandmother was now in heaven, or failing that, to have lamented that she was no longer with them. But she felt neither solace nor sorrow, only a guilty pleasure that she was going to Grandfather's in the winter. She'd tried to convince herself that she was bereaved. Grandmother Bird was, after all, Papa's mother. But Papa had been matter-of-fact in telling them of his mother's death. Isabella had looked at him quizzically as he was speaking to Mama.

"If ever there was a person who we can be certain ascended in glory, that person is Lucy Bird."

And Mama had echoed his "Amen."

The family had stood at Grandmother's grave site in the savage January wind while Grandmother's nephew, the bishop of Chester, had recited, "I know that my redeemer liveth, and that he shall stand at the latter day upon the earth, and though this body be destroyed, yet shall I see God."

Isabella had lifted her bowed head and glanced at Grandfather. He looked old and feeble. He was the only male in the family not wearing clerical garb. Without his boutonniere, his features flushed, tears streaming down his cheeks, he looked the face of grief, so exposed, so vulnerable. To see Grandfather in pain plowed her heart.

When the service was concluded, she went to him and pressed her wet cheek against his. "Oh, Grandfather, I'm so sorry."

Grandfather embraced her, sobbing, "My dear child," his eyes red with cold and loss.

Isabella, responding to his embrace, repeated, "Dear Grandfather."

"Your grandmother smelled so sweet. Not a day in her life that she wasn't as good and as sweet as she smelled," he sobbed as if the words were rent from him. Poor, poor Grandfather.

"Oh, Grandfather," Isabella cried, hugging him closer. Grandfather could never again speak to Grandmother nor smell her sweetness. There was no calling her back. That was the power of death.

And now, Grandfather himself had taken that journey, he had crossed that border, and she could never again go for early morning gallops or play late-evening games of chess with him. To Hennie she cried, "I can't bear not talking to him. Grandfather was always so cheerful. Oh, he can't be dead."

"He's not really dead, Isabella. He's in heaven with all the angels, and with Grandmother, and Flag," Hennie said with assurance.

The thought of Flag thumping his tail at Grandfather's arrival made Isabella smile. "But, Hennie," she cried, "I want to see him. I don't want to go to Taplow Hill if Grandfather's not there."

Papa instructed the wagon drivers to proceed to Birmingham with the furniture, and the family took the carriage to Taplow Hill. As they departed, the melodious bells of Saint Albans were pealing, calling the faithful to prayer.

"Mama, you won't have to have new mourning clothes made," Hennie said, referring to the black bombazine that Mama had donned when Grandmother had passed. "And Papa can keep on wearing his black armband."

During the journey Isabella fretted about the funeral service. At Grandmother's funeral, the open casket had stood in the drawing room, and everyone filed past it. She had looked so uncomfortable in that bare box. Grandmother's hands were crossed over her chest and were at rest, which wasn't at all the way her hands had usually been. Would Grandfather look like Grandfather? Would his eyes be closed? Grandmother's were, and it made Isabella feel like an intruder disturbing her sleep. She had never seen Grandmother nor Grandfather lying down. When the cold caused a little ball of mucus to gather under her nose, she struggled to dig out a handkerchief from her small reticule, afraid the phlegm would drop on Grandmother as she leaned over the open coffin.

At Taplow Hill the air vibrated with the sound of church bells.

"Mama, why does that bell keep tolling?"

"The bell rings nine times for the passing of a man."

"Don't they ring it for women? I don't remember any bell for Grandmother."

"It did ring. Six times to indicate a woman."

"But this bell has tolled more than nine times."

"Yes, it rings once for each year of Grandfather's life, and Grandfather lived a long life, eighty-four years."

Isabella had not anticipated the crowd of people who had come to mourn Grandfather. The Bird family alone filled the drawing room, but in addition were Grandmother's family, including the two bishops, and neighbors, friends, the indoor maids, the outdoor hands. Isabella was curious as to whom everyone was and kept questioning Mama until she had everyone properly identified, but Hennie was overcome with shyness and clung to Mama's side with her face hidden in Mama's skirts.

A moonfaced man in black, carrying a staff wrapped in crepe, moved through the throng, incanting, "Viewing is in the library. Kindly step this way. Viewing is in the library."

"Mama, who is that?"

"Isabella, I've told you, you are not to point. That man is from the funeral parlor."

Isabella was introduced to Papa's oldest brother, Uncle Robert Merttins, whom she had never seen before. He looked so much like Grandfather, even to the twinkle in his eyes and the dimple in his chin. He had just returned from India and repeated again and again how he had gotten home just in time, that if he had not changed horses at Banbury, he would have arrived too late, and he iterated his father's last words to him as he stood by his bed, home after so many years.

Grandfather had whispered, "What was it the old man Simeon said? *Nunc dimittis*, was it not? Lord, now lettest thou thy servant depart in peace."

"And so it has been," Uncle Robert concluded. "Father departed in peace."

So many aunts! Rebecca and Catherine, and Aunts Elizabeth and Lucy with their parson husbands and their children, who always spent part of each summer at Taplow Hill, and, of course, Aunt Margaret with Merttins and Hannah. Seeing this gathering from so many shires caused Isabella to regard the family as a living web spread over England, a web that trembled with sympathy if any member were in trouble.

Papa and Uncle Robert were off in one corner of the crowded room, but Mama and the girls joined the line of people threading into the library.

When Isabella saw Grandfather lying so still and solemn in the coffin, his eyes closed, no smile, no twinkle, she was racked with convulsive sobs. Mama handed her a handkerchief, put her arms about her, and drew her to her skirts.

"Isabella," she said, "he's gone to his reward."

Isabella could only sob, "I want him here. I want him here."

That same moonfaced man gave black scarves and black gloves to Papa, to Uncle Robert, to Aunt Lucy's and Aunt Elizabeth's husbands, and to two youngish men who Isabella thought were neighbors—or maybe they were the "mutes" from the funeral parlor that Mama had told her were sometimes sent from the undertaker's to stand about and look mournful, although surely no such mourners were needed here—and then the six of them lifted the coffin and carried it through the rooms to the waiting carriage. A pall, like heavy black smoke, settled over the crowd as the coffin was carried by.

Black horses with cockades of black feathers on their heads pulled the carriage at the head of the cortege. Isabella saw the feathers fluttering in the slight breeze through a blur of tears. She willed herself—she wasn't at this funeral; she wasn't in this procession; that wasn't Grandfather trapped in that casket. No, it could not be. She marched resolutely, each foot slapping the ground, until she suddenly crumbled, like a dam that gives way, the tears and grief pouring down.

Papa was at her side and gently lifted her up. "The good Lord does not give us more than we can bear," he said. Mama was dabbing a handkerchief at Isabella's cheeks, and Hennie was stroking her hair.

"I love him so," she sobbed.

"Of course you do," Mama said. "Remember Grandfather had a good, full life, and he is reaping the joys of salvation."

"Grandfather loved you, Isabella. You know he did," Hennie comforted.

"Do you think so?" Isabella asked, clinging to this hope.

"Yes, I know so."

"I wish he weren't in that box."

"Grandfather is not in that coffin," Mama intoned. "That is only his mortal shell. Grandfather's soul is above us this very moment, enjoying eternal bliss."

When the body was actually at the gravesite in the churchyard for burial, there was an additional tolling of the bells—the death knell—to let the parish know of the final laying to rest of the deceased. As the coffin was lowered into the ground and earth cast upon it, Papa officiated with "Unto Almighty God we commend the soul of our brother departed, and we commit his body to the ground; earth to earth, ashes to ashes, dust to dust; in sure and certain hope of the resurrection unto eternal life, through our Lord Jesus Christ..."

Isabella, numb with anguish, could listen no longer. She couldn't separate Grandfather's body, now being pelted with clods of dirt, from his soul, which was winging through the air nearby, trailing a long white gown. Her throat ached with the effort to control her tears. She wanted to fling herself into the grave, be covered with a blanket of sod, and stay with Grandfather forever and ever.

After the funeral, as people were turning away from the freshly rounded grave, the children were gathered together for tea while the grown-ups congregated in the drawing room to hear the reading of the will. Taplow Hill, all its stock and acreage, its house, stable, barns, dairy, and outbuildings, was left to the eldest son, Robert Merttins. Robert immediately caused a stir by announcing that he had no interest in maintaining the farm, even if it were the family seat. Since only his youngest brother had had a male issue, who at present was a minor and whose mother was not capable of supervising the farm, he intended to sell Taplow Hill as soon as possible. He and his wife planned to live in the South of England, at Torquay, where his sisters and his sister-in-law and children would find a home.

Like a tongue that worries a loose tooth, touching it, causing it to rock back and forth, Isabella's mind kept returning to Grandfather. She assumed that Taplow Hill, like Tattenhall, was conversationally off-limits, that she and Hennie were not to talk about the farm nor about Grandfather. His boutonniere, his eyes, his dimple, his sunny disposition, his warmth, his pleasure in the good things of life, Taplow Hill itself became a treasure trove, sealed in the honeycomb of memory. That was the past. What would the future reveal?

CHAPTER 11

BIRMINGHAM

After Grandfather's funeral, the Bird family, Edward, Emma, Isabella, and Hennie, proceeded to Birmingham, a journey of three days. Isabella grieved that each clop of the horses' hooves took them farther from Taplow Hill. Hennie looked bereaved. Isabella remembered Grandfather kissing her forehead. She seized Hennie's hand and brought it to her cheek.

"At least, Hennie," she declared, "we have each other."

Isabella knew she could not survive without Hennie. Tattenhall was gone. Taplow Hill. Grandfather. What if she were to lose Hennie? The thought was unbearable. She squeezed Hennie's hand and spontaneously thanked God for her sister. Then she squeezed it again with the excitement of something new and wonderful happening.

For the journey, Papa had leased a large carriage with four horses and a coachman, and their own carriage pulled by Shag and Trojan and piled with luggage followed.

Late afternoon on the third day, Papa gestured. "There's Birmingham, just ahead."

On their right, behind a high red brick wall, tall chimneys were belching black smoke. They heard the roar of machinery, the sound of hammers, the whistle of steam and fumes escaping from boilers.

"The Soho Works," Papa announced, "a manufactory founded by Matthew Boulton and James Watt. Their steam engines are sent all over the world."

"Was *Rob Roy* made there?" Hennie asked.

"I'm sure it was."

Papa directed the coachman to the rectory in Frederick's Road. He drove through crowded streets lined with small workshops and thronged with people. Isabella, accustomed to the friendly faces of Tattenhall, had never seen faces like these: faces that looked at the four-horse carriage and its occupants with hatred, faces that looked stern and discontent, sallow faces with dirty skin brown with smoke, scowling faces, not one merry or jovial, with emaciated bones.

Isabella had seen rural poverty, but in the country, people didn't look hungry. Ill-dressed, pale, thin people like this must be what Aunt Mary was describing in the streets of Calcutta. Isabella scrunched down in the carriage.

Mama, who was also troubled by the wretched-looking people and their ruffian aspect, said, "Sit up, Isabella. They won't harm you."

But Mama had misunderstood. It was not fear that made Isabella cringe; it was embarrassment to be riding in an elegant carriage through crowds of people who looked as if they had never sat down to a satisfying meal. She leaned as far back against the cushion as she could.

On Frederick's Road the houses were separated from one another by wide expanses of lawn. When the carriage stopped in front of an imposing three-story house, Hennie and Isabella were relieved that trees surrounded it. Isabella was surprised that after such a brief interlude, she could look at trees differently than she had looked at them even this noon.

As the sun set, the carriages were driven directly into the rectory's courtyard. The family was shown up steep, crooked stairs, down narrow corridors, and up more stairs to their rooms. As Papa and Mama were examining the feather beds and deciding which bed would be theirs and which the girls', Isabella pushed at the small window that opened like a door. Below were red tile roofs of different heights and, a short distance away, a church tower with a square in front of it.

"Hennie," Isabella suggested, full of the excitement of exploring a new town, "let's go down to the courtyard."

Hennie shook her head. "How will you find the way back to our room," and Mama answered, "You are to stay right here."

Isabella grumbled, but brightened when Papa said they would all promenade later.

In the parsonage at Tattenhall, Isabella and Hennie had shared a bedroom, but in Birmingham everything—the church, the congregation, the rectory—was much larger.

"Here," Mama announced, "Isabella and Hennie, you may each have your own bedroom. Isabella, as the older, you may have your choice of the two chambers."

"Do you mean that I can have either one?" Isabella demanded, unaccustomed to being allowed to make important decisions. Isabella went back and forth through the connecting door, considering the merits of each room. One chamber had windows facing the garden. "Look, Hennie," she said, "You'll be able to grow flowers." In that room the branches of an enormous oak tree brushed the panes. The other chamber was considerably larger; it had three windows, two with a view of a neighbor's roses, and the third overlooking the slate roof of the porte cochere at the side of the house.

"If I have my own room, how will I sleep? There's only the one bed?" Isabella asked.

"A bed from Taplow Hill is arriving for one of you to use," Mama explained.

"Which one do you want, Hennie?" Isabella asked, but she knew how Hennie would reply, for Hennie rarely declared her own preference.

"Either room is nice, Isabella. You take the one you like best. I'm only glad that we can walk from one to the other without going into the hall."

"This is what we'll do," Isabella announced. "We'll share a bedroom just as we always have. And we'll make the other room our sitting room, where we'll study, and read, and sew. What do you think, Hennie? Which room do you think should be for sleeping?"

Hennie's face brightened, and Isabella crooned, "You don't think I could sleep without my little pet, do you," for they had shared a bed since Hennie had been graduated from the cot. Mama objected that they were too big now to sleep in the same bed.

"Why," Isabella argued, "just because we're eleven and eight, do we have to have separate beds?"

Mama retorted, "Isabella, I don't want to reprove you. When I tell you something, that is explanation enough, more than adequate."

Isabella, undeterred, continued, "If we hadn't moved, we wouldn't have separate beds. We'd still be in the same bed in the same room." She curbed herself from adding, "I wish we had never left Tattenhall."

Mama found Isabella's logic irrefutable, but she rued, as usual, Isabella's intractable nature. She could, she complained, take care of a dozen Hennies to one Isabella. "Not another word, miss. This conversation is completely out of order. Since you choose to be difficult, I'll decide. You, Hennie, will have this bedroom, and you, Isabella, will have the larger room."

The Taplow Hill bed arrived, and was installed in the back room for Hennie, and their old bed put together in the larger room. That night Isabella was sitting up in bed, scribbling in her journal, and couldn't adjust to how big and how empty her bed was without Hennie. When she covered her ink and put down her quill, she stretched out. The sheets were cold. She could not fall asleep. Grandfather's death, his funeral, leaving Tattenhall, the journey, the sour faces of Birmingham, and now this strange house and bed without Hennie: it was all too much change.

"Hennie," she called. But Hennie was in the other room. It was so quiet. Only the *clop-clop* of an occasional horse could be heard on Frederick's Road. At Tattenhall there were always the crickets, and soft little noises, the wind rustling the grass, and the church bells of Saint Albans. *It's too quiet here,* she thought.

"Hennie," she called again. Again no answer. Isabella scratched on the wall, but even that brought no response. What if Hennie wasn't there? In a panic, she said to herself, "I don't care what Mama says. I'm going to sleep with Hennie," and she got out of bed and went into Hennie's room.

For once Hennie was awake. She threw back the quilt for Isabella. "Oh, Isabella," she said, "I'm so glad to see you!" as if they had suffered a long separation. "I don't like sleeping alone."

"Nor I. We'll just make our own arrangement. There's no need to upset Mama. I'll join you here after we're both in bed."

"What if Mama catches us?"

"We'll keep it a secret. Our secret."

"Shouldn't we tell Mama?"

"If she finds out, she won't let us."

Night after night, Isabella got into her bed to write in her journal. When that was finished, she tiptoed into Hennie's room and snuggled into bed with her.

Hennie, confident that Isabella was coming, was just about asleep, but she patted Isabella's shoulder. "Good night, dear sister."

Mama, of course, discovered this ruse. She had so much on her mind in helping Edward that though she knew she should insist, she decided that for the time being, she would ignore it. The girls, she reasoned, were experiencing many changes, and they were refraining from lamenting the move. Eventually, Hennie's bed was moved into Isabella's room, as it could accommodate two beds, although the girls continued to share one bed, and the back room was designated their sitting room.

"This is a good arrangement, Hennie, because the back room is brighter, and most of the time when we study, it's daylight."

A room for work and a room for sleep was ideal. When Isabella couldn't sleep, she slipped into the sitting room and lit the lamp with no fear of disturbing Hennie, and yet they always had one another for the intimate talks that were the soul of life to both.

The Atrium, as they soon called the sitting room because the branches of the oak tree scraping against the windows made them feel the open air, was, they thought, the best room in the house. A highboy, a large round table with little drawers all around the edge, and a Regency sofa with arms in a treble clef design, were carted from Taplow Hill to furnish the room. In that same wagonload were special gifts from Grandfather: the mahogany pedestal chess table, with its sixty-four squares of rosewood and satinwood and its hidden drawer underneath with the Indian chess set, for Isabella; and for Hennie, a beautifully woven Persian carpet in soft shades of blue, beige, and rose.

At first, the tables and carpet and sofa recalled Grandfather and the rooms at Taplow Hill where the furniture had stood, and it made them sad. But soon, the Atrium was a refuge they could call their own.

On their first morning in Birmingham, Papa took them to nearby Saint Thomas. As they approached, Hennie asked, "What's wrong with the fence? Why don't they repair it?" Thirty feet of the iron railing was missing; the gap was made more evident because at either end, a loose rod hung at a discordant angle from the other palings.

Isabella added, "Saint Thomas looks gloomy, doesn't it, with the missing railing and its dirty brick."

Before Papa could reply, Mama said, "I want to talk to you girls." Her voice had a penetrating edge. It would be many years before Isabella realized how brave Mama had been. Mama must have been appalled at this large, dismal church whose only grounds were two small patches hedged in by the broken railing, sandwiched into a working-class district. Saint Albans had presided over a spacious churchyard, it boasted beautiful stained glass, and five cheerful bells tolled the hours.

Mama gestured to Papa to go ahead, and right there with people passing, Mama lectured the girls, reminding them of their pledge not to make comparisons. "I told you girls you were not to make denigrating remarks."

"Yes, Mama."

"Your father is undertaking a difficult and noble service in answering the call to come to Saint Thomas. This is not an easy parish; even the bishop thought Papa was asking too much of himself. Papa is going to need my help, and he is going to need your help, and he is going to need it every moment. I want you to ask Jesus to guide you, just as Jesus and the good Lord guide Papa."

"Yes, Mama."

Mama took a deep breath and plunged on. "Saint Thomas in Birmingham is where God has led Papa, and it is our Christian duty to help him. Keep in mind, if you can't say something nice, say nothing at all. You, particularly, Isabella, mount a seal upon your lips. Do you understand?"

The girls were too intimidated to do more than nod. Mama set the pattern of absolute trust in her husband's decision. No one ever heard her complain; no one ever heard her wish that she was back in peaceful Tattenhall. The girls whispered occasionally to one another how much they missed Tattenhall, how much they grieved over Grandfather's death, and how much was wanting with the loss of Taplow Hill. No summers to anticipate.

One hot July day, Isabella was remembering wading in the stream at Taplow Hill, and, of course, Grandfather. "Oh, Hennie," she lamented, "my heart is bursting. Whatever would I do without you?" Isabella felt like a ship stripped of sails and mast by a violent storm, but thanked God she had her anchor, Hennie.

CHAPTER 12

BIRMINGHAM BAZAAR, JUST AS YOU ARE

Edward Bird's unsparing efforts, his piety, his religious passion won converts to Saint Thomas in Birmingham, and the congregation began to swell. Unlike the dairy farmers of Saint Albans, the urban laborers of Birmingham embraced the idea of a work-free Sabbath.

Dora's every moment was given to the church: she taught in the Sunday school, she was in charge of home visits to the sick and the needy, she organized the sewing circle to help overseas missions, and she also supervised church dinners and was in charge of the annual bazaar. Papa pressed Isabella into teaching Sunday school classes. Although she was no taller than her students, her command of scripture and of language gained her pupils' respect.

The girls were given singing and piano lessons—the universal practice for daughters of nineteenth-century middle-class families. Despite Isabella's utter lack of musical aptitude, Papa placed her in charge of the choir, which she had both to rehearse and to direct. As a female, however, she was not allowed to sing. Eventually, when Papa hired a curate, Isabella was relieved of her choir duties. Hennie tagged along after Mama and became a reliable and gentle shadow, and, eventually, she, too, taught the infant Sunday school class.

The years passed, dominated by the Christian calendar: Christmas, Epiphany, Purification, Lent, Ash Wednesday, Annunciation, Good Friday, Easter Day, Ascension Day, Whitsunday, Trinity Sunday, Transfiguration, Michaelmas, All Saints', Advent. Isabella and Hennie, without a tutor but with the guidance of Papa, continued their studies: the Bible, of course, Milton, Shakespeare, history, and in a radical departure, French, for which Papa hired a master who also taught music and drawing.

The pain in Isabella's back, which throughout the years had been like intermittent thunder, became a constant tempest without respite. She continued faithfully performing her duties, putting on her cloak and bonnet and going forth no matter the weather, no matter the pain. But there came a day when the pain became intolerable, a great beast crunching between his giant molars the sinews of her spine. Walking was impossible. She became so paralyzed that even lying on the couch was an ordeal. Finally, when Isabella was sixteen, surgery became necessary.

These were the years in which physicians usually excused themselves from surgery, considering it manual labor, fit only for barbers, not for professional men of intellect. Isabella's doctor, however, removed, without ether or chloroform, a fibrous growth from her spine that had been pressing against the sciatic nerve. The surgery relieved that pain, but since the incision was made without antiseptic conditions, Isabella soon developed (as did most surgery patients) infections and abscesses. Her eventual recovery was painful and protracted. Isabella, still unable to walk, despaired of ever moving about.

At Saint Albans in Tattenhall, where the entire congregation had numbered three hundred souls, the annual bazaar for the benefit of the Daughters of the poorer Clergy in Cheshire was more a tacit exchange of necessities—such as pen cleaners, pot-holders, linen towels, tea cozies, and egg warmers—than a genuine bazaar. Even a zealous housekeeper had a limit to the number of pincushions she needed. But at Saint Thomas, with its flourishing congregation, the annual bazaar was an event that exhausted the energies of a full-time committee. For weeks preceding, Mama talked nothing but bazaar, which boasted more than twenty booths, each presided over by a committee member and each offering an assortment of fancy work. As no large department stores or shops existed, a well-stocked bazaar under the aegis of a good cause offered women a social function, a shopping excursion, and a trip to an exhibition.

In addition to practical necessities, there were christening dresses, pillow shams, table runners, shawls, afghans, nightdresses, mob caps, knit stockings that demanded ingenuity and talent to fashion, as well as gewgaws and knickknacks: Berlin-worked reticules, bags, and needle books; a stunning variety of pincushions, some draped with lace in the shape of a heart, a swan, a star, a lyre, others of velvet, embroidered with pearls, all with pinheads adding additional decoration; yellow silk watch cases embroidered with pansies; ink wipers; samplers in cross-stitch spelling "Religion Is Our Guide and Industry Our Support" or "Home, Sweet Home" or "Give Us This Day Our Daily Bread"; silhouettes snipped from black paper; flowers of tissue; embossed cardboard lampshades; painted hand-screens; a profusion of broadcloth, ribbon, and gilt-paper keepsakes; mother-of-pearl card cases; drawings of allegorical figures and landscapes—"Bolton Abbey in the Olden Time" was a favorite—and a booth of fresh flowers already wired into the massed, stiff bouquets of circles of flowers edged with myrtle leaves that was in favor. All, silent testimony to the number of hours leisured women had to fill.

There was a "Cozy Corner" where one could buy a pot of tea with a choice of cucumber, watercress, egg-and-chutney, chicken-with-mayonnaise, or sardine-butter sandwiches and wedges of simnel, seed, plum, marble, or Genoa cake, as well as rusks and scones and gingerbread. The bazaar was the highlight of Saint Thomas's fall calendar, and the undertaking of the entire church community, but its center was the rectory. No family contributed more than the Birds, supervised by Mama.

Hennie presided over a booth of watercolors—portraits of heliotropes, tulips, pansies, pinks, geraniums, and shrub roses, each with its foliage—that she had been painting all year and had framed with borders of tiny shells. Her flowers were always sold out by midafternoon, for they were exquisite and accurate renderings.

Mr. Trimble and Mr. Lovett, the two curates, hammered together the booths, set up trestle tables, and rounded up chairs for the Cozy Corner. Today, with the bazaar in progress, Mr. Trimble drove a charabanc to fetch the ladies, while Mr. Lovett ran errands, took turns at a booth, and made change or refills of scrip.

Ann Wilson, Mama's aunt, and her three daughters, took complete charge of the Cozy Corner. Mrs. Wilson was a diplomat in getting women to donate the cakes, assuring each woman that her specialty was exactly what was needed to make the bazaar a success. All day the Wilson women cut sandwiches, supervised the making of the tea and the washing of the cups, and contributed their own gaiety so that the Cozy Corner, with a cup of tea accompanied by the Wilson smile, comforted everyone.

In former years Isabella had had charge of a booth with worsted footstool covers and fire screens, until Mama discovered Isabella's abilities as an organizer. It was Isabella who devised the system of how the booths were allocated so that none of the ladies felt slighted if her booth was in the back of the hall or in a draft. It was she who persuaded the committee to sell scrip tickets so that all the money handling was centralized, and she who hired pony-cart rides for the children in front of the church. Each year Isabella had assumed a larger role, sitting on the committees with Mama, writing innumerable notes, inspiring the women to produce the large and varied flow of merchandise, and advising about pricing. All of which made Mama's job much easier.

This year, Isabella was the only drone in this beehive of activity, spending the day, as she had spent every day for weeks, lying on the sofa in the rectory. She was without the energy to swat a fly. The rectory was empty, everyone was across the way at the bazaar, and Isabella felt particularly useless. She brooded about what Papa's visitor, the Reverend Doctor Caesar Malan, the gifted Swiss preacher, had asked her a few days ago:"Do you consider yourself an experimental Christian?"

After her months of pain and lethargy, Isabella resented the question. "You will forgive me, I'm sure," she answered, "but religion is a matter that I do not wish to discuss."

"No, you forgive me," he said and took her hand in his own. "I certainly shall not pursue the subject if it displeases you. Since my conversion ten years ago, I have had such sweetness that I cannot resist the temptation to share that joy with you." Dr. Malan, a man of many accomplishments, and of striking appearance, brought her hand to his lips in a gesture that quite embarrassed Isabella. "I shall pray that you give your heart to Christ and become a useful worker for him."

"There's nothing I can do," Isabella said, indicating the pillow under her head and the robe over her lap. "I do not know how to find Christ."

"Come to him *just as you are*," Dr. Malan answered, looking at her with his penetrating eyes. "This is a new hymn that you may not have yet heard." He handed her a printed leaflet and bid her good-bye.

At the time Isabella had only idly glanced at it and then had been interrupted, but now she picked up the sheet.

Just as I am, without one plea
But that Thy blood was shed for me,
And that Thou bid'st me come to Thee,
O Lamb of God, I come.

Just as I am, and waiting not
To rid my soul of one dark blot,
To Thee, whose blood can cleanse each spot,
O Lamb of God, I come.

Just as I am, though tossed about
With many a conflict, many a doubt,
Fightings and fears, within, without,
O Lamb of God, I come.

Just as I am, poor, wretched, blind;
Sight, riches, healing of the mind,
Yes, all I need, in Thee to find,
O Lamb of God, I come.

Isabella's soul soaked up the words like gentle rain on parched soil. Her feelings of uselessness dropped away, replaced by purpose and energy. Taking a sheet of paper from the table beside her, she began to write.

From that day until her death, her pen was at the service of good causes, active in true "never-rest, never-weary" Evangelical style. Later, when she wrote her travel books, she felt guilty that both the traveling and the writing were selfish indulgences. In compensation she gave every pound she earned from her travel books, which over the years was considerable, to hospitals, missions, and other worthy projects.

CHAPTER 13

THERE MUST BE SOMETHING A WOMAN CAN DO

The claws of the table as they settled deeply into the carpet looked as if they were scraping the woven flowers. Hennie, her workbasket at her elbow, was embroidering a pattern she had copied from the rug: satin-stitched petals in shades of blue. She held the hoops with taut linen close to the gas lamp that she had just asked Isabella to light. Isabella scratched the lucifer, and the gas ignited with a quiet purr. The flame weaved and danced with the draft from the windows until Isabella replaced the globe. The last of the raindrops pinged softly against the marble sill, and through the open windows the girls could smell the rich earth that John had upturned that morning, and they could hear the occasional clip-clop of a carriage on Frederick's Road.

Isabella was writing, and the nib of her pen, with its faint rasp, flowed across the page. Every few moments she dipped the quill into the glass inkwell with its silver-hinged lid. Words flowed from Isabella like water in a downhill stream, and her pen flew across the paper. She could always be interrupted when she was writing, for she started in again as if she had never been stopped. The times not to interrupt her were the intervals when she lifted her head, as now, and her gaze was abstracted.

Hennie knew that although her eyes were focused upon "Mount Vesuvius in Eruption," Isabella was not seeing the steel engraving but was perceiving an interior landscape. Hennie waited. Isabella's pen was again moving as if of its own volition.

"What are you thinking about?" Hennie asked.

"That volcano looks remarkably staid and comfortable for something spewing forth its innards."

"No, seriously. What are you thinking about?"

There was a pause. Then Isabella replied, "I'm thinking about what Lord Chancellor Brougham said about hospitals."

"What was that?"

"That hospitals for the support of old men and old women are injurious in their effects."

"Why does he think that?"

"He argues that they are injurious because if a man knows there is a hospital for his old age, that man won't do what any prudent man must do, and that is, save for his infirm years."

"There are many operators and unemployed men not able to save."

"Lord Chancellor Brougham's theory doesn't allow for those people. Actually I am writing another pamphlet." And Isabella once more bent to her work.

On her seventeenth birthday last October, Isabella lighted the gas jets on both sides of the mirror and looked long and earnestly at herself. She saw a petite figure with small hands and feet and an abundance of soft dark hair, straight dark eyebrows, a clear complexion with pink cheeks. Those were the assets, and oh yes, small ears close to her head.

The liabilities were that although her eyes were fringed with dark lashes, they were undistinguished, as was her nose, and worst of all, her teeth were too prominent. Or maybe the worst was that she looked so sensible and, well, capable. Not a bit helpless, the way a woman should look. Hennie looked grave and sweet and as if she needed protection. Hennie also had clear blue eyes that were large and innocent. Isabella counseled herself, *If I can't be a beauty, what is important for me to do is to develop my mind.* She added botany to her lists of studies and resolved to write articles for Christian journals.

"Isabella," Hennie again interrupted, "what do you think of Papa's new curate?"

"He acts as if he were afraid of his own shadow."

"Oh no. He just has proper respect for Papa. I like his being deferential."

"You can call it 'deferential,' but I think he's obsequious."

"Isabella, you're too harsh."

"Anyway, I don't like the way he looks."

"Why, he's a well-favored young man."

"Oh, I suppose so. His skin's just too damp," said Isabella, ready to drop the topic. But a sudden perception made her ask, "Do you like him?"

Isabella glanced at her sister. She wondered if Hennie were attracted to the young man.

"Truthfully the only conversation I've had with him has been about the selection of hymns." Mr. Trimble had been Papa's curate for three months, but then, Hennie was painfully shy.

Isabella thought of the conversations she had had with him, about the repeal of the Corn Laws, about the Chartists, about the selection of the new bishop, about the Bull Ring Massacre. "He's an intelligent man," Isabella offered in a conciliatory tone. "By which I mean that he agrees with me about Cobbett and O'Connor. I have no interest in young men, Hennie, none whatever,"

"Isabella, you can't mean that. Of course, someday you shall marry and have children."

"Never."

"But what can you do? That's what a girl is meant to do."

"And that's precisely why I won't do it," Isabella bridled. "No, I don't mean that. But I do mean that I shan't marry. Look at Mama."

"Mama's a wonderful model of a woman's role."

"If that's the kind of life you want, a vine clinging around a tree, then get married. But it's not for me. Mama doesn't do a thing unless Papa approves. She has no life without him. No opinions. If Papa were to die, Mama would wither and expire too."

"Isabella, how you talk. Mama takes charge of the rectory. She teaches in the Sunday school. She taught us. She organizes the annual bazaar for overseas missions."

"Exactly. Everything she does is related to the church and to Papa."

"But Mama had a full religious life before she even met Papa."

"Yes, and her father was a minister too, and she took care of him until Papa came along. No, everything that Mama does is because Papa is rector of Saint Thomas. But Mama's not the only one. What married woman do you know who has a truly independent life?"

"But that is the way God made Eve, as a helpmate to Adam."

"As for me, I don't want an Adam in my life. I'm too disagreeable and selfish anyway. I'd make a wretched wife. No, you're the one who will be married, and I shall content myself with my nieces and nephews."

"You wouldn't make a wretched wife, Isabella. I think you're wonderful. You're clever, and you have all kinds of courage, and you always think of things to do and say, and I love your glistening eyes."

"You're my pet, too, Hennie," Isabella laughed and leaned across the tabletop to pat Hennie on her arm. "But I know how disagreeable I am."

"No, you are not." Hennie paused, counted to herself four threads on her linen, inserted her needle, and then said, "I don't plan on marriage either."

"Nonsense! You'll succumb to the first man with melting brown eyes."

"Let's make a pact. I'll get married only after you do."

"No, Hennie, that wouldn't be fair. I tell you, I'm never going to be anyone's wife."

"Then I won't be either." Hennie put down her embroidery hoop and held up her palm as they had when they were children.

Isabella touched her hand to Hennie's. They tapped one another three times and clutched their fingers together.

"Good, it's agreed. I'll be your wife until you discard me for a Romeo who will take you to the ends of the earth," Hennie teased.

"Never. Not if I have to darn his socks and cook his omelets. You'll be the only wife I'll ever want."

"Seriously, Isabella, I've given it much thought. I'm perfectly happy just living at home and being your sister. I don't want anything more."

Isabella looked up at Hennie's tone of quiet determination. "You do mean it, don't you, Hennie?"

"I do. Furthermore, I want to serve God in my own way. I know it isn't much, but selecting the hymns, arranging the altar flowers, pressing the cloth, teaching the little ones the Gospel, helping Papa visit the bedridden, and trying my best to brighten my little corner—I just want to keep on doing these things."

Isabella heard the conviction in her sister's voice. "Hennie, you're as good as you are beautiful. I know I'm not beautiful; I'm plain. But even if I were a Helen of Troy, I would still want my own life. And I shall never be like you. I don't know what it is, but I am filled with this restless urge." Isabella tightened her hands into fists. "There must be *something* a woman can do."

CHAPTER 14

SABBATH BATTLE IN BIRMINGHAM, SCOTLAND

Tolerance was not Edward Bird's temperament. The empty pews at Saint Albans in Tattenhall had not influenced one iota his determination to make Sunday the Lord's Day. The same determination inflamed him in Birmingham, where the shops and the alehouses were open on Sunday. He made it his crusade to see that they were closed. His earnestness and sincerity made some converts among shopkeepers. Patiently he visited the various merchants in his congregation. He formed a league in Birmingham with like-minded ministers and urged them to conduct similar campaigns. He preached, he extolled, he persuaded, and one by one, he got the merchants to give up Sunday trading. That is, the merchants each promised that they would close if, and it was a big if, all the other merchants closed also.

Edward said to his wife, "Our efforts will be crowned. All the merchants, save two, have now agreed to Sunday closing, to serve God, not Mammon."

"Who are the two? Van Burg and Hay?"

"Yes, they are still resistant."

"They are stubborn men. If those two hold out, will the others agree?"

"They say they will."

"Be cautious. All your efforts may not be successful."

Dora looked at her husband. Edward was in his midfifties, but he looked old. His face was lined, his shoulders stooped, his hair white, but a radiance of disinterested goodness and blamelessness gave him, she thought, the look of a saint. Recently, while visiting his parishioners, he had caught scarlet fever, which both the girls had caught from him, and he still looked ravaged with the illness.

"I'm near success because I am going to serve a summons on Van Burg and Hay that will prohibit them from opening their shops on Sunday."

"How can you do that?"

"Mr. Bright can arrange it. He is a warden, you know, and he is firm for Christ. It can be done."

Edward Bird pursued his plan. As the rector, he served the summonses himself. The two small businesses, one a greengrocer and one an alehouse, were in the same block, a few doors apart. He went first to Mr. Van Burg in his alehouse. The heavyset, scowling man was rolling casks in front of his shop when Rector Bird approached.

"A word with you, Mr. Van Burg."

The man stopped his job, turned, put his hands on his hips, and said, "Well, Reverend Bird, what will it be?"

"You have one last opportunity to serve Christ. I entreat you, for your own salvation, to close your shop on the Lord's Day."

"And I've told you, time out of mind, that I'm not doing it."

"Then it is taken out of your hands. I have here a summons that I am now serving on you that will compel you to close your shop on the Sabbath." The rector handed the man the summons.

Mr. Van Burg took the paper, glanced at it, tore it in half, and spat on it. "Where did you get this phony document? You think that carries any weight? There is no city ordinance that prohibits Sunday retailing. You and your busybody ministers! Now I'm telling you, Reverend Bird, get out of here, and get out of here fast." The big man stepped menacingly in front of the rector. "I'm giving you one last opportunity. Get."

"Consider your soul, Mr. Van Burg," the reverend said without a trace of fear.

"I'll consider my soul, but you'll not tell me how to run my business."

"Give it to 'em, Fred," a bystander called. A knot of men, patrons of the alehouse and idlers, crowded round the two men.

"These men of the cloth, they always be putting us down, telling us what to do," another called.

Emboldened by this display of support, Van Burg muscled up to Bird, whom he towered over. "I don't want to crowd a runt like you, but I mean it. Get."

The rector adjusted his hat, clasped his hands, and said, "I shall serve you another summons, for the Lord's will shall be done. You will not profane the Lord's Day with your filthy intercourse."

He turned to go down the block to the greengrocers, but his speech had aroused the men. "Filthy intercourse, huh?" They followed him with catcalls and jostled his shoulder.

"Who do ya think ya are, to be telling us the Lord's will?"

"Is it the Lord's will that the foundries closed?"

"Yeah, is it the Lord's will that my bairn be starving?"

The crowd had enlarged by now, and Mr. Hay, the greengrocer, came out to see what was the disturbance. Van Burg called to him, "Raymond, our dainty rector here wants to give you a summons."

"You can serve Christ, Mr. Hay, by voluntarily closing your shop on the Lord's Day, or I shall serve you with this summons that will compel you to do so."

"It's not worth the paper it's written on," Van Burg interposed. "There's no city law about Sunday closings."

"We've talked about this, Bird. I've told ya, I'm not closing on Sunday," Mr. Hay said.

"Get, I tell ya. Get out of here," Van Berg insisted.

One of the men picked up a ball of mud and tossed it at the rector. Another took a clump of mud, and another seized a tomato from the stand, and they heaved them at him. He was pelted with mud and insults. Just before the incident got out of hand, Bird squared and faced them, his back to the vegetable display.

The rector let his glance slowly go over them.

"You, John Stubblefield," he said, recognizing one man and fixing him with his eye, "you put down that mud and ask the Lord to forgive you." Bird's chin lifted, and he looked squarely at the men, but few were willing to meet his eye.

"You're good men, all, but you know not what you do. Now put down your rubbish, go home, get on your knees, and ask the Lord to protect you."

The rector stood silently, looking at each man in turn. "Go home, I tell you, get on your knees, and ask the Lord's forgiveness." With that, he walked quietly away.

This debacle marked the end of his Sabbath campaign. He had put so much pressure on the merchants that many of them had agreed just to get him to stop harassing them. Now they turned against him. Many of those whom he thought were on the side of righteousness became, in his mind, turncoats and forsook him and the church for Mammon. He had believed he had led these men to God. His defeat was bitter. This trial to his spirit broke his endurance, and once again he was sick.

This illness lasted so long that the doctor urged him to take months of complete rest. The family took lodgings near the sea for a few months, during which interval, Dora prevailed upon her husband to resign his charge at Saint Thomas's. When he recovered, he was given in the autumn of 1848, through the good offices of the bishop of Winchester, the living at Saint Margaret's in Wyton, on the river Ouse in Huntingdonshire. They left Birmingham with little regret.

The Bird family was bruised in health and in spirit. Isabella had never completely rallied from the back surgery, and had not fully recovered from the scarlet fever; she spent hours on the sofa. She did some writing, or botany studies, or fancy work, but the pen, or the book, or the needle often fell from her hand.

Hennie had not yet regained her color or vigor, and Dora Bird was worn-out from nursing the other three. Edward Bird felt humbled and punished with the pelting and what he considered the betrayal he had suffered in Birmingham. These considerations made Edward and Dora decide to avoid the low-lying mists of the river Ouse in Wyton and go to a lake in the Scottish Highlands for the summer.

Isabella and Hennie spent long days in a skiff exploring nearby shores, or scrambling over the hills, Hennie painting the flowers, Isabella classifying plant specimens. By fall the family's health had much improved. Summers in Scotland became an annual event. Edward Bird particularly appreciated the faithful observance of the Sabbath in Scotland and returned to England more determined than ever to see Sunday celebrated as the Lord's Day.

CHAPTER 15

TO LONDON, UNCLE LAWSON, COUNTLESS DOCTORS

Isabella found it hard to sit still on her way to London. England in the 1850s was crisscrossed with railroad tracks like the web of a giant spider, and she was on one of the filaments traveling to the center. She waved to Mama, Papa, and Hennie as the train shuddered, expelled its breath, and with a backward tremor finally began to roll. This was her first trip alone, with preparations to stay away for several weeks.

To think that she had almost forfeited the trip by arguing. She had antagonized Mama, altogether too easy to do, by declaring, "I'm perfectly capable of traveling by myself."

Mama had replied, "That's not the issue. It is not proper for a young, unwed girl to travel unescorted."

And the argument was launched. "Stuff and nonsense," Isabella retorted, jutting out her small chin. Her eyes followed the early morning wraiths of white mist in the meadows outside the rectory windows.

"Young lady, watch your language." Papa joined the fray.

Isabella hastened to apologize. "I'm sorry, it's just that any-one would think I was a blathering idiot who needed constant watching."

Mama answered as if she were snapping down pound notes, "John's instructions are to accompany you on the train and deliver you to Uncle Lawson's door."

Mama's prim voice set Isabella's teeth on edge. "Deliver me! What am I, a package?"

Knowing that further argument was useless, Isabella nonethe-less continued, straightening her back despite its pain, ready for combat. "I'm not a child. I am an adult, perfectly capable of board-ing a train and getting a hansom."

Mama sighed. "Very well, Isabella, if you must resist me, you can stay home and forget about going to London." Mama, a blue vein throbbing in her temple and her eye twitching, folded her embroidery. She had said the last word.

"Oh dear, I didn't mean—"

Papa interrupted. "Let's not do anything hasty. Isabella, you need sound medical advice, and it's not available here in Wyton. Despite that operation, your back is still painful, and it seems to me that a young woman like you should not be troubled with sleep-lessness and headaches." Papa picked up a book, signaling that the discussion was over. He spoke emphatically, "John will accompany you to your uncle Lawson's door in London, and Uncle Lawson will see that you are suitably chaperoned there."

Mama had opposed the London excursion until she realized that Isabella might meet a bridegroom. Isabella was already twenty-one years old, and in this remote parish, no appropriate husband existed. Marriage, Mama prayed, was the answer to Isabella's en-nui and to her headstrong temperament, and would end Mama's embarrassment that her daughter was a spinster. In London, Uncle Lawson had two married daughters who received people and gave dinners. Isabella might find a suitable Evangelical cleric who, after a proper interval, would propose marriage. Mama deemed it prudent to keep this hope hidden. As for her intractable nature, Isabella needed to be governed by a man more austere than her father, a man who would speak with authority, who would not brook any nonsense.

Mama had yet another reason for wanting Isabella out of the house, a motive that she did not admit even to herself: jealousy. Edward appeared to value Isabella's opinions more than her own. Whether it was a sermon, a tract, a book, or a recital, Edward always turned first to Isabella to discuss it.

"Won't it be wonderful, Isabella, to be pain-free?" Hennie chimed in.

Isabella's back ached almost all the time, and she had a list of other ailments; nonetheless, consulting doctors did not ignite her daydreams. London did: the Crystal Palace, Saint Paul's Cathedral, the Houses of Parliament, the Tower of London, and Madame Tussauds famous waxworks.

Accompanying her on the train, John made no difference: he was somewhere in the third-class carriage, and she had the first-class compartment to herself.

Or she did have. A young man diffidently opened the door from the corridor. "Excuse me," he said, consulting his ticket, "I believe I am billeted for this seat," and he sat down opposite her.

Isabella covertly looked at him: satin-pink cheeks, a large tawny mustache almost covering his mouth, tiny round spectacles. He took a paperback book with a yellow cover from his satchel. A French novel? Without doubt Mama would disapprove of that and also of his loosely tied cravat. When he looked up, Isabella quickly averted her eyes, although she would have liked to speak to him. She was only minutes away from Mama's strictures: a rector's daughter certainly did not talk to an unknown young man. She must be a model of decorum at all times. Isabella turned her gaze out the window to watch the white plume following the engine like the tail of a kite, to hear the whistle shriek at the crossroads, and to duck involuntarily at the rattling black cinders hurled against the window. The wheels made a satisfying *click-click-click* as the train sped over the tracks.

Isabella smoothed her new magenta skirt and checked again if her ticket was in her reticule. She knew it was; she just wanted the pleasure of holding the London, Brighton and South Coast Railway ticket in her hand. In her chest an exhilarated humming-bird was beating its wings.

Isabella rotated her shoulders to find relief from her backache. She was, in fact, nervous about the medical examinations and, in a habitual gesture, twisted her handkerchief. Since physicians were not required to attend medical school, Uncle Lawson was instructed to make appointments only with doctors who were members of the Royal College of Physicians and graduates of either Oxford or Cambridge.

Through the window Isabella saw Hennie's sweet face. Hennie, with her very first steps, had attached herself, a golden shadow, to her four-year-old sister. They had not been apart for even one day. When Isabella suggested that Hennie come to London with her, she was not surprised that Hennie preferred to stay home, saying she was frightened by crowds. She was too shy to be comfortable with an uncle she didn't know. She would rather Isabella write letters and tell her about everything than to go herself.

Through the steam and smoke, the barren fields were a parallel to her own life with its succession of dreary days, round after round of stitching hems, of calling upon the bedridden, of teaching Sunday school. Or of lying limply on the sofa trying to study French with no one to correct her, trying to learn the fundamentals of chemistry with no one to guide her. Nothing to look forward to, nothing of interest, nothing to relieve the tedium.

Individual houses began replacing the fields and hedgerows and the distant church towers. Houses soon gave way to streets of row houses, and these melded into block after block of gray stone buildings, into thoroughfares clogged with wagons, carts, hansoms, and barouches.

"Almost there," the young man said, carefully inserting a bookmark on his page.

Isabella nodded yes and smiled.

Abruptly the rapidly passing panorama shrank to a stone-faced embankment, a dark shed, and the platform of Brighton Station as the train, with a final tremor, stopped.

On the platform Isabella walked to the front of the train to find John openmouthed with wonder. He put his hand on the railroad carriage as if it were the flank of a horse.

"T'ain't like a stagecoach," John, whose job was driving a coach, said. "Soon me 'n' the horses 'n' the coaches will be on the shelf, a row of old relics."

They redeemed her trunk, emerged coughing from the sulfurous fumes of the station, hailed a hansom, and were driven to Kensington, one of the outlying suburbs, where her uncle Lawson lived.

Uncle Lawson himself came to the door only steps behind the parlormaid. "There you are, my niece. Welcome to Kensington Manor. I've been looking for you. Come in. Come in." He took Isabella's hand in his and looked lovingly into her face.

Turning his attention to Isabella, he said, "I'm sorry, young lady, that you're below par, but I'm delighted to see you." He tucked her arm into his and led her toward the stairs. "I'm lonely in this big house with both my girls gone. Wait and see," he said, his rosy face beaming, and patting her forearm. "We'll have you right as rain."

Isabella's anxiety melted. As he guided her upstairs, two maids following with the small trunk and hatbox, he said, "I wouldn't have known you. You've been transformed into a lady, and," he amended as if it were a welcome discovery, "you don't look a bit like your mother."

Isabella was not accustomed to comments about her appearance. She knew that Hennie was pretty, and she knew that she was not. What Uncle Lawson saw was a neatly turned-out young woman, small and dainty, with a quick smile, heavy chestnut hair, and wide-awake brown eyes with the look of intelligence. Not exactly pretty, but petite and comely.

"You don't either," Isabella dared to say, looking at his round, cherubic face with deep laugh wrinkles around the eyes and mouth. He deepened those lines with a loud guffaw.

"We're putting you here," he said, indicating a large corner bedroom with a bow window. "Now you do whatever it is you ladies do, and meet me downstairs for tea when you're ready. Marie," he said, indicating one of the maids, "will help you feel at home and show you to the back parlor." Isabella watched him descend the broad carpeted stairs.

This, she realized, was a much grander home than the rectory. On the landing were a tapestry and a suit of medieval armor, and rooms that she assumed to be bedrooms, which opened up into a large gallery with oil paintings, statues, and settees.

Maria, making a small curtsy, said, "Please, ma'am, let me help you put away your clothes."

Isabella, ashamed at the scantiness of her wardrobe, but not daring to refuse, nodded assent. Maria was younger than Isabella, and they chatted amiably. Isabella soon learned from her the routine for meals, Uncle's habits of entertaining, of his leaving the home and returning, of his daughters' visits. Noting the size and comfort of the house and the heavy furnishings of the bedroom, Isabella had a twinge of worry that her wardrobe, which had seemed so splendid at home, might not be adequate. She was appeased when Maria smoothed her hands over the silk fabric of her navy blue and her gray dresses as she hung them in the wardrobe.

At five-o'clock tea served in the blue parlor, Uncle Lawson explained, "I trust you won't mind, Isabella, that I serve short rations at tea. We have an early dinner, as you'll see, so best not to have too ample a tea."

Looking at the food spread on the table, Isabella could only stammer, "No one could want more." Potted meats, deviled sardines, rounds of toast with eggs and minced ham, celery salad, and both almond sponge and seed cakes, jam, and Indian tea that Kathleen poured and brought to her in a dainty porcelain cup: Did Uncle truly regard this as a light repast?

"I trust it is all right with you, Isabella, but I've made your first appointment with a Harley Street practitioner for next week. Let you get acquainted here in the city, first. He's an Oxford man as your father requested. Oxford or Cambridge men clearly must be the best."

"I don't mind at all." Isabella thought it safe to add, "But I confess to being anxious about seeing physicians." She brought the cup to her lips and inhaled the enticing aroma of the Darjeeling tea.

Uncle accepted this matter-of-factly. "Yes, of course you are," he said, adroitly heaping minced ham on buttered toast. "No one really likes physicians poking around. But don't you worry. I've scheduled you with a good man. We're going to start with Dr. Graham, one of the foremost nerve specialists in the country. Then I want you to see a few more men. We'll get a consensus of their diagnoses, and we'll follow whatever that regime is. That ought to work."

Thus Isabella, twisting her handkerchief into a rope, sat at the side of a large mahogany desk a few days later, being questioned by the eminent nerve specialist, Dr. Graham. He asked her to unpin her brooch, remove her lace collar, and unbutton the top buttons of her bodice while he thumped and listened with his stethoscope, which he explained was a recently invented instrument. Acutely embarrassed at unbuttoning her waist in front of a man, Isabella was grateful that a female attendant had remained in the room.

She could see that the foot of Dr. Graham's chair was carved into a lion's head that held in its jaws a globe that enabled his chair to swivel. Subversively, she thought that Dr. Graham probably believed that he belonged on top of the world, borne aloft by the king of beasts.

"Have you been vaccinated?" the doctor asked Isabella.

"Yes, when my sister and I were children."

"Your parents are to be commended. A bill is pending in Parliament now that makes smallpox vaccination compulsory, but it is arousing considerable controversy." Finished with reporting that information, and sparing his smallpox lecture, Dr. Graham turned to the business at hand.

"Now, Miss Bird, tell me about your problems."

Isabella listed her grievances: the suffocating lassitude, the persistent backache, the headaches, the chronic insomnia.

Dr. Graham listened, nodded, and asked, "Have you undergone any surgery?"

"Oh yes, indeed," Isabella answered ruefully. "I had an operation to remove a fibrous tumor from my lower back, but my back aches more than ever."

Dr. Graham busied himself with some papers and said, "My guess is that you are suffering a lack of adequate nerve energy."

"Nerve energy?" Isabella repeated, startled at the concept.

"Let me clarify," he said as he pushed back his chair. "A woman's function in life is to reproduce. Where would we be," he laughed artificially, "if this were not true?" He leaned back, his hands clasped. "Nature, therefore, has made the woman's systems different from the man's. Consider this: one quarter of each month, during the best years of a woman's life, is given to the depletion of her constitutional capital. Miss Bird, I must ask you: Are your 'monthly cycles' especially heavy and painful?"

Isabella blinked at hearing her "monthly cycles" spoken of so openly, and with no connection to the "original sin" for which

Mama said women deserved this burden. And how was Isabella to know if her "monthly cycle" was "especially heavy and painful"? Did this doctor think that women discussed and compared such things? Wildly embarrassed, Isabella stared at the floor.

"I thought so," said Dr. Graham, taking her discomfiture for an affirmative answer. Once again set on his rail, the doctor steamed ahead. "All of us have a limited, let me say, a finite fund of energy. If a woman must spend so much of her energy in her monthly replenishment, she is bound to suffer. Mental health depends upon maintaining adequate supplies of nerve force. Now, of course, one woman varies from another. You, obviously, are having difficulty sustaining your stock of nerve force."

"Are you saying I need a nerve tonic?"

"That would be an excellent idea. Unfortunately none are available, save the fraudulent potions of quacks and mountebanks. What I suggest is that at the onset of each of your 'monthly cycles,' you cease all activity. Take to your bed or couch, and stay there." Dr. Graham underscored this by shaking an authoritative finger at her.

Isabella thought, *But that's why I'm here, because I don't want to stay on the sofa all day.*

"Give your body every opportunity to recharge itself," said the doctor. "That is an easy remedy, but sometimes the simple ones are best. Basically it is only a recognition of the female structure. We find that often a woman's symptoms diminish as she begins to bear children."

Isabella failed to see the logic of this, but Dr. Graham continued, "Perhaps in ways we don't yet fully understand, as a woman fulfills the role she was clearly meant to perform, her body establishes a healthy balance of nerve force." He gave her a directive for a mild sedative to be filled at an apothecary.

Isabella departed considerably confused. Her major complaint was that she spent too much time on the sofa, and this doctor had prescribed more! And what if she never bore children? Was she doomed to suffer headaches, backaches, and insomnia her entire life? Her observations of married women with children did not suggest any superior "healthy balance" in them. The liveliest woman in the parish, a bundle of energy who volunteered for everything, was a spinster. No, she didn't follow Dr. Graham's thesis; so when Uncle Lawson asked what Dr. Graham had prescribed, Isabella did not have the vocabulary to explain it. She could only blush.

She saw several doctors that Uncle had chosen for her. They all gave roughly the same diagnosis, and Isabella understood as much as she wanted.

"Uncle Lawson, I don't think I need to see another doctor."

"There's one other fellow I want you to see. I promise you, he will be the last."

"They have all told me the same thing: spend more time lying down, and take a sedative. I spend too much time right now lying down. I don't want to feel groggy; I want to be alert."

"Just let this last doctor have his say. There's a good girl."

A few days later, Isabella wrote in her journal:

Uncle has certainly been conscientious, dragging me to all these nerve specialists. They've all done essentially the same thing: nod as they write a prescription for a drug, and tell me to rest—which is precisely what I don't want to spend my life doing. Yesterday, though, one of them, Dr. Jamison, surprisingly had a sensible suggestion: "Pack her off on a sea voyage," he told Uncle Lawson. Now there's a doctor I can listen to! But there is as much chance of my going on a sea voyage as there is for a frog to turn into a prince.

Not only did Uncle Lawson arrange doctor visitations, but he also kept Isabella's calendar as full as possible, often enlisting his daughters' help with teas, calls, receptions, and dinners. Uncle Lawson meant so well that Isabella did not want to disappoint him, and she did her best, but privately she had had enough "social frumpery" to last a lifetime. She found herself growing more and more weary, a weariness that lightly covered anger.

The invitation to a proper London dinner party had initially excited her, but soon she began to fret. She didn't have appropriate clothes. But even if she would have had a rich purple velvet gown with a collar of Brandenburg lace, she resented wasting her time. In London she discovered women dressed for dinner in rich velvets or light-colored silks with plunging décolletés. She had only her navy silk or her gray gown, adequate for occasions at home. She felt like a crow amid a bevy of brilliant popinjays. She wished that women were required to wear identical smocks and never had to give a thought to clothes.

Certainly the drawing room looked splendid with its crystal chandeliers, and the food presented as if it were an artist's palette. A pompous young man, looking as if he had swallowed a flagpole, escorted her into dinner. He had a supercilious look, and she longed to say to him, "I think you are as tiresome as you obviously think I am."

At the table were ten other guests, none of whose names she remembered. She did her best to ignore her aching back and to make conversation, although this was difficult, as she was sandwiched between two men who seemed enraptured with the women on the other sides of them. She couldn't think of anything to say, and she refused to comment about the weather. *I can't sit here as if I were the Sphinx,* she lamented. Finally she was ready with a gambit about the Duke of Wellington's funeral, but she had only a well-tailored shoulder to talk to.

The woman opposite her sported long, dangling earrings; all the women except her were adorned with sparkling gems. She had only a modest cameo with her grandmother's likeness. Women, she learned, were expected to keep the conversational ball rolling.

They, themselves, were not to expound, but were to give conversation a nudge in the direction of a man. It was the man who made the observation, told the anecdote, or related the experience that provided the substance of the dialogue, or more often, the monologue.

When the men withdrew for their port and cigars, and the women retired to the sitting room, it was almost worse because the women prattled about their new Irish servant, or how to make a raspberry shrub, or about a clever dressmaker. Finally she was home, sated with the social scene.

Isabella and Uncle Lawson were playing chess, their favorite game. Isabella said, "Chess has constant surprises, and there is always something to learn."

Uncle Lawson cleared his throat. "Isabella, I feel awkward about this, but your aunt Barbara is arriving tomorrow."

Isabella stopped thinking about her next move and dropped her hands to her lap. "Aunt Barbara? You mean Mama's sister?"

"Yes, and my sister too."

"Is someone coming with her?"

"Why no. What do you mean?"

"She is not married and travels alone?"

"Yes, she is not married and seems to enjoy the single state. After Barbara's unfortunate defection from the church, I had nothing to do with her for many years. But now…" He faltered, then jumped ahead. "She is quite the independent woman."

"Mama still doesn't see her."

"True, your mama still harbors ill will. She would not want you to meet Barbara."

"That's probably true," Isabella agreed slowly, remembering Mama's tight lips whenever there was even the slightest allusion to her sister, "but I am of age now."

"For the past dozen years, I have told Barbara that she can come anytime she wants."

"Where does she live, Uncle Lawson?"

"She lives in Brighton, but she is accustomed to coming up to London, sometimes for a few days, sometimes for weeks. She makes her home here."

"How long is she staying this time?"

Uncle Lawson pulled out a letter from his suit pocket. "She says she will be staying a few weeks. But you stay as long as you like. I'm glad to have you here."

Taking off her frock that night, loosening her stays and removing her whalebone corset, unlacing her shoes, pulling out the pins from her hair, Isabella shook herself with relief, glad to get into her loose-fitting nightdress, her hair tumbling over her shoulders. Freedom. She was fired by Aunt Barbara's impending visit and eager to know what she was like. An independent woman! Mama would expect her to leave in the morning, before Aunt Barbara's arrival. She knew she was not going to do that. She felt that her life had definitely taken a turn for the better.

CHAPTER 16

AUNT BARBARA, MISS EVANS, TRIP TO AMERICA PLANNED

The next morning, before Uncle Lawson had departed in his carriage, he said to Isabella, "I may be delayed getting home. I'm depending upon you to do the honors, to see that your Aunt Barbara is welcomed and comfortable." He peered over the rim of his glasses at her, and she managed to nod her head in acknowledgement, but that didn't prevent her stomach from churning.

She was nervous about Aunt Barbara, and her nervousness increased throughout the afternoon. Uncle hadn't yet come home when, late in the day, a vigorous woman in a striking gray-and-white traveling costume strode into the drawing room at the heels of the parlor maid, who barely had time to curtsy and announce, "Miss Barbara Lawson, miss."

She came right over to Isabella, who rose from the sofa, and before she could greet her, Aunt Barbara took both of her hands and said, "I have long wanted to know you, Isabella."

Isabella, aware that Mama had disowned her sister and forbidden any contact between them, removed her hands and, blushing, twisted them together. She remembered the dolls that Aunt Barbara had sent long ago.

Glad to have something pleasant to say, she blurted out, "Remember those dolls you gave us? Adele and Louise? Oh, of course you don't know what we named them."

"You mentioned their names in your thank-you notes."

"They were the most wonderful gifts Hennie and I ever received." She warned herself not to mention that Adele had been transformed into the cabin boy Allen, who on a pirate ship circled the globe in search of adventure, although there was something about Aunt Barbara's manner that tempted her to think that this caution wasn't necessary. She had warmth and a sense of the open air about her that made Isabella believe that she could be trusted.

"I confess," Aunt Barbara said, "I had hoped that the dolls would be harbingers of a friendship between us. Well, we can make up for it now."

"Will you be in London long?" Isabella knew what Aunt Barbara had written to Uncle Lawson, and she chided herself for asking something banal, but her awareness of Mama's disapproval so embarrassed her she didn't know what else to say. Then, realizing that the question sounded rude, she said, "I mean, what brings you to London?" and then blushed furiously as she became aware that that also was not a question that someone younger asked someone older.

"My work brings me to London," Aunt Barbara answered matter-of-factly, "and I stay until I have accomplished what I need to do. I anticipate being here a few weeks."

Surprised at herself, Isabella felt a faint tide of hostility. What manner of woman was this? Women didn't work, at least not outside the home, unless it was for a church bazaar or for missionaries.

"What kind of work do you do?" Isabella asked, hoping the question didn't sound too challenging, but she had never heard a woman talk about her work.

"I am a professional writer." Seeing the mystified look on Isabella's face, Aunt Barbara explained, "I write articles for publication in periodicals, articles for which I get paid. I also earn commissions translating German and French books into English. I come to London to read and to do research, primarily in the British Museum. And to see my friends, go to theater, concerts, visit art galleries. You know what they say about all work and no play."

Isabella nodded, although she didn't know what "they say." Instead of admitting her ignorance, she said, "May I ask what you are working on now?"

"Of course. I usually write articles about science. In fact, I have just completed an essay in the *Edinburgh Review* on geology, arguing against the neptunists, who believe that water and not heat is the agent for change. Forgive me," Aunt Barbara said. "You probably have not heard of Werner and his followers. I tend to get carried away."

"Not at all. It sounds fascinating." Isabella had no idea what Neptunists were, but she did understand that geology was a topic of intense debate. In cutting through hills to lay railway tracks, many fossils had been exposed. She had heard Papa say that God had placed them in the embankments when he had created the world, as a test of man's faith. "Are you writing another science article?"

"No, I'm giving myself a treat and am writing an essay on the novels of the 1840s, to be published in *Household Words*."

Isabella drew in her breath. Her parents had not allowed her to read fiction, although they knew that during those far-distant summers of her childhood, Grandfather had permitted her to read novels. She had argued long and strenuously, but her parents had drawn the line: fiction was by definition false.

Aunt Barbara went on to defend fiction. "Good novels hold up a mirror to society. They ask profound questions. They expose the true relationship between master and servant, between husband and wife, between father and son or mother and daughter."

To herself Isabella vowed that from now on she would read fiction. "What novels are you writing about in your essay?" she asked.

"I am using *Mary Barton* by Mrs. Gaskell, Charles Dickens's *Dombey and Son*, Thackeray's *Vanity Fair*, Charlotte Brontë's *Jane Eyre*, and her sister Emily Brontë's *Wuthering Heights*. Three of the five, please note, are by women."

Isabella was concentrating on memorizing the list. "I haven't read them," she confessed, "but I'm going to."

"I envy you, reading them for the first time. *Household Words* is presently publishing *Cranford*, a charming memoir by Mrs. Gaskell. And they have begun monthly installments of Charles Dickens's new novel, *Bleak House*. You expect Dickens to be in the periodical, as he is also the editor," Aunt Barbara laughed. "I can let you have my copy." Digging into her reticule, she handed Isabella a magazine with a pale-green cover.

"Thank you." Isabella stumbled over the words as if she were on the verge of an unknown world. Only as a child with her grandfather had she been in a conversation with someone who attached importance to novels.

"Forgive me," Aunt Barbara said again. "I'm like a full bucket of water. At the slightest touch, I slop over."

"No, Aunt Barbara, I like hearing about your work and your ideas." Isabella thought about last night's dinner party and how disappointed she had been. She had hoped that conversations at London dinner parties would be stimulating; but they weren't. Here, as in Wyton, or Birmingham, or any other place Isabella had lived, women spoke only about their experiences, mostly anecdotes about domestic affairs. Aunt Barbara was quite different. "I'll look for Barbara Lawson and read your essays."

"You won't find her." In answer to Isabella's look of surprise, she continued, "I use a nom de plume, 'Paul Roberts.' If I didn't have a male name, it would be much more difficult to get published." Isabella was ingesting this when Aunt Barbara resumed. "Yes, I want my essays published, and I want to support myself. I've taken a saying of Thomas Carlyle for my motto: 'An endless significance lies in work; properly speaking all true work is religion.'"

"I like that," Isabella said.

Aunt Barbara rose, embraced Isabella, and kissed her on both cheeks in the European fashion. "We're going to get along famously, I just know."

Chewing on the end of her pen that night, Isabella was re-reading her journal entry, an entry almost completely about Aunt Barbara:

At dinner Aunt Barbara quoted Carlyle again. "Not what I have, but what I do is my kingdom." Papa would agree with that, but Papa would be opposed to an independent woman. He'd insist that the natural order of the universe was violated by a woman who did not look to her husband for authority—or her brother-in-law if she was unfortunate enough not to be married.

So much of what she says is singular. She certainly has a different point of view. Imagine taking a male name! I don't think I would ever do that, but she is right; women are not treated fairly. Although, in truth, many women seem content with their situation. Not me. I still am furious that I can't go to Cambridge, and that lump of a Merttins does. But Aunt Barbara is educated. She even translates books. And she didn't go to college.

She and Mama don't look a bit alike. It's not only that she is taller and has a roundish face, but her entire appearance is different. She walks purposefully; her voice and face are much more animated; she laughs; she has more energy. Poor Mama has a tic that twitches one of her eyes when she is tired. She is always serious. Oh, she smiles when she is pleased, but her lips don't part. In fact, biting on her lips and folding them into her mouth is her most characteristic expression. Aunt Barbara is like an out-in-the-open, fast-flowing, sun-sparkling river, and Mama is more of a quiet, tree-shaded brook.

To tell the truth, as pleasant as Aunt Barbara is, I am not completely comfortable with her. I don't want her to know that I am as ignorant as I am. I find myself shaping questions and sentences in my mind before I say them out loud.

A few days later as Aunt Barbara was helping herself to breakfast kippers, she said, "If you can fit it into your schedule, Isabella, perhaps you'd like to go with me to the *Westminster Review* office today."

Isabella was flattered that Aunt Barbara thought she had a schedule, and that she had invited her to accompany her. She nodded.

Aunt Barbara explained, "One of the editors is a friend of mine, and I would be pleased to introduce my niece."

Stepping down from Uncle's carriage, Isabella matched her step to Aunt Barbara's healthy stride and soon found herself mounting well-worn stairs in Paternoster Row and along a corridor to a door with a glazed window lettered "Westminster Review," where Aunt Barbara gave a vigorous rap. Admittance found them in a small room with a harassed-looking little man sitting in front of the most cluttered rolltop desk Isabella had ever seen.

He waved familiarly at Aunt Barbara while saying, "She's in. Just putting her to bed."

Mystified, Isabella followed Aunt Barbara down the hall, past three glazed-glass cubicles. At the fourth one, she knocked, and a cheerful voice said, "Enter." The voice belonged to the only oc-cupant of the room, a young woman who rose and greeted Aunt Barbara, her face alight with pleasure. "The very person I need to see!"

Aunt Barbara made the introductions. "Miss Evans, may I pres-ent my niece, Isabella Bird. Isabella, this is Miss Evans."

Isabella made a curtsy, and Miss Evans laughed and said, "We dispense with formalities here." She removed a stack of books from a chair. "Make yourself at home while I confer with your aunt." Miss Evans continued as the two women sat close together at the desk, "I'm still working on my translation of Feuerbach, and I've reached a critical juncture. Glance at this passage. You see how im-passioned the German is. If I translate that literally, do you think it will be misunderstood? You recall the brouhaha that greeted Froude's *The Nemesis of Faith.*"

Isabella was mesmerized by the young woman's voice. She tried to describe it to herself. It was warm, but it had a slightly rough quality, something like a brook purling over sharp stones, or deep, like the held notes of an organ while the melody danced above. Her appearance was not intimidating. Older than Isabella but younger than Aunt Barbara, she had large eyes, a long face and nose, and a rather melancholy expression that was animated when she spoke.

Miss Evans continued to Aunt Barbara, "Of course I respond to his bold humanism—*'Homo homini deus est'*—but this paragraph is his definition of love; that is the heart of the book. He makes this distinction between 'self-interested love' and 'the true human love' that vibrates as an almighty force through all living, which impels the sacrifice of self to another."

"Miss Evans, this passage is, as you say, central to an under-standing. It is what Feuerbach means when he calls his book *Das Wesen des Christentums.* Let me go over your translation carefully."

As the two women worked, Isabella noted their mutual respect for one another: it was the talk between equals, an uninhibited exchange of ideas. Neither interrupted. Each listened and considered what the other had said. And each had impressive scholarship. How had Miss Evans and her aunt become so learned? She wondered if she could ever possess such knowledge. She pulled out the *Household Words* that Aunt Barbara had given her; in the presence of their industry, she did not want to appear idle.

As they were saying farewell, Aunt Barbara said to Miss Evans, "Please don't think I am rude, but we've known one another for five years, isn't it? Ever since you translated Strauss's *Leben Jesu.* Do you think we could advance to a first-name basis? I wish you would call me Barbara."

"It's a privilege, Barbara. I have long wanted to. I so treasure our friendship. Do call me Mary Anne."

The women kissed each other, and Aunt Barbara said, "I'll see you at the concert." Soon Isabella and Aunt Barbara were once again on the sidewalk.

Isabella asked, "Did you decide to see the editor another time?"

"My dear, Miss Evans is my friend. I wanted you to meet her. She is the assistant editor."

As Isabella sat down to write that evening, her head was in a whirl. She scribbled:

Aunt Barbara and Miss Evans are the most wonderful women I have ever met. Uncle Lawson told me that Miss Evans had been Evangelical, and she had had an experience with her family similar to Aunt Barbara's when she broke with the church. Miss Evan's family, like Aunt Barbara's, disowned her. "Mind you," he added, "I don't agree with Barbara, but we have agreed to disagree, and I am always pleased when she comes to visit." Neither of these women have husbands; they live alone. And furthermore, they are not dependent upon a brother, or a father. Both support themselves with their writing. I never heard of anything so remarkable. But to look at them, they seem like perfectly normal women. I mean, they're not eccentric or queer. They appear to have friendships with other women and with men. And even more remarkable, they are both autodidacts. If they could educate themselves…Maybe Papa will hire a tutor for me. He would if I were a boy. Neither of them could go to college. Now that I have met them, I hate even more to go home. But I've already overstayed my visit, so like it or not, I've got to fold myself up and ship myself back to the parsonage and be a rector's daughter. I wish I knew how to live an independent life like Aunt Barbara. Uncle insists that his coachman, Edgars, accompany me. It is completely unnecessary.

Aunt Barbara had an appointment the next morning, so they said good-bye before she left. Isabella did not dare suggest that they write to one another, but when she said that she knew she would often think about her, what she truly meant was that Aunt Barbara was a beacon, a ray of light. Then the time came to say good-bye to Uncle Lawson.

"Well, little lady, it looks to me as if you're in better shape than you were when you arrived, eh?"

In fact, Isabella realized, she had barely thought about her back the past few weeks.

"Yes, Uncle, you're just what the doctor ordered. I wish I could stay here even longer." To Isabella's embarrassment, her eyes misted with tears. The Bird family was not given to displays of emotion, but Isabella flung herself into Uncle Lawson's arms and said, "I've had such a wonderful time. I shall treasure it all my life."

"You're welcome anytime, my dear, anytime," Uncle said, holding her close while patting her shoulder.

On the train going home to Wyton, Isabella quickened with resolution. Her health would improve, she would make a schedule for herself, she would read in a systematic way, she would apply herself to French so that she truly had command of the language, and, above all, she, like Aunt Barbara and Miss Evans, would earn her living as a writer. A startling idea.

I write easily, she told herself. *I have already published two pamphlets and had essays in religious journals. I am going to think of my writing as a serious ambition. But I won't risk telling Mama and Papa that I have met Aunt Barbara; I will just say that I met this woman writer at a dinner party because I know that I can't keep it all to myself.*

As she came through the ticket barrier, there stood Hennie. The two girls locked arms and looked at one another thirstily. "Oh, Hennie, I have so much to tell you!"

Alone that night in their room, Isabella poured out everything, about Aunt Barbara, about her ambition to be a writer, about her determination to study and to follow a disciplined course of reading. Hennie was completely understanding, saying that she, too, had been thinking that their lives should have more direction, and she volunteered to study with her.

"It will be like when we were girls, and we can quiz one another. Let's learn Latin and maybe even Greek. I'm sure Papa has books. And I think we should add the Bible to our studies. When you are writing, I'll study drawing and painting."

"Oh, Hennie, I never anticipated that you'd study along with me. I'm so glad. Of course we can study the Bible. I'm going to let my chemistry slide, but I'll take up history."

Still flush with the idea the next morning, the girls, with Mama's permission, fixed up Isabella's bedroom as a study, asking that a large table, a suitable lamp, and chairs be moved into the room. Then they bent their heads together and devised a schedule, after which they begged Papa for texts. He delighted them by saying that he would send off to his book dealer for any books that he lacked. When Isabella had the temerity to suggest a tutor, he was quick to say no. Even on practical grounds, he explained, it wasn't feasible. There was no one in Wyton to fill that office. But he could help them with the languages.

No sooner had they gotten under way, feeling self-important, as if they had had a new coat of paint, when Isabella's back screamed with pain. "No, I'm not going to heed it," Isabella vowed, but the need to rest her spine was overpowering. "Not one of those doctors did me a bit of good. I'm going to ignore it."

But the pain proved imperious, and Isabella found herself once again on the sofa, from where she continued to study, but serious work from that position was difficult. She longed to read a novel from Aunt Barbara's list, but she didn't dare flaunt such disobedience. *If only Hennie and I could live together independently,* Isabella despaired. *If only I could earn enough money with my writing!* Spurred by this dream, she did her best to concentrate on the text in hand.

When the newness of the schedule had worn off, but Isabella and Hennie were still diligent, Papa declared, "If I can disturb you scholars, I'd like to see you in my study this morning."

Mama was already there, her hands busy as always with her needle. "A family gathering?" Hennie said.

Isabella, looking at Mama, said, "Let me get my knitting. I'll bring yours, too, Hennie."

Soon the three women were occupied, but so accustomed were their fingers to this work that they were able to give Papa parade-ground attention.

"Yes, a family gathering, for what I am about to say affects all of us," Papa started. "Most of all, Isabella, it concerns you."

Isabella ran a quick inventory in her mind. How had she been remiss? She wasn't aware of anything she had done.

"Uncle Lawson and I..." Papa continued.

Oh no, Isabella thought, *he has found out about Aunt Barbara!* Her heart turned a somersault.

"Your Uncle Lawson and I," he repeated, "have been in steady communication, and after consulting with your mother and asking the good Lord for guidance, I have been persuaded that what I am about to propose is a rewarding course of action."

Please, Papa, Isabella silently pleaded, *please get to the point.*

"Uncle Lawson tells me that Dr. Jamison proposed that you embark on a sea voyage."

"Yes, Papa," Isabella assented.

"As you know, I have begun work—my magnum opus," he said, "on the religious revival. I have collected much evidence from England and Scotland, and Keble has kindly given me copious notes from Ireland. What is lacking is information from the New World. I am in no position to travel, but I would like to commission you, Isabella, to be my surrogate. Does that appeal to you?" Papa spoke earnestly, but his eyes sparkled.

"Papa, you don't mean..." Isabella began, and then her mouth fell agape with the enormity of it.

"Yes, I mean for you to go to the Americas in my stead."

Isabella saw that Mama was jabbing her needle into the linen. "Your mother has agreed—" Papa started, when Mama interrupted.

"I've agreed, yes, but with certain stipulations. I don't intend you to run..." Here Mama sputtered as if unable to finish, then, shaking her head, said, "Hog wild."

What did Mama mean, "hog wild"?

"Of course not," Papa said to Mama in a conciliatory voice. "Isabella is a level-headed, sensible twenty-three-year-old young lady. She is not going to do anything irresponsible."

Isabella gathered that Papa had been over this ground before with Mama.

"I know she is young, but I'll personally guarantee that she will be chaperoned every leg of the journey." Turning toward Isabella, he added, "I mean for you to go to the Americas in my stead and to garner as much intelligence as you can on the spreading of the Word. You'll spend your time with men of the cloth and in churches. It is not possible for me to vacate my post here, but I believe that material on the New World will significantly increase interest in my book."

"I can't think of anything more wonderful," Isabella said, thinking of Aunt Barbara's independence and that she would write a book about her travels in America.

"Your doctor has prescribed a sea voyage. Very well. With this mission in mind, you will have your sea voyage combined with Evangelical labors."

Isabella's face clouded. "What about Hennie? I don't want to go if it means that Hennie feels left out."

"Isabella, I don't feel left out. Truly I don't. I'm delighted for you. You know I do not like to speak to strangers. I guess I'm just a dull old homebody."

"You're not dull," Isabella protested.

"Hennie doesn't have a selfish bone in her body," Mama interjected, and Isabella immediately translated that into "Hennie isn't selfish the way you are."

"You can be assured that Hennie will harbor no resentment. That's not in her nature. You are my brave flag, and she's my demure violet." Papa smiled. "I have learned that distant cousins of mine are returning to Prince Edward Island in Canada this spring, and you can accompany them. Of course, I shall provide you with letters of introduction, and we shall work out an itinerary and arrange for chaperones to escort you."

Isabella merely smiled. She wasn't going to let the thought of chaperones darken her trip. "But, Papa, can we afford it?"

"Let me worry about that. I shall entrust you with one hundred pounds. You are to budget and spend it exactly as you wish. I shall provide the passage and whatever additions your wardrobe requires for the journey, but every other expense must come from this fund. How long you stay in America depends upon how you manage your hundred pounds."

The winter flew by. Isabella applied herself to her studies with renewed vigor. Letters were written, arrangements confirmed, her wardrobe refurbished and an unyielding whalebone corset provided for her back, tickets bought, boxes and trunks packed and corded, and here at last was the morning of the day she was to depart.

CHAPTER 17

1854, ACROSS THE ATLANTIC

On a sparkling Saturday morning in April 1854 Isabella, to her amazement, found herself on the deck of the *Canada*, a paddle-wheel steamer of the British and North American Royal Mail Steam Packet Company, headed for the New World. She fluttered her handkerchief to Papa on the wharf and then walked across the deck to look at the crowded Liverpool harbor: frigates and clippers, huge square-sided timber ships, high-sterned green galliots, the long black hulls and tall raking masts of American whalers, the *East Indiaman*, the *Flying Cloud*, and most inspiring of all, the screw troopship *Himalaya*, its decks packed with a cheering regiment of Scotch Greys en route to the Crimea.

To think that she was actually a voyager and not a mere spectator.

She located Papa once again, once again waved her handkerchief. He raised his arm in salute, two guns were fired, the lashings were cast off, the Stars and Stripes, the Union Jack, and the rampart lion ensign of the steamship company flaunted gaily from the fore, the bell rang, the paddle wheels revolved, and the *Canada*, with 186 passengers, crew, mail, and cargo, left the Mersey, outward bound for Halifax and Boston, and she was abroad.

If I hadn't gone to London, Isabella mused, *I wouldn't be on my way to America.* She didn't know that her journey had actually started with Mama's grim realization that her twenty-one-year-old daughter was not married and appeared to have no prospects of getting married.

Early last fall Edward and Dora had had this discussion, germinated from Papa's worry about Isabella's lassitude and her many physical complaints, and from Mama's concern about Isabella's nervous prostrations and her combative disposition.

"If Isabella were to meet a suitable young man to whom she could devote herself..." Dora left the thought unfinished. "I know that in a real sense, my life began only when I met you," she added.

"You must not say that, Dora. Your life began in the service of Christ."

"Oh, of course," Dora hastened to agree. "But the fulfillment of marriage, the privilege of bringing up children...Yes, I am sure that wedded bliss is the solution for Isabella." From that seed the visit to Uncle Lawson had flourished.

On board, Isabella wrote the first of many letters to her sister, with the private determination that they would be a resource for a book about the New World.

April 9, 1853

Dearest Pet,

"Stateroom" is a misnomer; "broom closet" is more accurate, and I share these confines with a Mrs. Bundy. Fortunately she has the bottom bunk. "Fortunately" for if not, I would be in imminent danger of her descending upon me. Mrs. Bundy was presiding over a boisterous farewell party in the stateroom and was rivaling her guests in nips of gin. I made a quick retreat. With the judicious help of the purser all the visitors were persuaded into the launch, and Mrs. Bundy collapsed on the lower bunk. Sensible Papa had stayed on the wharf throughout, and I waved my handkerchief at him until he was just a speck.

Reflecting on the farewell scene, Isabella was seized with regret. How could she have left Hennie!

Bidding good-bye to Papa and seeing the green of England melt into the horizon made me wish I were not outward bound but were coming home. I had to remind myself I would be with you again by late autumn.

This is a small vessel, less than three hundred feet long and only thirty-five feet wide. I am surprised that with such small accommodations all the passengers and crew fit on board. Many of the passengers are berthed in dormitories.

Amusements are left to the passengers' own devices, but I can see that the pattern of the day for most will be eating and sleeping. Some of the men are stretched out supine on the salon sofas; it is remarkable the degree to which they have made themselves comfortable. The energetic are playing deck shuffleboard, groups of five and six abreast are walking on deck, some passengers have disappeared to their cabins, and the rest of us are reading, writing, or playing chess or cards or backgammon. A chess tournament is being organized, and I have been assigned to play a Mr. Ross.

Colonel and Mrs. Sawyer seem like agreeable companions. They are homeward bound to Prince Edward Island after eight years in India. We all eat at a long table without regard for social rank. I found myself sitting with an Irish pork merchant, a Jew who regards pork as an abomination, a French cook who speaks no English en route to Toronto, another English army officer, a French Jesuit, a rough Californian who wears nuggets of gold for buttons, and a woman who claims she is a French duchess.

April 10

Before braving Mrs. Bundy and the upper bunk last night, I took a few turns on deck. The wind held steady, and the sails that by day looked dingy were white at night.

Fair winds prevail, and the studding sails assist the steam engine. Today is Sunday, and I attended services, pleased to see many other worshipers. Not Mrs. Bundy. As I was reading my Bible, Mrs. Bundy said, "I wish you'd pitch that book overboard; it's enough to sink the ship." An inconsistent point of view since she has already told me that she is an atheist.

The dressing bell rings at eight in the morning, and breakfast is served between eight thirty and nine thirty. The long table is profusely adorned with cold tongue, ham, Irish stew, mutton chops, broiled salmon, crimped cod, eggs, tea, coffee, chocolate, toast, hot rolls, and bottles of Perrin's Sauce and Gentleman's Relish. I marvel at how people pitched into it when late supper—served after a bountiful lunch, tea, and dinner with large quantities of soup, fish, game, venison, meat, and poultry, French side dishes, jellies, puddings, pastry, and a dessert of fresh and preserved fruits, as well as wine, spirits, liqueurs, and ale—was offered between nine thirty and ten thirty last night!

In her journal she wrote:

> Mr. Ross proved a poor chess player. I was fortunate in play-
> ing white, and I never lost my advantage. My next opponent
> is Mr. Hunt. A Miss Goodman has also signed up—the only
> other woman, but she impresses me as being of inferior in-
> tellect. Most people would judge her to be handsome, but
> she talks nonstop nonsense, and she is an outrageous flirt.
> She is going to write a book about America, so she says, after,
> I imagine, a whirlwind three-week visit. I have read all the
> books on the subject recently published, as well as books by
> the earlier travelers: Frances Trollope, Harriet Martineau,
> and Charles Dickens. I hope to stay at least six months, and
> even then my impressions can only be superficial.
>
> I was admiring the sea, staring at its heaving surface, listen-
> ing to its restless surge, marveling at its immensity. Dark as
> the night was, the white sails were visible above like spectral
> wings. The tiny ship skims over the water, leaving a dissolv-
> ing path in the trackless waste. But my heart was like an
> incandescent beacon ahead of the ship, beckoning her on,
> to go west toward the unknown.

That evening Isabella was standing on deck listening to the deep
surge of the water, to the creak of the timbered hull, to the lazy flap
of the sails. All traces of regret at leaving Hennie had disappeared.

Mr. Ross came and stood at the rail next to her side. "I hope I'm
not intruding," he said, "but allow me to congratulate you on how
well you play chess, Miss Bird."

Although Isabella was proud of her command of the game, she
tried to reply with becoming modesty. "Thank you. I had a good
teacher. My grandfather," she explained, "taught me when I was a
child. I spent my childhood summers with my grandfather, who

was teaching chess to my male cousins. When he saw how interested I was, he included me in his demonstrations," Isabella said. "How long have you been playing, Mr. Ross?"

"As is apparent, I have really just started since I came down. At Balliol, crew caught my fancy, and that's a demanding diversion."

If he went out for crew, Isabella thought, *there is more muscle on that lanky frame than is apparent.*

"Did you 'come down' last year?" Isabella hoped that was the right expression and that she did not sound as impressed as she felt, or as envious.

"Yes. I had intended to take Holy Orders, but at the last moment, I had what I guess you'd call a crisis of faith." He laughed ruefully. "I'm on this voyage to figure out what direction my life will take."

"My father is a rector of a small parish in the South of England," Isabella said, but not wanting to continue in the vein of clergyman's daughter, she asked, "What part of England do you come from? I can't quite distinguish your dialect. It isn't pure North of England."

"You have a good ear, Miss Bird. It's Nottingham, close to Yorkshire."

"I was born in Yorkshire myself."

"Were you! That makes us neighbors. Neighbor, would you care to join me for a savory in the salon?" Mr. Ross laughed.

That night she wrote in her journal:

April 12

This morning I took a turn on deck before breakfast. I was rewarded with seeing the sun peer over the horizon and vault into the sky. Mr. Ross was also on deck, and when he lifted his hat to greet me, his red hair and beard caught the fire of the sun. His coloring is dramatic, as his face is thin and ascetic and almost excessively pale. Such is the informality of shipboard life we chatted like old acquaintances.

I am so enthralled by the ocean that as we were looking at the restless, plumbless waters, I recited,

But thou art almighty—
Eternal—sublime—
Unweakened—unwasted—
Twin-brother of Time!
Fleets, tempests, nor nations
Thy glory can bow;
As the stars first beheld thee,
Still chainless art thou!

We discussed poetry, and he urged me to read Matthew Arnold's *Empedocles on Etna*. Imagine having my reading directed by an Oxford graduate!

At breakfast Colonel Sawyer told me that Mrs. Sawyer was feeling ill-disposed and would be staying in the stateroom today. I wonder if "ill-disposed" translates into "supercilious." She certainly is unhappy with the eating arrangements and pointedly spoke only to the other officer and to the countess. I overheard her say to her husband, "There doesn't appear to be anyone nice on board," excepting herself, of course. She acted as if the poor Californian had lice. He, bless him, seemed utterly oblivious to the snub and continued to shovel food into his mouth with his knife.

Mrs. Bundy occupies our closet night and day; she claims that gin is a great remedy for boredom! But I much prefer to walk on deck or be in the salon than to remain in such close quarters.

The sky is still perfectly cloudless, and the sea has a peculiar deep, clear, greenish-blue tint that the mate tells me only occurs far from land. After breakfast, people promenade on deck, watch the wind, suggest how it has changed, look at the course, and ask the captain when he expects to be in port. Bets are afloat as to how many days the crossing will take from Liverpool to Halifax. Then we retire to the salon, interrupted only by meals, until eleven at night.

Isabella had just started her stroll on deck when Mr. Ross appeared. She wondered for a moment if he had waited until she emerged, but told herself that that idea was nonsense. She certainly did not lie in wait for him. Nonetheless, his companionship was most agreeable. They circled the deck side by side.

"Your father, you tell me, Miss Bird, is a clergyman."

"Yes, he is a fervent Evangelical."

"I envy him. Not necessarily the Evangelical but assuredly the 'fervent.'"

"Oddly enough, Mr. Ross, I understand what you mean. My father and mother are both fervent, and my sister has a purity of faith that never wavers. But I have not been so blessed. I have often found myself in the dark, as it were, questioning God's ways, and even…" But here Isabella broke off, appalled that she was speaking with such candor to a stranger.

Mr. Ross took no notice of her abrupt interruption. "Yes, my own faith has been severely tried. Oxford is still reverberating under the shock caused by Newman's secession to Rome."

"I am sure that is troubling. Even my father, whose faith is beyond questioning, regards the Oxford Movement as a dangerous tendency. Although I must acknowledge that despite Newman's later apostasy, 'Lead, Kindly Light' is one of my favorite hymns."

"If only Newman had left his faith unexamined! Perhaps that is what I should do. If only I could. One would not, after all, take apart a flower."

"That is certainly my sister's way, but speaking for myself, I prefer faith buttressed by the light of reason."

"John Keble may be the man for you."

"I know him only as the writer of sacred verse."

"He is. For a decade he was professor of poetry at Oriel, but I am thinking of his volumes of *Spiritual Counsel.* He is a remarkably steadying influence. Still." Mr. Ross fingered his gingery beard. "Well," he continued inconclusively, "maybe this voyage will point me in the right direction."

"I trust that it will," Isabella said and then confided, "I am investigating the revival of Evangelical faith in Canada and the United States for a book my father is undertaking. Perhaps such a project would be helpful to you in your present dilemma, if you'll forgive my boldness."

"By George, that's a remarkably noble enterprise. You're right, I do need a sense of purpose, and it is good of you to suggest it. Amazing," he said, "the sun is already far advanced. We best hurry down to breakfast. I trust you will forgive me for imposing upon you in this fashion."

That evening they met again on deck to admire the sunset. When Isabella climbed up to her bunk that night, she chided herself on her impatience to see him again. "Why, I hardly know him," she told herself, but she was full of eagerness to continue their discussions.

April 15

When I climbed up to the poop deck for my stroll, I anticipated seeing Mr. Ross to question him further about the

Oxford Movement. As I pushed open the door, I heard Miss Goodman's vacuous laugh, and there she was with Mr. Ross, next to her, laughing too. I hastily retreated—I don't think I was observed—and took my walk on the afterdeck.

I am disappointed in Mr. Ross, as Miss Goodman, with her ridiculous chatter, has become the laughingstock of everyone. As might be expected, she didn't advance in the chess tournament beyond the first round. I had thought Mr. Ross was a more serious young man. I compelled myself to walk until my agitation passed. I don't know why I'm upset; it isn't as if I had known him for any length of time.

Mr. Hunt was a disappointing opponent. He led with the queen's pawn, which I think is an inferior opening. I managed to engineer a knight's fork, and he was faced with the choice of losing either his king or his queen. Since the king must move out of check, his queen was my captive, and Mr. Hunt soon surrendered. The people watching gave me the impression that they would have preferred to see Mr. Hunt victor. A superior woman chess player is apparently against their taste, but I am not going to make a deliberate mistake in order to satisfy them. The next, and semifinal, round is against Monsieur Vallard, who speaks little English but is a hard campaigner. So am I. I regard those sixty-four squares as a field to control and to conquer.

April 16

Mrs. Sawyer put in an appearance at dinner where again she directed her remarks only to those she deemed her social equals or superiors. She signaled a look to her husband that said as clearly as words, "Not our kind, dear." I am going to find it a trial to be their guest. She said to me, I thought with malice, nodding to the table where Mr. Ross and Miss Goodman were eating together, "I see that that pretty little Miss Goodman has made a conquest." I answered with what I hoped was coolness, "We know about shipboard romances, don't we?" I am hurt, but I shall not let her know it. It's scorching to have Mr. Ross's preference flaunted in confines from which there is no escape.

Monsieur Vallard is a chess player. His mannerism initially distracted me as his small white hands fluttered over the board aligning and realigning his pieces, but I soon became inured to it. A crowd gathered early. This time, perhaps it was national honor; I felt the sympathy was for me. The game was intense. I captured his queen with mine, and then mine was in jeopardy. He declined; instead his knight took my rook, and two plays later, he had my king in check. However I was able to extricate myself, and eventually he declared *échec et mat*, the French term for "checkmate," meaning that he had no moves to make that would not cost him the game. When I thanked him, he said, "Je vous en fais mes felicitations." Despite the fact that all Jesuits are arrogant, he was a gracious loser. The final round is tomorrow. Chess remains a game of great beauty, and I am thankful that last winter Uncle Lawson and I played so often.

Tonight several people approached to congratulate me. Mr. Ross came to my table and said, "I never knew women played so well."

I accepted this civilly, answering, "Thank you. Women are full of surprises," but I thought, *tant pis*, for an opinion like that.

On April 19, she penned a letter to Hennie:

Dearest Pet,

Allow me to introduce you to the chess champion of the Royal Mail *Canada* outward bound for Halifax and Boston! It is a slight achievement, I know, and I risk the sin of pride in even writing about it, but Grandfather would be pleased, wouldn't he? My final round was against Major Rogers, who is an intimidating presence. He has square shoulders, a white walrus mustache, and wears a monocle. And it was a hard-fought game, lasting nearly three hours. It has taken me the entire trip to adjust to the weight of the pieces. In addition, the chessmen are the new Staunton design, so instead of my beloved elephant as counselor to the king and the queen, the piece is a bishop who looks as if he were wearing a visor.

We are nearing land; a pod of seals kept us company this morning. Do our faces look as identical to them as theirs do to us? We also had a strong head wind for the first time, and most of the passengers were seasick. My back may be my Achilles' heel, but I am favored with a stable stomach, and I enjoyed the almost-deserted deck. I even felt sorry for Mrs. Bundy, who looks a pale tint of green that has not, however, improved the coarseness and vulgarity of her tongue.

The voyage, I am almost sorry to report, has been uneventful. No Russian pirates, no icebergs, not even fog. A lottery has been started on the hour of our arrival; the rigging has been tightened, the railings polished. A Yankee skipper, his genial countenance beaming, has just announced, "Come, there's a glorious country, and no mistake, a great country, a progressive country, the greatest country under the sun," and I looked where he pointed. No white cliffs or verdant hillsides, but a low, gloomy coast, barely visible through the mist.

We docked in Halifax—in nine days and five hours—just as the evening sun was setting in floods of purple light, the breeze fragrant with pine. As I write this, I am ensconced at the Waverley House, and although it is utterly cheerless, it boasts of being the best inn in Halifax. I can see the colored lights of the *Canada* disappear around the head of the harbor as she steams to Boston. Disembarking was completely chaotic, but three hours later, there she was, on her way.

I want to send this letter with the outgoing steamer, so I close hastily. I love you and miss you sorely.

That night, Mr. Ross, on a black charger of magisterial size, invaded Isabella's dreams. She was mounted on a French pony. They had several skirmishes, after each of which he leaped from his steed, removed his visor and plumed helmet, and with an elaborate flourish bowed deeply. In return, Isabella also dismounted to give a full one-leg-behind-the-other curtsy. Then they remounted and skirmished again, all according to some ritualized pattern.

April 19

Despite my winning the chess tournament, which I am ashamed to say I take pleasure in, and despite the Sawyers, who are chaperoning me, this passage has been a solitary interlude with time for observation and reflection. Mrs. Sawyer stayed in her cabin almost the entire voyage—which might have been just as well, as I am to travel with them to

Prince Edward Island and to be their guest for a week, and I'm not at all sure I like her. Her only remarks about her eight years in India have been about the servants and their untrustworthiness. Colonel Sawyer met some Anglo-Indian cronies, and I barely saw him.

I am upbraiding myself for thinking, even for a moment, that Mr. Ross was interested in me. When will I learn? It is a hard lesson, but a necessary one, and the sooner I go about it, the better. I feel such a failure. At the same time, I resent feeling that way. Why should I feel a failure because a man doesn't pursue me? I am not well educated, I know, but I am intelligent. A woman is successful only if she has a man at her beck and call. That means she must be a flirt and act helpless and stupid. At least I didn't act like a coquette. I refuse to conceal my curiosity and learning.

Why am I hurt at Mr. Ross dropping me? And in such a fish bowl! I had truly thought that he liked me for my intellect and my understanding. Isn't it possible for a man and a woman to be companions without the woman always demurring? Mama does not have an opinion that is not Papa's, and that deference, I notice, is a matrimonial talisman. Women lose their independence when they get married. Aunt Barbara and her friend Miss Evans are women of strong opinions, of humor, and of wonderful vitality, but would they be if they were married? I like the company of men—they're more interesting than women. My reaction to Mr. Ross alerts me that I don't have control over my feelings. Talk about contradictions! To be honest, I want a man to be in love with me, but I don't want to be beguiled by him. I just wish my heart didn't feel so raw and my pride so bruised.

I feel let down. Irrationally I had expected that this voyage would culminate in the foreign and the exotic, but as reason might have told me, everything is familiar: the soldiers wear the well-known scarlet, the voices are English, the faces have an Anglo-Saxon cast, and the Sawyers are dull. I yearn for novelty; I am tired of English accents.

CHAPTER 18

LETTERS HOME—ISABELLA IN AMERICA

Two days in Halifax were more than ample to explore every resource the town had to offer. Then, Colonel Sawyer, his wife, and Isabella rode a lumbering public coach across Nova Scotia, endured a wild passage on the turbulent waters of the Northumberland Strait, and docked at Charlottetown, where the Sawyers enjoyed a tearful reunion with their family. Isabella wrote to Hennie:

June 1, 1853

Dearest Pet,

I set out this morning with Mr. Kruger and his sister. We shall be gone several days, not knowing each night where we shall stay, but begging lodging wherever we find ourselves. So far the trip has primarily been boring and disappointing. I know I should be ashamed, the Sawyers mean well, and they are generous to me, but I feel positively stifled.

Despite their hospitality I have had more than enough of them. They ape all the sterile mannerisms of the English without any of their innate dignity.

There are endless calls, endless discussions on servants, turnips, and plovers, endless stories of political puerilities. Everyone seems to flit around reporting or seeking news of their neighbors, anything that has been done or said, and a great deal of what has not been done or said.

What a welcome change! Mr. Kruger, his sister, and I left this morning in a light wagon with little baggage a chess-board, some books I doubt we'll read, heavy buffalo robes in case we don't find shelter) to go to the northwest corner of Prince Edward Island to visit an Indian village. Miss Kruger and I are wearing straw bonnets, and all three of us are determined to laugh and to enjoy ourselves. We stopped in the woods and unpacked our hamper of cold meat pies and bread, only our horse next to us contentedly eating his oats. From birch bark we fashioned cups that leaked almost as fast as we could drink. In refilling mine from the creek, I fell into the water, which provided my companions with so much merriment they couldn't rescue me. But I soon dried out in the brilliant sun.

We are already in an isolated part of the island and had about decided that the buffalo robes would be put to use when we came upon this small house with its single inhabit-ant, an émigré from the Scottish Highlands who has been here for five years. Within minutes he had laid a repast of tea, scones, raspberries, and cream. He was genuinely glad to see us and has retained such a vivid interest in Scotland that he kept us up late with his questions. I so enjoy the genuine warmth of Scottish people. What a glorious day.

Yours devotedly,

Isabella

In the days following, they trapped for lobsters and then boiled them in a rude shipbuilder's cabin discovered deep in the woods a remote spring, and helped with the housework in exchange for lodging with the keeper of a small store, until they arrived at the Indian village. The village consisted of fifteen wigwams made of poles tied together at the upper end and thatched with large pieces of birch bark. Fierce dogs announced their presence, and scantily dressed children with long, lank hair kept the dogs company. But the dogs were silenced, and Mr. Kruger was welcomed, as his medical knowledge had been of assistance when he had been here before. Only one small plot was under cultivation.

"These Indians," Mr. Kruger said, "dig for oysters, fish, hunt, and collect berries, confident the earth will provide. Their attitude is to disturb the earth and its spirits as little as possible, using only what they need. We have to remember that we are trespassing on the very ground we walk on. Prince Edward Island belongs to the Indians."

To enter the wigwam, Isabella followed Mr. Kruger on her hands and knees and crawled through an aperture. Inside, the earthen floor was brushed clean, a pile of neatly stacked furs the only "furniture."

A fire was burning in the middle, over which hung a kettle of fish that a young woman was stirring. She had a dark complexion, with glossy black hair and magnificent eyes. She was wearing a cap made of scarlet beads that she must have known set off her hair

Judith Jordan

and eyes to advantage. She had recently given birth to twins, "papooses," who were tightly strapped onto boards and who looked like exotic idols.

A few days later, Isabella and the Krugers returned to Charlottetown, where the consensus was that the danger of cholera was over and it was now safe to travel. The Sawyers were concerned that the delay had disrupted the carefully arranged sequence of chaperones. They asked a friend, Mr. Martin, to accompany Isabella as far as Portland, Maine, and entrusted him to find a replacement for the next lap of the journey. Isabella lost no time in being on her way. The chain of chaperones broke down at Portland, and Isabella did not reestablish it. She wrote Papa, "No country in the world gave more respect to women than the United States, that the presence of a lady was a beneficial restraint upon manners and conversation."

June 20

Dearest Pet,

I haven't had an ill day since I've been here—that, despite this intense heat, which I do believe rivals the tropics. Give me cold anytime!

New York City is teeming with immigrants with their kettles and blankets and large blue boxes or corded chests. I am told they arrive at a rate of one thousand a day. They are pathetic; so many are emaciated, pallid, huddled together in close, ill-ventilated spaces, with insufficient water to keep clean.

Probably in no city in the civilized world is life so fearfully insecure. The practice of carrying concealed arms, if

166

illegal, is perfectly common. Terrible outrages and murderous assaults are matters of such nightly occurrence as to be thought hardly worthy of notice even in those prints that minister to man's taste for the horrible.

New York City is subject, as are other American cities, to numerous fires, whereas we English scarcely know a fire engine by sight. New York has also adopted the novel plan of numbering streets. Broadway is well paved, but a great part of the city is indescribably dirty.

From here I shall dip into that nefarious region of slavery, the South, and then travel as far west as I can. The West, that verge illuminated by the setting sun, calls to me in a mysterious way. I do know I have developed a raving appetite for a packet of letters from you, and I shall not budge until they arrive.

July 1

Dearest Pet,

To my immense joy, your letters have arrived. I'm happy to hear that the bazaar was an outstanding success, as well as your garden. What did you plant in remembrance of me? Something wild and gaudy?

Everyone here is talking about Harriet Beecher Stowe's recently published *Uncle Tom's Cabin*, which I have just read. It is powerfully written, and I much admire the benevolent intentions of Mrs. Stowe, for surely slavery violates the undeviated law of moral right as laid down in divine revelation.

Going to Virginia I sat next to an abolitionist on the train and struck up a conversation about *Uncle Tom's Cabin*. "That book," he said, "has thrown the cause back for many years."

"Why?" I asked.

"Her most despicable villain is a Yankee overseer from Vermont, and she vents her sharpest ridicule on a Yankee woman."

"But certainly," I argued, "the book is a condemnation of slavery and a contribution to the cause of abolition."

"Mrs. Stowe has always avoided approving our cause. You've read the book. Who does she depict in the most admiring colors? The true southern gentleman and the genuine southern lady, that's who."

"Still, the effect of the novel is intensely antislavery."

"Tell me, then, why the warmest praise for the novel has been from southern critics?"

As you can tell, as in most disagreements, neither of us influenced the other, but our discussion is a microcosm of the controversy the book is generating here.

An interesting aside on the economic rewards of the slave-owning, cotton-growing South is this story. I ventured into one of the opulent Broadway emporiums in New York, where I asked the price of a bracelet flashing with diamonds.

"Twenty-five thousand dollars," the clerk told me.

I gasped! That's about £5,000 at today's exchange. "Who would buy such a thing?" I asked.

The clerk said, "I guess some southerner will buy it for his wife."

August 15

Dearest Pet,

In Illinois, on the *Lightning Express* en route to Chicago, warranted to speed sixty-seven miles an hour(!), two "prairie men" were sitting in front of me. Fine specimens of men, they were, with handsome faces and a reckless bearing: tall, broad chested, and athletic, with aquiline noses, piercing gray eyes, and brown curling hair and beards. They wore leather jackets, slashed and embroidered, leather knee breeches, large boots with embroidered tops, silver spurs, and caps of scarlet cloth, worked with somewhat tarnished gold thread, doubtless the gifts of some fair ones. Each of them wore two pistols stuck into their leather belts, gold earrings, and costly rings. They kept all of us fortunate to be nearby amused by their drolleries, an endless procession of racy Western stories, whistled melodies, and comic songs. Blithe, cheerful, chivalrous.

I tried to imagine myself as free as those men, but it was a feat beyond me. I was sorry to see them leave the cars in Davenport, Iowa, for they relieved the tedium of a long journey.

A very different kind of man slumped in the seat next to me, and I knew from my knowledge of physiognomy that he was a "lowlife." I am sure that a phrenologist examination would confirm my suspicions. Knowing that I could not keep awake the entire journey, I took the precaution of removing my money and tickets from my purse. Sure enough, I shortly felt the man's hand in my pocket, withdrawing my purse in which I had left only my luggage checks. In the train shed in Chicago, when the baggagemaster came through the car and asked for checks, I bowed to my neighbor, and said to the baggagemaster, "This gentleman has the checks for my baggage."

September 30

Dearest Pet,

Every town of large size has from ten to twenty daily papers, every village has its three or four, and even a collection of huts produces its one "daily" or two or three "weeklies." They are bought by the dozen everywhere, and are greedily devoured by men, women, and children. Almost as soon as the locality of a town is chosen, a paper starts into life.

Mammon is the idol, which the people worship. People work harder than slaves—sacrificing home enjoyments, pleasure, and health itself to the one desire: the acquisition of wealth. None dare to pause in this race, which they so madly run. All are spurred on in their headlong course by avarice, ambition, or eager competition. But, despite this, the Sabbath is universally observed, and I marvel at the liberality of the philanthropic societies.

My plans are to return to Montreal, to Quebec, then down to Albany, and across to Boston, where, despite the onset of winter, I hope to embark on the *America*, reputably the slowest and wettest of the whole line. Now that I have started the journey toward home, I find myself more eager than ever to see your sweet face.

October 15

Dearest Pet,

I am on the Saint Lawrence River en route to Quebec. You'll find it difficult to believe that the steamers on this noble river regularly shoot the rapids. The river becomes more and more turbulent until we enter what might be termed a sea of leaping waves and raging waters, enough to engulf a small boat. The idea of descending it in a steamer is an extraordinary one. It is said that from the shore, a vessel looks as if it were hurrying to certain destruction. Still we hurry on, with eight men at the wheel. Rocks appear like snags in the middle of the stream—we dash straight down upon rocky islets, strewn with the wrecks of rafts, but a turn of the wheel, and we rush by them in safety at a speed of thirty miles an hour, till a ragged ledge of rock stretches across the whirling stream. Still on we go—the flood roars louder; the descent appears steeper; earth, sky, and water mingle together. I involuntarily took hold of the rail—a madman attempted to jump over; a flighty lady screamed and embraced more closely her poodle dog. We reached the ledge—one narrow space free from rocks appeared. Down with one plunge went the bow into a turmoil of foam, and we had "shot the cataract" of La Chine. The exploit is one of the most agreeable that the traveler can perform.

I am sorry my trip is about over, but I am heartened by the thought that I shall soon be steaming toward you.

On the train to Boston on the final lap of her journey before embarking, Isabella shut her eyes and mused about her trip. The voyage out, the chess tournament, the Sawyers, Mr. Ross were now a long eight months ago. Mr. Ross, like a deeply buried fishhook, still rankled. What tightened her throat was that he had spurned her in favor of a shallow woman, and she had been so eager. She shook her head at the memory. She had not gone as far west as she had wanted. Dare she dream of another trip? Still, she had been as far as Iowa and had seen the father of waters, the mighty Mississippi. For Papa she had visited innumerable churches and the comfortable homes and drawing rooms where Papa had ensured she had introductions, but she had also visited schools, hospitals, cemeteries, and slums. And the people she had met! Most of her trip had been spent in actual travel—clipper, stagecoach, "cars," as the trains were called, paddle boat, buckboard, horse and buggy— and she had talked to and listened to whomever she met: slaves, itinerant peddlers, hunters, western men, freed Negroes, adventurers, editors, wives, and clergymen. She had page after page of notes, material for her own book. She gloated like a miser counting his coins.

Astonishingly, even in a stagecoach over corduroy or plank roads, she had not suffered one backache or sleepless night—unless she counted just a few weeks ago in Quebec when she had been ill. She was sure it was the cholera.

Her mind leaped ahead to the rectory, but superimposed on that image was the young Indian squaw on Prince Edward Island. Her wigwam was bare of any of the comforts to which Isabella was

accustomed, but she envied the simplicity of her life: no tight cor-
sets, no laced shoes, no burdensome bonnets, no furniture to dust,
no maids to interrupt her, no calls to pay, no choir to rehearse, no
rectory duties to perform, but sitting literally on nature's bosom
and taking from Mother Nature only what she needed. Hennie
would have liked that Indian girl.

Hennie was like a dollop of honey or balm, she thought ruefully. *I'm not ready yet to go home.* Of course, she corrected herself,
she would be glad to see Mama and Papa and Hennie. But after
the freedom of her travels, during which she experienced no en-
nui, sleeplessness, or back pain, and after seven months of being
accountable only to herself, the rectory would seem like putting on
a garment several sizes too small and entering a prison.

CHAPTER 19

1854, BACK HOME TO WYTON

"Oh, Papa, how good to see you!" Isabella squeezed Papa's arm and shyly kissed his cheek. "You didn't have to come to meet me. I didn't expect you to come to Liverpool." She was surprised to see him, delighted really, and yet, glancing at his ramrod figure, his being here meant that her wonderful trip ended this very instant, not, as she had anticipated, at the rectory doorstep.

"You don't think I'd let my girl travel alone, do you?"

"But, Papa, I've been doing that for seven months. I wrote you how a young woman traveling alone in the Americas is always treated with courtesy and deference." But from the look on Papa's face, she knew that her days of freedom were over. What she did now, what she said must again be rigidly controlled. Isabella felt a spate of anger but immediately thought, *How can I feel that? Papa is kind to make this long trip to meet me.*

"Papa," Isabella said as she took out her purse, "let me pay for our railroad tickets to Wyton. I still have ten pounds."

"Isabella, you do manage money ably. I am pleased," said Papa. Isabella glowed. He continued, "You keep that. I'll buy our tickets."

On the train Isabella told him about the great revival in progress in America, how she had attended religious meetings of every

174

creed and heard 130 sermons. She told him she had voluminous notes. The most impressive service, held in the African Baptist Church in Richmond, Virginia, was when a former slave, called upon to pray, did so with such a reverent and eloquent manner and such a fullness of petition that she was deeply moved. Isabella saw his lined face, his mat of white hair, and felt warmth toward this man whose life had been in bondage.

"Let us pray that this awakening spirit comes to England," Papa said. He shut his eyes. "Lord, revive thou thy work in the midst of the years."

"Amen," Isabella answered, but her spirits drooped. She wished she found the Lord's work more gratifying. *Something is wrong with me,* she thought, *that I rebel at doing what I should do joyfully.*

"My modest endeavors will be substantially enriched by your contribution, Isabella. I'll work on my book this very week."

At Euston Station they had to wait to redeem Isabella's small trunk and cases. "In the United States, Papa, you can check luggage at the beginning of a journey to your final destination, and, surprisingly, it shows up when you arrive." A bitter wind swept through the open platforms, and Papa and Isabella were thoroughly chilled before the luggage was claimed.

In the cab to Brighton Station, Isabella said, "The city looks imperial with its gray stone buildings. Most American cities have wooden structures."

They settled in the carriage of the Wyton train, yet were unable to get warm. The conductor apologized for the malfunctioning heating system.

"I haven't been this cold the entire trip!" Isabella exclaimed. Papa's eyes were tearing.

They were still shivering when they arrived at the rectory. The gaslights turned low, Papa, Mama, Isabella, and Hennie sat around the fireplace, talking late into the evening. *Homecoming,* Isabella thought, *is sweet.* Isabella gave them gifts: a painting of Niagara

Falls for Hennie, a beaver muff and collar for Mama, and a book of American hymns for Papa. She told them her adventures, and she listened to the news of family and parish events.

"And how has your health been, Isabella? Have you been well?" Mama asked, handing her another cup of hot tea.

"Other than that time in Quebec when I think I must have caught the cholera, I've hardly had a moment's pain. My health really has been quite remarkable."

"Praise God. We have also had good health. In fact, Papa said just last week that he has never had a season in which he felt better."

Papa nodded. "I attribute my good health to abstinence from drink. I have been so distressed to witness the ruined lives and the debasing influence of alcohol among the agricultural laborers that I have started a temperance league here. Shortly after you left, I took a public pledge that I will no longer accept even a glass of wine with my dinner."

"But, Papa, why did you do that? Surely you can allow yourself that modest pleasure, as you have all of your adult life." In the familiar terrain of self-denial, Isabella knew that she was truly home.

"I did not want to be accused of hypocrisy, and, furthermore, I want to reach their consciences by setting a good example by forgoing that glass. I think it is doing me a world of good."

"How is the work progressing for Sunday observance?" asked Isabella, steering the conversation away from the troubling waters of self-denial.

Isabella and Hennie kept smiling, each so glad to see the other that their lips curved and their eyes beamed. Finally, when they were upstairs in their bedroom, Isabella clasped Hennie to her. "I've had a wonderful time. But, oh, my pet, it is good to see you."

"I didn't anticipate what it would be like with you away, Isabella. I'm content to stay at home, but it is hard when you're not here. Everything loses its flavor."

"My dearest pet."

"I've prayed for you morning and night."

"I know you have, and I am confident that kept me alive. On Lake Huron I was on a jetty waiting to board a steamer. As the boat was approaching, somehow I got jostled over the edge of the pier and found myself in cold, deep water."

Hennie drew a sharp breath.

"Yes, had it not been for your prayers, I would have drowned then and there. A tall red Indian jumped in and pulled me out. But as the waters closed over me, I was called before the Day of Judgment, and I had a vivid illumination of my life. Do you know what I remembered?"

"What?"

"That day I danced with the primroses." Isabella turned from the dressing table where she was brushing her hair and faced Hennie. "Twenty years ago, when I was sick and everyone was in church, I went outside to gloat over the flowers. I never told anyone, not even you, about it. In fact, I had long forgotten it. But that disobedience arose to stab me on what I believed to be Judgment Day."

Hennie nodded sagely. "Yes, the utmost vigilance is required to assure salvation." Hennie loosened her corset ties and was pulling her nightdress over her head before removing her undergarments. "Your letters were so full of detail and observation, Isabella. Just as if I were right by your side."

"That's what I wanted. I had your picture, that lovely miniature, in front of me as I wrote. It was as if I were talking to you. You know, Hennie," Isabella confided, buttoning her flannel nightdress, "I have been thinking that I might use those letters and my journal as the basis for a book about my travels."

"What a wonderful idea, Isabella. You could use the letters almost as they are. I am sure you can get the book published."

"Yes, I am eager to start. People want to read about America. I even have a title, *The Car and the Steamboat*."

John Murray IV, later Sir John Murray IV, would publish Isabella's book on her American journey in 1856 under the title *The Englishwoman in America*. Murray and Isabella became close friends, and many of her letters to him, written from her famous excursions, became the foundation for many of her books. The prestigious publishing house he headed was to become her life-long publisher.

CHAPTER 20

1857, BACK TO AMERICA, PAPA'S AND MAMA'S DEATH

B y the spring of 1857, Isabella's health was again in decline, and her doctor recommended a second journey to America. She left that same year, on her second journey to America, a planned six-month tour that stretched out to nearly a year. In an 1858 letter, she summarized her activities on that second trip:

> I remained a fortnight at New York, which I had visited be-fore from which point my route was new and three weeks in Philadelphia; two months in the slave states, Virginia, South Carolina, and Georgia; a fortnight at Washington during the session of Congress; a month in the neighbourhood of Boston; a week at Longfellow's; two months in a beautiful village in Western Massachusetts; two weeks at Albany; a week at Niagara; two weeks at Toronto; one month in the bush; two weeks at Detroit; six weeks in making a tour in the far, far west over the prairies of Illinois and Wisconsin, forty miles beyond railroads, up the Upper Mississippi, into the Minnesota Territory, to the Falls of Minnehaha, up

Lake Huron and to the extreme end of Lake Superior, and into the Hudson's Bay Territory among the wild Indians a journey altogether of 2,000 miles, during which I did not remain stationary for four weeks, as it was considered that frequent change was the most likely to benefit my health.

Isabella returned to Wyton on April 3, 1858. That she had not seen her family in nearly a year seemed incomprehensible to her. Papa had elevated, to a feverish pitch, his battle against the two causes that defined his life: strict observance of the Sabbath, and temperance. His pamphlet on temperance, as yet unfinished, would spread his message beyond his congregation, to distant, wider audiences. This prospect excited Isabella as it did the Reverend Bird himself.

It was a joyful homecoming. Isabella felt a warmth at being with her family again. Dear, quiet Hennie was always a comfort, no matter how far apart they were, and her parents, whose unyielding beliefs she had come to respect—if not fully share—seemed resigned to, even proud of, Isabella's eccentric lifestyle.

But the joy was short-lived, for Edward Bird took sick that very evening. The next morning Edward was not able to eat breakfast, and he confessed that he had had a feverish night.

Dora suggested that he might rest, but he protested, "No, I must not forgo my duty."

By late afternoon, however, he could not continue. Dr. Bradley was summoned and diagnosed an attack of influenza. When a painful abscess developed on Edward's neck, Dr. Bradley explained, "His lungs are filled with such abscesses. I can hear them through the stethoscope. The lungs sound like stones grating together." Edward's breath was short and harsh, his distress acute. The doctor lanced the deep-seated abscess, bringing local relief, but Edward's sufferings were severe.

Dora and the girls tried to make him comfortable, but finally Edward whispered, "Please kneel where I can see you." He asked them to speak to his flock. "Tell them," he said, "my sole desire has been to bring them to Jesus, the friend that sticketh closer than any brother." Then he commended them in prayer to God and "to the hope of reunion in that inheritance that fadeth not away." That night, May 14, 1858, Edward Bird died.

Isabella was rent to the core of her being. Despite his harsh and controversial views, Papa was, she said, "the mainspring and object" of her life. Mama and Hennie were sustained in their grief by their conviction that Papa had only preceded them, that he was waiting to greet them in the stately halls of the Lord. Isabella was unable to voice her doubts that such a reunion awaited, or, if it did, her serious misgivings that she would be admitted to the sacred precinct of heaven.

After Papa's funeral, Isabella lay awake a long time. She remembered when Papa's hair was brown, and his arm circled her, with the clip-clop of Autumn's hooves steady under them, the bells of Saint Albans pealing overhead, and his voice in her ear, pointing out the new growth on the tips of the hedgerows, the woodcock's nest, the shimmering cobweb.

She finally fell into a deeply troubled sleep. A wildly turbulent night followed, of fierce nightmares and emotional convulsions. She awoke early the next morning with an urgent need to write, to tell all of Britain, perhaps the world, about Papa's sacrifices, that he may never be forgotten. She began with a memorial sketch detailing Papa's unswerving crusade to harvest souls for Christ, his indomitable spirit to have the Sabbath recognized and to keep it holy. She felt acutely she was not able to do him justice. When the memorial sketch was finished, she turned to the completion of Papa's manuscript on the great religious awakening, trying with all of her abilities to keep her father alive with her pen.

As she undertook these frenzied labors, the familiar pain crawled into her back. She put down her pen and bowed her head, rested her forehead in her hands. She had wanted to write about her travels that now were a distant interlude. The days and months and years, struggling against pain, struggling to be good, stretched ahead in a gray, featureless vista. Was this all life had to offer?

She felt an instant shock of shame for thinking of herself instead of Papa. She prayed, "Lord, forgive me. Christ forgive me."

After Edward Bird's death, Dora and her two daughters were compelled to vacate the Wyton rectory. The question was, where should they go? Returning without Edward's position to the places where he had been rector held no appeal.

"Mama," Hennie asked, "wouldn't you like to move back to Boroughbridge, where you first met Papa?"

"No, the family are dispersed, and the Hall has new tenants now," Dora answered as visions of her tight-lipped mother and her exceedingly reserved father came to mind. "It is kind of you to suggest it, but no."

"We all like the Hebrides," Hennie mused.

"Yes," Isabella agreed, "but in the winter, Tobermory is isolated."

For years the Birds had been spending summers in Scotland in the belief that the Highlands would dispel Isabella's lassitude. Every summer the family had gone farther westward, until for the past several summers, they had rented a cottage in Tobermory, on the Isle of Mull. Tobermory, nestled in a cove between the arms of two ridges that descended into the sea, was a small fishing village with twice-weekly ferry service, weather permitting, to Oban on the mainland. From the Cottage, which the Birds leased, they could see the woods of Arus on the opposite ridge, the fishing boats bobbing in the gleaming waters of the sound, the islands barring the harbor mouth, and the distant sea.

"But," said Isabella, her dark eyes sparkling with a new idea, "we could go to Edinburgh. We already know the Cullens. We can write to them to rent rooms for us until we find suitable quarters."

"That's a lovely idea," Dora responded. "Dear Edward was so happy in Scotland, where the Sabbath is strictly observed. Do you remember how often he was asked to be guest preacher in various kirks?"

"Yes, that is a wonderful idea," Hennie concurred. "And from Edinburgh we could get to Tobermory much more easily than from southern England."

Without a settled home, the Birds stayed with friends or relatives for months and then in rented rooms in Edinburgh until they found a comfortable flat. The move was finally accomplished, and they were ensconced at 3 Castle Terrace.

After the Bird women moved to 3 Castle terrace Mama's health began to decline. Though the changes were slow at first, she became increasingly confined to her bed with respiratory ailments.

Still, Dora's austere will demanded that her failing body do her bidding, compelling her to rise, to sink to her knees in prayer, to cross herself, and to offer thanks to her Savior. Racked with coughing, spitting up clots of bright blood, too weak to lift her head, nonetheless, Dora exacted of herself morning devotions. Witnessing this trial, Isabella and Hennie tried to persuade Dora that the Lord could see into her heart, but the habits of a lifetime were not to be altered.

One afternoon, Dora asked the girls, as was her custom, to sing her favorite hymn, "Just as I Am." After they sang the last notes, Dora Bird's soul went home to its Maker. At her request, engraved on her tombstone, with Edward Bird's coffin reburied next to her, was the epitaph that she had chosen, "With Christ, which is far better."

CHAPTER 21
NOTES ON OLD EDINBURGH

The sisters now had only each other. That the bond was close, intense, and carried the cargo of Isabella's heart was true. Hennie was Isabella's intellectual equal. She taught herself, for instance, Hebrew and Greek—the better to understand the Bible, which she knew intimately. Hennie, however, had a more compliant nature and a more devout character than her older sister. Hennie's friends were chosen for their need—the poor, the sick, the housebound—whereas Isabella's friends were chosen for their interests. Hennie assumed her duties with loving piety.

Isabella still compared herself unfavorably to Hennie and wished that she, like Hennie, might be content with Sunday school classes, tending to the poor, quiet friendships, and sketching familiar scenes. When Isabella, however, tried to live Hennie's life, she became ill. Her illness, in turn, activated her ever-vigilant guilt. What she did not recognize was that Hennie's life, by using only a tiny part of Isabella's own energies, made her profoundly bored, with boredom's attending lassitude. Isabella had a desire to enjoy life, a desire she had been trained to call selfish. She could never alter her character to fit into Hennie's self-effacing clothes. Try as Isabella would to be like Hennie, the effort made her ill.

Isabella's humanitarian undertakings were of a wider scope than were Hennie's parish duties. Increasing the availability of water in poor neighborhoods of Edinburgh was one such mission. The scarcity of water, one well or spigot for an entire overcrowded area, made cleanliness impossible. Women had to haul water from one well that served hundreds. There was rude jostling and a long wait before she could fill her bucket. Then there was a climb of 150 steps up a narrow, winding street before she even reached her building.

"An economy of water" but unlimited whiskey at every corner for a few pence without shoving, without waiting, caused, Isabella wrote, "a prodigal expenditure of human suffering." Isabella petitioned landlords and city councilors to coerce them into action. Failing there, she tried to start a private subscription for washhouses. She spent five weeks in London visiting washhouses in the East End. Her plan was to hire rooms in the poorest neighborhoods and furnish each with a boiler, a mangle, an ironing stove, and ironing boards. Twelve or more women every day, on paying for their soap and a trifle for fuel, could have clean clothes without having wet garments strewn about their cramped rooms. The plan did not succeed. She was successful, however, in having additional water spigots installed near several tenements.

Another of her plans, cabmen's shelters, did open on Princes Street. Drivers of hacks and carriages could relieve themselves, wash, eat a hot meal, and enjoy one another's company in a cheerful room for the cost of a meal.

Isabella spent three weeks in Ireland researching the religious revival. She sailed to the islands of the Hebrides, inspected the schools, and she wrote a learned series on the history of Christian hymns. She continued to write numerous articles of a religious nature, most of which were published in *The Leisure Hour*, *The Family Treasury*, *Good Words*, and *Sundays at Home*.

Isabella's most ambitious literary and charitable endeavor was the inspection of how the poor lived. She published twenty-six detailed pages of their condition entitled *Notes on Old Edinburgh*. It sold many copies. Full of indignation, it was addressed to the respectable citizens who called themselves Christians. Her basic position was that divinity, in part, was the compassion we feel. After this booklet, people could not plead ignorance of the wretched rooms in which the poor struggled for life.

Isabella visited thirty-seven rooms in tenements at noon and again at midnight. She said that she did not pick out the worst nor the most scandalous.

In no other city could tenements be found without gas, without water-pipes, water closets, or sinks, or temporary receptacles for ashes, and entered only by one long dark stone stair, which return such enormous profits to their owners as 45 to 60 percent. Tenants complained of rapacious landlords, no repairs, no gaslights, a want of privacy, the distance of a water supply, and dark stairs.

The entrance of the close which we selected is long and narrow, and so low as to compel a man of average height to stoop. It is paved with round stones, and from the slime in which they were embedded, and a grating on one side almost choked up with fish heads and other offal, a pungent and disgusting effluvium was emitted. The width of this close is four feet at the bottom, but the projecting stories of the upper houses leave only a narrow strip of quiet sky to give light below. A gutter ran along one side of the close against the wall, and this, though so early in the day, was in a state of loathsomeness not to be described.

Ragged children, infinitely more ragged and dirty than those which offended our eyes in the open street, were sitting on the edge of this gutter, sitting as if they meant to sit there all day; not playing, not even quarrelling just stupefying. Foul air, little light, and bad food had already done their work on most of them. Bleary eyes, sore faces, and sore feet were almost universal. Their matted hair and filthy rags were full of vermin. Their faces were thin, pinched, and precocious...There they sat, letting the slow, vile stream in the gutter run over their feet, and there they were sitting three hours later.

The rooms, 9'x 5' or no larger than cubicles, housed entire families. Many of them had access only through other rooms or through passages like the galleries in a coal pit. Many had no windows whatever, requiring candles in midday, and had only thin partitions separating them from their neighbors. The stench of disease, refuse, waste, was overpowering. At night, the stairs and rooms were full of people brawling, or unconscious with drink. Many of these people had known better times, but they had lapsed. A few had jobs, but to keep decent, and to pay exorbitant rent was impossible. There were alms, but a shortage of affordable housing.

Isabella made it clear that circumstances had made these people what they were. She did not share the common Victorian attitude that to be poor was a sin.

Isabella's fortieth birthday passed. She continued to fulfill her moral duty with various humanitarian causes, and as always, she suffered lassitude, and her back pain was again so severe that she was persuaded by Hennie to consult a physician.

Dr. John Bishop was one of the most highly regarded practitioners in the city; and Isabella already knew him. She had taken a class on microscopes from him at the Edinburgh College of Medicine and had been quite impressed.

When at last, Isabella found herself in his office, sitting across from his desk, and saw his soft brown eyes warm with friendship and admiration focused upon her, she felt that at last she had a doctor with whom she could be frank. "I want to speak with utter candor," she began. She told him of her back ailment, of her periods when every action seemed to require too much energy, and of her weariness.

After he had examined her and questioned her in detail, he said, "What you are struggling with, Miss Bird, is a problem in physics. No wonder you are discouraged. Your spine has a burden placed upon it that it is unable to perform. As a child your back was weak. Then you had a fibrous tumor removed, and that invasion has further weakened your spine. Now you ask this infirm backbone to support your body and your head, and it is sending signals that the task is too much."

Isabella listened to his gentle voice and felt a burden lifted. An oasis opened before her. It wasn't her fault. She didn't need to feel guilty.

"All the willpower in the world is not going to help your spine," he continued. "What I would suggest is that we devise a brace to support your head, to relieve the weight on the spine, and see if that will alleviate your pain. It will be an experiment, you understand, but I think it is worth undertaking."

Dr. Bishop took out calipers and tape and made precise measurements. He designed a steel brace and sent the detailed sketches to a small manufactory. The day came when he showed it to Isabella. She had thought that it would be shiny and was surprised at its dull dark color.

"It almost looks medieval," she said.

"On the contrary," Dr. Bishop said. "It is the very latest made-to-measure technology. I suggest that you start wearing it for a short while each morning and gradually increase the time. Here, let me help you."

He put it around her neck and adjusted the leather straps. "We may have to make another hole here," he said.

Standing so close, Isabella could smell his bay rum.

"Now, rest the back of your head against that spoonlike piece. There," he said, "how does that feel? You take it off and put it on by yourself."

That was one of Dr. Bishop's characteristics that Isabella liked. He never rushed, he never acted as if he had other patients waiting, but he gave her his full, unhurried attention.

"Come in next week, and let me know how it is going."

Despite adjustments and the addition of padding, Isabella found the brace uncomfortable. She began to feel that her body, imprisoned in her brace, a prisoner of pain, was a perfect partner for her soul that could not soar, carefree, above the burdens of the world. Why could she accept herself only when she was helping the less fortunate?

CHAPTER 22

THE SANDWICH ISLANDS

"This is such an aimless life," Isabella told Dr. Bishop. Though she had been his patient for nearly two years, worn the brace as often as she could tolerate, and faithfully followed his several prescriptions, she felt, at forty-two years old, near mental collapse. "I'm suffering from pain in my bones, pricking like pins and needles, excruciating nervousness, exhaustion, inflamed eyes, sore throat, swelling of the glands behind each ear. I'm taking three bromides a day, and I still feel a shaking all over and am oppressed with an undefined terror. I'm such a miserable being."

Dr. Bishop listened sympathetically to Isabella's litany of symptoms. "I am going to prescribe a radical remedy," he said, his keen brown eyes looking at her over the tops of his spectacles. "You've suffered all these years. Now it's time we get to the heart of the matter. I want you," he said, his forefinger tapping the paper in front of him, "to take a trip. Your previous trips helped. But this time, be bolder. You're blessed with the stomach of an ostrich. You tell me you're never seasick. Circle the globe." To Isabella's astonishment, he said, "I mean it. Go around the world. Now, that's doctor's orders."

Itineraries, maps, shipping schedules, ticket agents, deciding where to go, designing and stitching a light gray-and-white wool traveling outfit, deciding what to take filled the following weeks. On each voyage Isabella had reduced the luggage she carted with her. This trip would satisfy curiosity and take her where she'd not been—Australia, New Zealand, California.

The day of departure dawned under an unhappy sky. In Liverpool, Isabella toted a needlepoint carpetbag, her shawl, and her reticule with her steamer tickets. Hennie, carrying Isabella's knitting, boarded the *Odysseus* and accompanied Isabella to her tiny cabin. Isabella directed the porter where to place her small trunk and gave him a tip.

The unwelcome gong sounded, and the steward called, "All visitors ashore. All visitors ashore."

Isabella clutched Hennie. "Oh, Hennie, I can't leave you!"

Hennie comforted her, as always, putting her arms around her, patting her. "There, there, Isabella. The time will go quickly, you'll see. And you'll come home, strong and healthy."

"My pet, my own pet, I don't want to go."

"All ashore who's going ashore," the steward called.

"You'll be fine," Hennie said, and with a long, tight hug, she was out of the cabin, walking resolutely down the narrow corridor.

Isabella, however, was not fine. On the trip out, she rarely left her cabin. She was still a semi-invalid. Australia and New Zealand failed to interest her. She complained of the dust, of the heat, of the trees smelling like drains. As she was soon to discover, it was not travel itself that she craved, but escape from the stultifying conventions of British society.

In Auckland, New Zealand, she boarded the *Nevada*, which, when she first saw it out in the harbor, for there was no wharf, she did a double take. It was tall and decrepit, a steamer of the old paddle-wheel type. During the voyage its belabored engines lost their boiler tubes, and the entire superstructure listed more and more to port. When it rained, the eight passengers ate meals in waterproofs and rubber shoes since the deck above leaked. Isabella concluded that the boat was definitely unseaworthy and was, in fact, a peril.

The clear sky of the first day gave way to a steady drumming rain and a heavy swell on the second day. Rain and waves quickly became extreme as the *Nevada* steamed headfirst into a hurricane. Isabella's long-dormant psyche woke up. Like a discarded cloak, her ennui vanished. How would this ancient ship confront this violent storm? Isabella made her way to the salon to discover it deserted. Outside the heavy windows, all was invisible. Intense black, night, day, sea, sky, horizon—everything was obscured.

A pale, distraught Mrs. Inwood, who was traveling with her son and who was the only other female passenger, labored into the room.

"Oh dear," she screamed, barely audible above the shriek of the wind. "Oh dear, I must get some tea." She sank onto the sofa, biting her lip.

Seeing no attendant, Isabella gestured that she would find someone. With the boat lurching spastically up and down or suddenly shivering from side to side, she made her way, arms outstretched for balance, to the nearby galley, where a messboy was clinging to the counter.

"Not possible," he shouted. "Not possible."

Back in the salon, Mrs. Inwood was crumpled forward, her eyes closed, her lips compressed.

"Here," Isabella called, "let me help you," and she lifted Mrs. Inwood's feet to the sofa and placed a cushion against her back. Then she sat stroking Mrs. Inwood's forehead while she listened to the boat strain and grumble and crack and heave, to which, after a violent lurch and reeling of its bulk from side to side, was added a heavy clang. She listened to the constant howl of the wind. No attendant appeared, and hours passed before the storm abated.

"It was," the captain later declared, "the worst hurricane I have seen in my eighteen years as captain. It almost boxed the compass! The ocean was leveled, absolutely leveled. Nothing like these rollers now."

Isabella felt much better. She wrote Hennie:

At last I am in love and the old sea-god has so stolen my heart and penetrated my soul that I seriously feel that hereafter, though I must be elsewhere in body, I shall be with him in spirit! It is so like living in a new world, so free, so fresh, so vital, so careless, so unfettered, so full of interest that one grudges being asleep; and instead of carrying cares and worries and thoughts of tomorrow to bed with me to keep me awake, I fall asleep to wake to another day in which I know that there can be nothing to annoy me—no door-bells, no "please ma'ams," no dirt, no bills, no demands of any kind, no vain attempts to overtake all I know I should do. Above all, no nervousness, and no conventionalities, no dressing. If my clothes drop into rags they can be pinned together...I am often in tempestuous spirits. It seems a sort of brief resurrection to a girl of twenty-one.

Isabella's youthful vigor continued, even when the ailing engines stalled completely in the Tropic of Capricorn and the *Nevada* sat there limp and sizzling. She helped to shape the activities of the day: reading aloud *Idylls of the King*; playing chess, checkers, and quoits for exercise; taking turns fanning and nursing Mrs. Inwood's son, who had had a lung hemorrhage; writing letters; conversing.

At the mess table, an old Scotch doctor who had kept both to himself and to his bottle, in a state of chronic intoxication, abruptly announced, "That young Inwood, his hour is close."

Indeed, all the passengers were apprehensive as Mr. Inwood lay in the deckhouse, white and unresponsive. Their talk and movements were dominated by his condition and their fear of his dying.

Mr. Baylor said, "Mrs. Inwood must disembark at Honolulu and get competent help. Her son will never survive all the way to San Francisco."

"Yes," Mr. Stuart agreed. "It is astonishing that he is still with us. If you concur, Miss Bird, perhaps you'll undertake to tell Mrs. Inwood that it would be best if she secured medical care in the Sandwich Islands."

Isabella had privately come to the same conclusion. She was gratified that Mr. Baylor and Mr. Stuart were of this opinion since she had a high regard for both of them; they were tireless in caring for Mrs. Inwood and had completely taken over the night nursing duties. But when she broached the idea to Mrs. Inwood, Mrs. Inwood reacted with panic. She knew no one in the Sandwich Islands; in fact, she had never heard of them. Isabella did not want to dwell on the fear of the young man's dying if he continued without proper medical care, but she told Mrs. Inwood what she knew of the islands' salubrious climate, and that a hospital and an elegant hotel had recently been constructed in Honolulu.

Mrs. Inwood continued to feel timid about this unexpected development until she got the idea that if Miss Bird would land with her, she would feel quite comfortable. Her pleas were so urgent that Isabella could not refuse, and therefore, she found herself about to disembark.

Listing so far to port that the right paddle wheel was almost out of the water, and with its bilge pumps working ceaselessly, the *Nevada* steamed into Honolulu Harbor. Isabella had been on the high seas for six months. From a distance, Oahu seemed a disappointment with its barren gray peaks. But as the boat entered the harbor, Isabella beheld a colorful scene:

We looked down from the towering deck on a crowd of two or three thousand people...Such rich brown men and women they were, with wavy shining black hair, large, brown, lustrous eyes, and rows of perfect teeth...

Outside this motley, genial picturesque crowd about 200 horses were standing, each with the Mexican saddle. Every now and then a flower-wreathed Hawaiian woman sprang astride one of these animals, and dashed along the road at full gallop, sitting on her horse as square and easy as a hussar.

The women seemed perfectly at home in their gay, brass-bossed, high peaked saddles, flying along astride, bare-footed, with their orange and scarlet riding dresses...a bright kaleidoscopic flash of bright eyes, white teeth, shining hair...

Isabella's attitude toward the native population was an abrupt and sympathetic contrast to Victorian empire builders, missionaries, explorers, and other travelers who shared an assumption that they were of a higher class, that natives were to be saved and to be made like the English. She was able to accept all people, and was able, as a herder said of her, "to take people as she found them." She observed and admired the natives. She did not have the prejudice of those English who felt contemptuous of others, or of those who were bent on converting the heathens into Christians. She asked where were the hard, angular, careworn, sallow, passionate faces of men and women such as formed the majority of every crowd at home, as well as in America and Australia? She continued in a pertinent statement, "The conditions of life must surely be easier here, and people must have found rest from some of its burdensome conventionalities..."

The "burdensome conventionalities" were an oppressive weight to Isabella, and the escape from those onerous duties gave non-English peoples part of their appeal. Isabella was particularly struck by the behavior of the women. Later she wrote, "Used to the downtrodden look and harassed, careworn faces of the overworked women of the same class at home and in the colonies, the laughing, careless faces of the Hawaiian women have the effect upon me of a perpetual marvel."

There was nothing of the superior, of the condescending, of the take-me-as-the-model in Isabella's attitude.

The *Nevada* was to be in port for only a few days and was then to toil on to California. Two of the men on board who were continuing the voyage were going to hire a carriage to drive to the Nuuanu escarpment. Would Miss Bird care to accompany them? Would she go to the Nuuanu Pali? Yes. A small incident, but recall that she was disembarking only because of Mrs. Inwood. One of the passengers offered to take Mrs. Inwood and her son in charge, and he would also arrange for Miss Bird's room at the hotel. Mrs. Inwood assured Isabella that she would be comfortable. Isabella preferred to explore far more than she preferred the conventional: accompanying Mrs. Inwood, arranging for a room, seeing what the hotel was like, unpacking. Under these halcyon skies, Isabella could discard the self-sacrificing, self-effacing role, assure herself that Mrs. Inwood was well looked after, and go off to the new and the unknown, a choice that allowed a healthy selfishness to be asserted, a choice impossible in that "dim, pale island," as she called Great Britain.

She was on her way back to the hotel when friends approached her and told her that a lady friend of theirs, anxious for a companion, was going to the volcano on Hawaii, that she was a most expert and intelligent traveler, that the *Kilauea* would sail in two hours, and that "unless I went now I should have no future opportunity during my limited stay on the islands…that in short I *must* go, and they would drive me back to the hotel to pack!"

Isabella's only regret, other than leaving Mrs. Inwood, was that she was not able to study about volcanoes or about the big island of Hawaii before embarking. Her eager interest in the natural world instantly impelled her to agree. Having only two hours to get ready, traveling with a total stranger, going to an area about which she knew nothing, with no prior arrangements made—all of these were insignificant in the face of the opportunity to see more of the world.

On board the *Kilauea* she noticed, as had Mark Twain a few years earlier, that there were very few trunks and portmanteaus, but that the aft end of the saloon was heaped with Mexican saddles and saddlebags, which she later learned were the essential gear of every traveler on Hawaii. In preparing for their ascent of the volcano, her host suggested that she do as the native Hawaiian ladies do, use a Mexican saddle and ride astride.

That a lady did not ride astride, but rode sidesaddle, was a truth universally acknowledged. Riding sidesaddle, a lady's limbs were covered and her skirts could billow demurely. Riding astride was unheard of. It was not done. Normally it was not even mentioned as a possibility. But her yearning for adventure left her no choice, as she wrote in her journal:

> It was only my strong desire to see the volcano, which made me consent to a mode of riding against which I have so strong a prejudice, but the result of the experiment is that I shall visit Kilauea thus or not at all.

This was a pivotal decision. Isabella allied herself with her sister and their conservative, high-minded friends: "a mode of riding against which I have so strong a prejudice." But the bedrock of convention yielded to curiosity, "my strong desire to see the volcano." This decision was the watershed in her life. Astride, she had no pain; astride, she could gallop up and down hills; astride, she could ride with mad abandon, with the reckless energy for which her nature had been starved.

The immediate result of this decision was the need for clothes— she could not ride astride without covering her legs. For this expedition she wore a borrowed riding costume, furnishing, she said, "the grotesque element." She quickly stitched light flannel bloomers, like Turkish harem pants, ending in a frill at the ankle, over which she wore a loose skirt—her bloomer suit, she called it, attire that was a step away from convention, a step toward comfort and freedom.

The next morning the party started out, Isabella, like the native ladies, riding astride. They set off at a full gallop. Isabella clutched the saddle horn. The horse, without guidance, careened along the trail, every corner a terror, and stopped abruptly, forcing her to grasp the mane to prevent being pitched over his head—to the immense amusement of a group of native women. The ignoble start was quickly corrected.

Her chapters on Mauna Loa render the experience so vividly that readers had the satisfying sense of being eyewitnesses.

> I watched the indescribable glories of the fire-fountain, its beauty of form, and its radiant reflection on the precipices, 800 feet high, which wall it in, and listened to its surges beating, and the ebb and flow of its thunder-music. Then a change occurred. The jets, which for long had been playing at a height of 300 feet, suddenly became quite low, and for a few seconds appeared as cones of fire wallowing in a sea of light; then with a roar like a sound of gathering waters, nearly the whole surface of the lake was lifted up by the action of some powerful internal force, and its whole radiant

mass, rose three times, in one glorious, upward burst, to a height, as estimated by the surrounding cliffs, of 600 feet, while the earth trembled, and the moon and stars withdrew abashed into far-off space.

Her book *Six Months in the Sandwich Islands* was received it with enthusiasm. Liberated from paralyzing convention, Isabella Bird was the ideal travel writer. She was an astute observer and recorder—of people, how they live and labor and worship, and of landscapes, flora, fauna, street scenes, architecture, and festivals. She was not insensible to danger, but the questionable engines of the *Nevada*, the "worst hurricane that the captain had seen in eighteen years," the proximity of two live volcanoes, raging torrents, all quickened her: "My eyes seek the dome-like curve of Mauna Loa...for it is as yet an unfinished mountain. It has...a pit of unsettling fire on its side; it throbs, rumbles, and palpitates; it has sent forth floods of fire over all this part of Hawaii and at any moment it may be crowned with a lonely light, showing that its tremendous forces are again in activity...for it is as yet an unfinished mountain."

That the mountain was in process, was alive, excited Isabella.

"It is most interesting to be in a region of such splendid possibilities." Isabella Bird, despite every appearance and condition to the contrary, was able to make those decisions that enabled her to release the "tremendous forces" within her and to become the woman she was capable of being, to realize "such splendid possibilities."

CHAPTER 23

COLORADO, ROCKY MOUNTAIN JIM

Crossing the seemingly endless and treeless plains, the journey became so monotonous that when the huge transcontinental train braked in Cheyenne, Wyoming, Isabella was ready for a change. But Cheyenne was a "God forgotten" collection of frame houses and shanties where fifty-six people had died from cholera during the past two weeks.

From Cheyenne, Isabella took "the cars" for Colorado, embarking on the plains "like the waves of the sea which had fallen asleep." Her intention had been to travel farther south to Colorado Springs, the little London of the West, where her friend Rose Kingsley, Charles's daughter, had given her a letter of introduction. Rose's uncle, George Kingsley, had told her about Estes Park, a secret valley somewhere northwest of Denver, an almost inaccessible park, girded by snow-peaked mountains. A settler, gesturing toward the high peaks, told her that was where Estes was located. That determined her; it was to Estes Park that she would go. From the plains she saw the entire sweep of the range, one elephantine hump after another right into the high-peaked giants. Longs Peak, which rises a mile, beckoned in sublime grandeur. As Isabella said, "I could look at and *feel* nothing else."

At Greeley, she transferred from the cars to a wagon and continued on to Fort Collins, twenty-five miles nearer the mountains. She saw prairie dog villages with nothing green to rest the eye on, and five thousand cattle driven by heavily armed men as a precaution against the Indians who were maddened by "the reckless and useless slaughter of the buffalo." The glaring sun compelled Isabella to use her white parasol.

The people she met cautioned her against going to Estes Park: September was too late; sudden storms were likely; there were no women; the trail was obscured; the entrance to Estes Park was patrolled by a desperado called Rocky Mountain Jim.

In a buggy Isabella was driven forty-five miles to a cabin at the mouth of the canyon. If this grim shack was an indication of her intent to get to Estes Park, that intent would brook no obstacle. The cabin was roofless, the logs unchinked, without window. Table, bed, lamp, basin, and towel, but with a nearby den of rattlesnakes. Isabella herself killed a snake with eleven rattles. And in the two weeks she was there, seven other rattlesnakes were killed. The premises, and a primitive sawmill, were owned by a man who had moved his family to Colorado for his health. Joyous, harsh, incompetent, of the narrowest theological views, his life was typical of the hard, unornamented existence of the pioneer settlers. Isabella rolled up her sleeves and made herself agreeable, helping from sunrise to sunset with the round of toil.

The man attempted to find the trail to Estes Park and led her up gulches and across ridges and through canyons until finally he acknowledged that he was lost. After this dismal failure, she bought a bronco from him and rode to another homestead and this time, a cultured family. Again she was "agreeable," washing the churn and the greasy pots and pans. When a man wanting to know where to ford the river happened by, Isabella enjoyed his comment: "Be you the new hired girl? Bless me, you're awful small." Being mistaken for the hired girl pleased her.

The next day she pulled a quarter acre of corn and wrote, "I much prefer field work to the scouring of greasy pans and to the washtub, and both to either sewing or choir-directing."

As the season advanced, surveyors and tourists came down from the mountains. Snowfall covered the peaks with its glistening mantle. Again the people she met cautioned her against going to Estes Park. Her host drove her twenty-two miles in a borrowed wagon to Longmont, at the mouth of the Saint Vrain and an obscure trail to Estes Park. Access to Estes Park was through the Saint Vrain Canyon. The Big Thompson Canyon was too rugged.

In the hotel the food was greasy and fly speckled. Her ailments, "neuralgia, enflamed eyes, and a sense of extreme frustration," began to recur. After a stuffy, fly-plagued night, her hopes of getting to Estes fell to zero. That morning she was about to take the train to New York and return to Liverpool, but the rosy red of the mountain range reflecting the rising sun put renewed spirit in her.

The hotel owner, to whom she had recited her woe, told her, "You're in luck. Two young men, Messrs. Platt Rogers and J. Downer, are going to take you with them to Estes Park." The two young men who'd been pressed into this service were not enthusiastic.

Platt Rogers later explained, "We were not at all partial to such an arrangement as we were traveling light and free and the presence of a woman would naturally operate as a restraint...however, we could not refuse and we consoled ourselves with the hope that she prove to be young and beautiful. Our hopes were dispelled when Miss Bird appeared wearing bloomers, riding cowboy fashion, and with a face and figure not corresponding to our ideals."

Platt Rogers and J. Downer, both twenty-three-year-old graduates of Columbia Law School, had conventional attitudes toward Bird. Their treatment of her was distant, critical, and bordered on uncivil. Had she been "young, beautiful, and vivacious," their response would have been cordial.

The landlord provided her with a surefooted horse. She strapped her pack, a flowered carpetbag, behind the Mexican saddle, and the three started out. In the saddle Isabella instantly revived, all ailments forgotten. The air was keener and purer with every mile, the horse a blithe, joyous animal. The blue of the sky, the pine-scented breeze, the cold waters of the Saint Vrain, sparkling and hilarious in its heedless rush, the bright-yellow-green cotton willow, the dark-green fir, the quiver in the yellow aspen, the crimson oak, the lemon of the wild grapes, the scarlet of the Virginia creeper all exhilarated her. They climbed higher so often, losing the faint trails, that Downer turned back. They mounted ridge after ridge, each with sudden inspiring views. Here were the familiar crested blue jays, and the chipmunks, but here also were elk who lifted their stately heads as if to question the intrusion, bighorn sheep who posed on rock outcroppings, and deer who gazed at them with quiet curiosity. Here was the haunt of the Rocky Mountain lion, of the grizzly bear, and of the wolf. Up one arduous ridge after another, they labored, often leading the horses, to a height of nine thousand feet, through Devils Gate, a seven-foot keyhole of rock, with an abrupt descent of two thousand feet, and a yet higher ridge beyond. To the left, range after range of snow-clad majesty touched the sky.

As they ate their lunch of cheese, crackers, and sardines, Mr. Rogers said, "I don't want to alarm you, but I've been warned that we might meet Rocky Mountain Jim. We *will* meet him if he's at home, for he is a squatter, and unfortunately his claim straddles the only entrance into Estes."

"Who is this Rocky Mountain Jim?"

"A bad one, I'm told. No one knows what his past really is, as he gives out different versions. Sometimes he's Irish, sometimes Canadian, sometimes southern. He may have worked for the

Hudson's Bay Company, but he has been a scout escorting wagons across the plains, killing Indians and buffalo. He also goes on sprees and shoots anyone within range."

Isabella's curiosity was piqued, and secretly she hoped to get a glimpse of this outlaw, but in deference to Mr. Rogers, she said, "Perhaps he will be out hunting.What does he do now?"

"He's a trapper, a hunter, a fly-fisher. Brings furs, game, and trout to Denver. He also runs some cattle. But certainly he is an outlaw. He challenges all comers. He has a reputation, though, for knowing these mountains like nobody else. Like the back of his hand."

Isabella certainly hoped he was home. She longed to talk to someone who loved the mountains as she did.

"Perhaps your being along," Mr. Rogers continued, "will be a good influence, for he is supposed to have a way with the ladies."

Back in the saddle once again, they traversed one steep ridge after another, scrambling around the base of boulders the size of the pyramids, threading their way up the rocky bed of dry creeks. After ten strenuous hours, they were in a broad, grassy gulch belted with pines, a gulch that narrowed at its distant end. A rude log cabin—the only inhabitation they had seen all day—stood close to the trail. A small Arabian mare was picketed nearby, and a collie barked his disapproval.

"Rocky Mountain Jim's lair," Mr. Rogers said.

As they drew nearer, "den" is what Isabella thought. The mud roof was covered with lynx, beaver, deer hide, and other pelts laid out to dry; the carcass of a deer hung from one end of the cabin; a skinned animal was on a nearby tree stump; horseshoes, antlers, bones, and offal littered the ground. Roused by the barking, a thickset man of medium height emerged, leveled a kick at the dog, saw Isabella, stopped in midswing, and doffed his cap, showing a magnificently formed brow and head.

"And what may I do for you, ma'am?" he asked with a voice of Irish cadence. He was wearing a tattered gray hunting suit from which all the buttons were missing, a red sash knotted around his waist in which he had stuck a knife to keep his outfit together. His revolver, "a bosom friend," protruded from his breast pocket.

At Rocky Mountain Jim's invitation, Isabella swung from her saddle, grateful to stretch her legs, but Mr. Rogers said that they had best press on. The collie started to advance but halted at Rocky Mountain Jim's command.

"Ring, sit." The tawny dog sat on his haunches and never allowed his gaze to waver from Rocky Mountain Jim's face. Isabella found her gaze drawn to it, too.

"May I trouble you for a drink of water?"

"No trouble at all. A pleasure, I assure you." He turned and went into his one-room cabin, emerging with a battered tin cup, which he handed to her. "My apologies that I haven't porcelain or anything fit for a lady. I'm sorry this is all I have."

"Please don't apologize. If I wanted porcelain, I would have stayed home."

Rocky Mountain Jim gave her a quick glance. He took the tin cup, nodded to Mr. Rogers, refilled it, and handed it to him.

"We need to press on if we're to get to Estes Park before dark," Mr. Rogers said.

"It's a short canter from here. You'll easily make it by sunset." Turning to Isabella he sympathized, "You've been in the saddle a long time. Allow me to introduce myself, James Nugent."

As Isabella moved toward the cabin, the collie started to advance but halted at Mr. Nugent's command.

"Ring, sit." In profile, with his unkempt golden ringlets curling on his shoulders, with his finely molded forehead, his straight nose, his full lips, Mr. Nugent was distinctly handsome. Isabella had never seen a more well-favored man. When he faced her, however, he was repugnant, for the left side of his face was scarred, and pink skin puckered the hollow where his eye should have been.

"'Tis a bit of a shock, that missing orb of mine," he said.

His startling two-faced appearance, his two-faced reputation as a desperado, his cultured speech acted upon her in a mysterious way. She dropped her eyes, embarrassed that he might think she was avoiding looking at his face. He was barefoot. His feet were well fleshed and remarkably small.

Rocky Mountain Jim continued about his eye. "If you just persevere a bit, ma'am, you'll find that you get accustomed to it. It is a souvenir from a close encounter, a too-close encounter, in fact, a bear hug. But don't allow me to bore you with my exploits. You'll want to get to Estes."

Certainly Isabella had never heard a gentleman talk in such a direct way about himself. She, in her deliberate fashion, avowed, "I certainly would like to hear about your contention with a bear, Mr. Nugent." At a motion from Mr. Rogers, however, she turned to remount.

Mr. Nugent hastened to her—she reached only his shoulder. He lifted her lightly by the elbows, and she easily regained the saddle. His teeth looked remarkably white in his tanned face, and once mounted, she saw a deep scar across his left hand.

"Are those the paws of a beaver?" Isabella asked, indicating small paws drying on the roof. In a moment the paws were hanging from her saddle horn.

"It's a beaver kit, ma'am. You won't find a softer fur." He went on courteously, "You are not an American. I know from your voice that you are a countrywoman of mine. I hope you will allow me the pleasure of calling on you."

Isabella acknowledged that she would be charmed and that she wanted to hear about the bear.

"If you'll be so kind, I'd enjoy the gallop along with you."

He turned to Mr. Rogers, who asked, "How far is it?"

"Not above four miles."

"We'll manage, thank you. Don't trouble yourself," Mr. Rogers answered, and wheeled his horse about.

Mr. Nugent averred it was no trouble and mounted his light-red mare, trotting at Isabella's side.

"Now, about the bear," he began. "It happened on my way from Grand Lake," he said, giving his Arabian a whack. "That's over the Snow Range on the Ute trail. I was deer hunting, and I was creeping up on a big buck with only my revolver and hunting knife, when along comes Ring, ears back, tail flying, a mother bear and her two cubs chasing him. There's nothing as meddlesome as a mother bear, ma'am."

Isabella looked at his profile, the blond curls, the aquiline nose, the firm chin, and nodded her head in assent.

"I managed to fire a few shots before that beast was on me, biting and clawing. I whipped out my knife and slashed right and left, but bears have got the advantage—so much fur and hide. And those powerful three-inch claws! She was on her hind legs, snarling and lunging and giving me a workout. My Bowie was hitting its mark, the blood pouring out. I could smell the warm, fetid odor of it. Excuse me, ma'am.

"I might have won the day if she didn't just rake me, pulling my scalp over my forehead, tearing out the eye. I fainted dead away. When I came to, I was in a pool of my blood, and she in hers. Ring here was licking my hand. I took stock. That bear had dislocated my shoulder, broken three ribs, chewed my arm, and mangled my thumb. She had slashed my neck, torn my scalp, and gouged out my eye. I wondered how I survived.

"But you can't keep a good man down," he continued with a laugh. "It was Ring and Freedom here. Freedom stood right there quivering with all that blood, but I managed to hoist myself up on her. When I fell off, Ring licked me till I came to. It took every bit of strength I had, but I managed to get to Grand Lake. There are two cabins there, and I gave a yell, but by the time I got to one of them, I was on the ground unconscious again from a loss of blood."

Isabella looked at him quizzically.

"I did manage to yell and arouse two Frenchmen in one of the cabins. They were highborn and knew nothing of the mountains. They heard me yell and thought the Utes were on the warpath, so they holed up in their cabin. After all was quiet, they got up their courage and crept out. When they saw me, they went racing to Wescott's—the only other cabin.

"'Indians are here, *certainement*. This man has been scalped,' they told Wescott; it was Wescott who saved me. He took care of me like a mother, and I owe my life to him." Jim spoke with solemn reverence. "It was two months before I was able to get back to Estes. The best-laid plans of mice and men..." he concluded with a wry laugh.

"Forgive me for being long-winded. People always want to know how I lost my eye." He checked his horse. "The top of this rise is Park Hill. You can see Estes from there." And Rocky Mountain Jim wheeled Freedom about.

"Thank you for your escort," Isabella said, "and thank you for your story."

Rocky Mountain Jim assured her it was his privilege and repeated that he would like to call. He lifted his cap, except for this gesture looking every bit a ruffian, and he galloped away.

Isabella's head reeled. She forgot both his reputation and his appearance, one profile desperado, the other profile Praxiteles, and thought only of his chivalrous manner and of his daring story.

Pratt Rogers's head did not reel. He wrote that "Miss Bird was interested if not impressed, and was quite willing to accept Rocky Mountain Jim at his own valuation."

At the top of Park Hill, at the head of Muggins Gulch, Isabella looked on the valley that she had sought, lying below, bathed in the glow of the setting sun. This was what she wrote:

It is an irregular basin, lighted up by the bright waters of the rushing Thompson, guarded by sentinel mountains of fantastic shape and monstrous size, with Longs Peak rising above them all in unapproachable grandeur, while the Snowy Range with its outlying spurs heavily timbered, came down upon the park slashed by stupendous canyons lying deep in purple gloom. The rushing river was blood red, Longs Peak was aflame, the glory of the glowing heaven was given back from Earth. Never, nowhere, have I seen anything to equal the view into Estes Park...The mountain fever seized me, and giving my tireless horse an encouraging word, he dashed at full gallop over a mile of smooth sward at delirious speed.

CHAPTER 24

ASCENT OF LONGS PEAK, CLOSER TO JIM

Isabella Bird and Platt Rogers were headed for Griff Evans's ranch, the only habitable cabin in Estes Park. His spread included a large, low cabin, several smaller ones nearby, two fenced corrals, a shed, and a dairy. Evans, a genial Welshman, greeted them and ushered them into his log cabin. The unchinked room was good-sized with two windows, furnished with a round table, two rocking chairs, a couch, and a small harmonium. Skins, antlers, Indian bows and arrows, and wampum adorned the rough walls; rifles were stacked in the corners. Huge pine logs blazed in the stone fireplace.

Seven men were lying about on the floor, smoking. A middle-aged woman sat at the table, writing. A sick man sprawled on the couch. Isabella asked if Evans could house her. To her delight, he led her to the most distant cabin, which she could have to herself. "So in this glorious upper world," she wrote, "with the mountain pines behind and the clear lake in front, in the blue hollow at the foot of Longs Peak at the height of 7,500 feet, where the hoarfrost crisped the grass every night of the year, I have found far more than I ever dared to hope for."

Her cabin, also unchinked, had a stone fireplace, one window, a warped door, a bed, table, basin, and for a wardrobe, one hook. Under the cabin a skunk, with whom Bird lived in amiable accord, had established domain. He chose the midnight hours to do deep breathing, to sharpen his teeth, and to heave against the floor. The skunk eluded traps, and Evans did not dare shoot it because the ensuing odor would make the cabin uninhabitable.

That first night in Estes Park, her goal realized, Bird nestled comfortably into her straw mattress, six blankets heaped on top of her, and saw views of the trip that day through the canyons of the Saint Vrain and the Little Thompson Rivers. She saw images of the desperado, with his musical voice, his courtesy, his red sash and revolver. She dreamed of a cavern in mountain fastness, lapped by water, and of a robber with blond hair curling to his shoulders, with amethysts sparkling around his neck, lifting supple furs from a chest, pelt after pelt in a seemingly bottomless supply, and with a sweep of his broad-brimmed hat, displaying their brown and sable richness.

Isabella learned that her host, Griff Evans, had come to Estes Park and staked his claim at the edge of a small lake and that the desperado, Jim Nugent—Rocky Mountain Jim—had arrived the following spring, in 1868, and staked his claim at the head of a gulch approaching the park. Both men were squatters, both were cattlemen and hunters, and both were intemperate whiskey drinkers who enjoyed boisterous sprees together.

Their camaraderie, however, unraveled when Griff Evans, initially a cattleman, discovered that he could make more money putting up hunters, prospectors, and consumptives than running cattle. He was lodging more and more guests in his cabins. One of them, after a recuperative visit, wrote for the *Chicago Tribune*,

August 15, 1871, that "Mr. Evans and others contemplate putting up a cheap hotel for the next season…I see no reason why this cannot be made a prosperous resort worth a dozen Saratogas to the invalid, especially delicate women and those troubled with lung complaints."

Here was a clash of interests. Jim's livelihood depended on hunting and trapping. Although Jim enjoyed bouts of conviviality, his brooding, complex nature preferred an isolated life in the mountains he loved. Thus his livelihood and his temperament made him oppose the encroachments of civilization. Jim's reaction was explosive.

"Why, you puffed-up banty rooster!" he shouted at Evans. "What the hell do you think you're doing? Bringin' in a bunch of dudes to ruin our hunting and fishing? And tramp down the grass for our cattle?"

"You can make more money off dudes than cattle," Evans replied.

After this episode, Griff's and Jim's friendship never regained its former companionable basis. Events of the winter 1873–74 were to alienate them to the point of murder. But while Isabella was in the park in the fall of 1873, there was no overt hostility between them. As it happened, most of that time Evans lived in Denver. The two men were uneasy with one another, but Griff recommended Jim as a guide, and Jim made frequent visits to the ranch. Nonetheless, Isabella wrote, "there is always the unpleasantly exciting risk of an open quarrel with the neighboring desperado."

Eight dollars a week entitled Isabella to the cabin, to a horse when one could be roped, and to all the food she could eat. "There's always bread and milk in the kitchen. Eat as much as you can. It'll do you good," Evans encouraged. Unlimited meat, a steer hacked away without regard to joints, or just-caught rainbow trout, oven-warm bread spread with newly churned butter, fried potatoes, brown molasses pudding hot from the oven, tea, coffee, milk, cream. Coffee and no pudding in the mornings; pudding and no coffee at noon and night. Otherwise, the menu was unvaried. The "poor" wives kneaded bread all day.

Isabella liked the good-natured Welshman, whose cheery presence in the house was like sunshine. Evans was careless, reckless, jolly, social, convivial, peppery. He was too fond of the bottle, and his pockets had holes, as he spent money as quickly as it came, but he made everyone welcome. The cabin rang with his laughter and his song, but Isabella's sympathy went to Mrs. Evans, "a most industrious wife...who has to work like a slave; and though he is a kind husband, her lot, as compared with her lord's, is like that of a squaw."

In the evening, with the snow forming miniature drifts on the floor, the pine logs blazing and crackling, Isabella was writing to "My Pet" or mending her clothes, "which are dripping to pieces." Others were playing euchre, cleaning rifles, casting bullets, making flies for trout fishing, repairing tackle, or waterproofing boots. They sang "D'ye Ken John Peel?," "Auld Lang Syne," "John Brown," and with the Evanses' sixteen-year-old daughter Jenny and the four younger children all singing parts, the rafters echoed with the choruses.

After this conviviality, Isabella went through hoarfrost or storm, hearing owls hoot, wolves howl, even the growl of a mountain lion, to her cabin, which she half expected to be occupied by a four-footed creature.

Isabella's tolerance of cold was remarkable. The frosty air, snow sifting through the chinks of her cabin, her ink freezing, even her hair freezing, caused no complaints. When Isabella said it was cold, the temperature hovered in the neighborhood of zero. It was the heat that wilted her.

With the exception of the morose hired man and of Edwards, also a Welshman and Evans's partner, who lived there with his wife and family, and whose disposition was the sour antithesis of Evans's, Isabella found the people at the ranch good company. The company consisted of a very intelligent and high-minded American couple, a young Englishman who gave himself airs and consequently was dubbed "the Earl," a miner prospecting for silver, a young man in poor health, and the grown-up niece of Evans. The group was often enlarged by elk hunters or by silver prospectors. (Precious ore was not found in Estes, thereby sparing it the boom and bust of mining towns.) Reading matter was scarce, newspapers old. Conversation centered around "The last great Aurora, the prospects of a snowstorm, tracks and sign of elk and grizzly, rumors of a bighorn herd near the lake, the canyons in which the Texan cattle were last seen, the merits of different rifles, the progress of two obvious love affairs, the probability of someone coming up from the plains with letters, Rocky Mountain Jim's latest mood or escapade, and the merits of his dog Ring as compared with those of Evans's dog, Pluck...topics which were never abandoned as exhausted."

They all talked about Rocky Mountain Jim, which pleased Isabella. Her curiosity was intense, and she was glad if she didn't have to steer the conversation in that direction.

Evans said, "When he's sober, Rocky Mountain Jim's a perfect gentleman, but when he's had liquor, he is the most awful ruffian in Colorado," that he had "ugly fits," "drank like a fish," was a "a wild man," and woe to the person who was in his way then. She need not worry about herself, however, for he respected "good women." "Treat Jim as a gentleman, and you'll find him one."

Mrs. Evans and Mrs. Edwards told her privately that before his tangle with the bear, the women of the territory idolized him, his sixteen (they had counted) golden curls, his Grecian profile, his courtly speech, courage—but he was not a chaser. His prowess against the Redskins, his skills as a hunter—a killer of Indians and animals—and as a guide were legendary. Evans added that his exploits caused mothers to hush fractious children with threats of

Rocky Mountain Jim coming to get them. But Isabella noticed that the children looked forward to his coming.

They didn't have long to wait. The next afternoon after her arrival, little Sam Edwards ran in, saying, "Rocky Mountain Jim wants to speak with you."

Rocky Mountain Jim, or Mr. Nugent, as she always carefully called him, was waiting to take a ride with her. Not a sedate ride but a barebacked gallop and race in the "intoxicating frosty air." And he was charming, respectful, and witty. He entertained her with Indian and frontier lore. He enthralled her with tales about Longs Peak, which towered a lofty 14,700 feet above them and which had been scaled for the first time only five years earlier.

Rocky Mountain Jim told her about Alice E. Dickinson, who two years earlier, with the F. V. Hayden surveyors, was the only woman to reach the summit. Jim did not need to persuade her. Longs Peak tantalized her, its peak ablaze with sunrise and sunset color; the sight of it, wrapped in almost inaccessible mystery, was enough to urge her on. If an assault were to be attempted, it would have to be now.

Evans did not encourage the climb. It was late September, winds were apt to be knife keen, snow to obliterate landmarks. But one morning he said that the weather was looking more settled, and since she was eager to go, it would be worth it, even if she got only to timberline. Platt Rogers and J. Downer, who had arrived from Longmont, made up the party, with Rocky Mountain Jim as a guide. Evans, Rogers wrote, "rendered us great assistance as cautioning Downer and me to keep our whiskey flask from Rocky Mountain Jim."

Mrs. Evans had baked a three-day supply of bread. They hacked off chunks of steer, and the four of them set out, the horses heavily loaded with blankets, quilts, camping gear. Rocky Mountain Jim, in his ragged leather clothes, "was a shocking figure...With his one eye, his one long spur, his knife in his belt, his revolver in his waistcoat pocket, his saddle covered with an old beaver skin from which the paws swung down; his camping blankets behind him, his rifle laid across the saddle in front of him, and his axe, canteen, and other gear hanging from the horn, he was as awful-looking a ruffian as one could see."

He led the pace at a hard gallop over the grasses and then reared his skittish Arabian mare on her haunches to ride at Isabella's side. Fording the snow-born streams, up steep ascents and down descents, through a series of "glories and surprises," they kept up conversation. Her low, measured voice, her knowledge of plants and trees, her recitations of poems, her stories of Hawaii, her response to the grandeur around them charmed him. His Irish tongue, his mellifluous voice, his courtly manners, his familiarity with literature and with the mountains charmed her. She forgot his missing eye. He was always careful to have his good profile next to her. She forgot his reputation as a desperado and drunkard; she was thoroughly captivated. As Rogers noted, "Miss Bird was quite taken with Rocky Mountain Jim."

All day they rode up and down the mountains skirting Longs Peak, until the sun was in level slants and they were on a steep trail through a thick pine forest. The three men walked their horses, which were breathing heavily in the rarified air, but Isabella kept her seat, concentrating on not being dragged off her horse by the pine branches. As they approached timberline, the trees grew smaller and sparse and then became dwarfed with stunted shapes, contorted by the winds. They dropped down to a meadow on the southwest slope, "toward a bright stream trickling under ice and icicles, and there the growth of the beautiful silver spruce marked out our camping ground."

Unsaddling and unbridling the horses, making beds of pine shoots, gathering branches for a huge fire kept them warm in the nippy air. They drank their tea in the battered tin in which it had been boiled, and ate the charred meat without plates or forks. Sitting around the fire, Downer sang a student song and two spirituals, and Rogers sang a hymn, "Sweet Spirit, Hear My Prayer." Rocky Mountain Jim sang one of Moore's melodies in a singular falsetto, and with Isabella joining in, they all sang "The Star-Spangled Banner" and "The Red, White, and Blue." According to Platt Rogers, Rocky Mountain Jim recited "all the doggerel which he had composed in the loneliness of Muggins Gulch...The principal theme of his poems was himself, varied by references to a fair maiden, of whom he seemed to be enamored."

Jim ordered Ring, part collie, part mastiff, to "go to that lady, and don't leave her again tonight." Obediently Ring came at once, and all night leaned against Isabella's back. Isabella wrote that Jim "was very courteous and even kind to me which was fortunate, as the young men had little idea of showing even ordinary civilities." Indeed, the young men openly regarded her as an "encumbrance." Nor did they take Jim at his own evaluation, for Rogers noted that he "represented himself as the son of an English army officer who had been stationed somewhere in Canada, and he made some pretensions to a former state of refinement. She was disposed to resent our want of faith in him, and the jollying we felt compelled to give him."

Nevertheless, the bower in the silver spruce, a blanket spread over the pine boughs, the horse saddle as a pillow, Ring next to her made a luxurious bed. Isabella, however, did not sleep; she was too excited. "To lie there, with no better shelter than a bower of pines. In the very heart of the Rocky Range, under 12 degrees of frost, hearing sounds of wolves, with shivering stars looking through the fragrant canopy, with arrow pines for bedposts, and for a night-lamp the red flames of a campfire" was pure heaven. She was too aware of the red-handed desperado sleeping nearby, next to the fire, "as quietly as innocence."

What had grown so suddenly between them, she wondered? Surely there was the attraction, she confessed to Hennie in a letter, but then added, "I put it away as an egregious vanity unpardonable in a woman of forty."

The attraction was certain, for Rogers observed it in his diary: "Rocky Mountain Jim took quite a fancy to her and she took quite a fancy to him." From Rogers's point of view, an inexplicable preference on both sides.

A dawn such as might have been made when God first created heaven and earth, all light and glory, rose in the sky. Rocky Mountain Jim had, in a gesture that appeared theatrical, involuntarily and reverently uncovered his head and exclaimed, "I believe there is a God!"

Today was significant for both: for her a test of her grit and pluck, for him a display of his strength and knowledge. The men walked, but Isabella rode until they got to the boulder field, where the horses were picketed, as they could go no farther. They clambered over the rocks and snow crevices. Isabella's feet were punishing her, as she wore a pair of Griff Evans's old boots, but under a rock, she found a pair of shoes, probably discarded from the Hayden expedition, that lasted the day. In her thin Hawaiian traveling dress, she felt cold.

The two young men disputed with Jim about the way: they thought they could continue directly on the knife-thin ledge, but Jim advised going down to the headwaters of the Big Thompson and then climbing by a less precipitous ascent. They separated. Isabella wrote that Jim "parted with his brusquerie when they parted from the students, and was gentle and kind beyond anything."

Had Isabella Bird known what was involved, she would not have attempted the climb. Her experience of climbing Mauna Loa had not prepared her for these "hours of terror." Of being reunited with Rogers and Downer at the "Notch," she wrote:

The real business of the ascent began. 2,000 feet of solid rock towered above us, 4,000 feet of broken rock shelved precipitously below; smooth granite ribs with barely foot-holds, stood out here and there; melted snow refrozen several times, presented a more serious obstacle; many of the rocks were loose, and tumbled down when touched. To me it was a time of extreme terror. I was roped to Rocky Mountain Jim...I wanted to return to the Notch knowing that my incompetence would detain the party, and one of the young men said almost plainly that a woman was a dangerous encumbrance, but the trapper replied shortly that "if it were not to take me he would not go up at all." Fatigue, giddiness, and pain from bruised ankles, arms half pulled out of their sockets, were so great that I should never have gone halfway had not Rocky Mountain Jim...dragged me along with patience and skill...which never failed. Ice, snow, rock trembling, slipping, straining...slipping, faltering, gasping...One slip, and a breathing, thinking human being would be 3,000 feet below, a shapeless bloody heap!

She clambered on Rocky Mountain Jim's shoulders, stepped on his cupped hands, was pulled by her arms with a lariat. She crawled on hands and knees, but she did not complain or turn back.

As we crept from the ledge around a horn of rock, I beheld what made me perfectly sick and dizzy to look at—the terminal peak itself—a smooth, cracked face or wall of pink granite...Ring howled and refused to go further. Scaling, not climbing, is the correct term for this last ascent. The only foothold was in narrow cracks of minute projections on the granite.

Another grueling hour passed, Isabella stopping often to gasp for breath. Platt Rogers wrote that Isabella was "So fagged that she was unable to make her way, unaided, up the last steep cliff of the

Peak. By alternately pulling and pushing her and stimulating her with snow soaked with Jamaica ginger we got her to the top."

The rarified air gave urgency to every movement. "But at last the peak was ours," Isabella crowed, but added, "as it is, I am only humiliated by my success, for Rocky Mountain Jim dragged me up, like a bale of goods by sheer force of muscle." Isabella was elated, however, to be on atop the mountain. She wrote:

> From the summit were seen in unrivalled combination all the views which had rejoiced our eyes during the ascent. It was something at last to stand upon the storm-rent crown of this lonely sentinel of the Rocky Range, on one of the mightiest of the vertebrae of the backbone of the North American continent, and to see the waters start for both oceans. Uplifted above love and hate and storms of passion, calm amidst the eternal silences, fanned by zephyrs and bathed in living blue, peace rested for that one bright day on the Peak, as if it were some region
>
> Where falls not rain, or hail, or any snow,
> Or ever wind blows loudly.
>
> We placed our names, with the date of ascent, in a tin within a crevice, and descended to the Ledge, sitting on the smooth granite, getting our feet into cracks and against projections, and letting ourselves down by our hands, "Jim" going before me, so that I might steady my feet against his powerful shoulders.

She was also bruised and exhausted. Breathing on the descent was not so painful, but footing was even more treacherous. Fatigue made her muscles tremble and not respond to her will. She suffered falls and bruises and "once hung by my frock, which caught on a rock, and Rocky Mountain Jim severed it with his hunting knife." Finally, after a tremendous effort, the boulder field was crossed, and Isabella was lifted onto her horse. Rocky Mountain Jim and Isabella reached the silver spruce campground, and there were the men, who had descended by the steeper brow, saddled and ready to return to Estes.

But Rocky Mountain Jim quietly said, "Now, gentleman, I want a good night's rest, and we shan't stir from here tonight." He lifted Isabella from the horse and carried her to the arbor, wrapped in a roll of blankets.

Isabella awoke after a few hours, her feet icy, and hugging the blankets around her she sat by the fire, Ring by her side, his master smoking, the students asleep. The pine knots sputtered and flared; the stars wheeled overhead. Rocky Mountain Jim sang Irish ballads in his soft tenor. They discovered that they both had an interest in spiritualism; Jim was even now writing an essay about it in his Muggins Gulch cabin. With the solemnity of the mountains around them, they promised that if either of them should die, the deceased would appear to the survivor—a promise that was kept.

It was Rocky Mountain Jim's determination that had gotten Isabella to the top of Longs Peak even when her own determination faltered: "Had I known that the ascent was a real mountaineering feat I should not have felt the slightest ambition to perform it." They had reached the summit, and Rocky Mountain Jim had seen that no harm had come to her. We can guess that Rocky Mountain Jim admired her courage, that his blasted life had left him even more idealizing of the "pure" woman, that he responded to her dependency on him, and there was "a fascination in all her ways." He told her about a thwarted youthful love that had led him to embark upon his desperate life. His voice trembled, and tears salted his cheeks. Was he genuine? Was he moved by his own eloquence? Isabella wondered, "Or was his dark soul really stirred to its depths by the silence, the beauty, and the memories of youth?"

As Isabella reached for the mug in which tea was steeping, Rocky Mountain Jim's small, muscular hand stretched out to cover hers. Isabella started to withdraw her hand, saw the tears glistening on his cheeks, and turned her hand to allow his hand the cradle hers. His fingers tightened around hers.

"God bless you," he murmured. "God bless you." In an age when gentlemen wore gloves while dancing to avoid touching a lady's bare skin, when even the flash of a lady's ankle was an aphrodisiac, the touch of Rocky Mountain Jim's hand caused Isabella's awareness to tremble like the waters of a still pond whose surface is broken by drops of rain. She had never felt a man's hand around her own. Rocky Mountain Jim gave her hand a long, hard squeeze, then withdrew his and gave her a tin cup of tea, repeating as he handed it to her, "God bless you."

By noon the following day, they were back at Evans's ranch. "But a more successful ascent of the Peak was never made," Isabella wrote, "and I would not now exchange my memories…for any other experience of mountaineering in any part of the world. Yesterday snow fell on the summit, and it will be in inaccessible for eight months to come."

CHAPTER 25

MISSING JIM

Isabella recovered from her Longs Peak exertions with enthusiasm. She planned to leave Estes Park to see other parts of Colorado, but each day she postponed her departure in her pleasure of racing horses with Jim and in need of the horse that Evans was buying for her. Griff Evans took his wife, who was expecting another baby, and children to Denver for the winter, leaving the somber Edwards in charge, whose only moments of liveliness came when he told about his march with Sherman through Georgia. Isabella had given Evans one hundred dollars to buy a horse for her, and she anxiously awaited his return. He was expected daily, but daily Isabella was disappointed. There were even rumors that infuriated Isabella that he had gone buffalo hunting on the Platte.

When Evans did at last show up, he had a French Canadian with him who played a vast repertoire of songs on the organ, letters for Isabella, but no horse and no money. Sheepishly, Evans explained that as he had been "very hard up," he had spent the hundred dollars. Banks, reacting to a financial panic, were closed. Evans insistently promised to pay her in November, with a horse as interest, which, Isabella carefully noted, he did.

The high-minded American couple was still there, and the industrious Mrs. Edwards still labored in the kitchen. Isabella again postponed her departure, as each morning before daylight, Evans rapped on her door and in his deep voice called, "I say, Miss B., we've got to drive wild cattle today; I wish you'd lend a hand."

Cattle must be hunted out of the canyons where they had strayed, and where they were in danger of being snowed in and starved, and driven down to the park. Off Isabella would go to drive cattle, riding twenty miles or more each day, splashing back and forth through the Big Thompson, Evans declaring that she was "as much use as another man." Yes, this Edinburgh invalid whose spine could not support her head without a steel brace!

Another day she would be determined to leave, but again Evans would tempt her. "Here's a lot of horses for you to try." Again she herded cattle, riding alongside a stockman on a great buck jumper said to be the "best rider in North Americay." With a "Head them off, boys!" and a "Go to it, boys!" to direct a surge of a thousand Texas cattle,

Away we all went at a hard-gallop downhill. The bovine waves were a grand sight: huge bulls, shaped like buffalo, bellowed and roared. Great oxen and cows with yearling calves, galloped like racers, and Isabella galloped alongside of them and shortly headed them, and in no time the cowhands were placed as sentinels across the mouth of the valley. It seemed like infantry awaiting the shock of cavalry as they stood as still as the excited horses would allow. Isabella almost quailed as the surge came on, but when it got close her comrades hooted fearfully, and they dashed forward and with bellowing, roaring, and thunder of hoofs, the wave receded as it came. Isabella rode up to their leader, who received her with much laughter. He said she was a "good cattleman," and that he had forgotten that a lady was of the party till he saw her "come leaping over the timber, and driving with the others."

Isabella loved it.

One day, careening down a sharp moraine, Winchester stumbled, and Isabella pitched over his head. She was bruised, and her prominent front teeth were broken in a surprisingly straight line. Her mouth ached, and her teeth ached. The accident was fortuitous, however, for it repaired her one major defect, her protruding teeth, and even improved her speech. Next day she was back in the saddle.

Evans was getting Bird's services as a ranch hand without charge, but after Mrs. Edwards left, he offered her six dollars a week to stay and do the cooking. She noted that "I should like playing at being a 'hired girl' if it were not for the bread-making! But it would suit me better to ride after cattle." The men, Bird observed, really did not like washing and ironing their own clothes. She had never seen men performing these functions and found an "incongruity" in the sight.

The bright days sped by riding after cattle and visiting with Mr. Nugent, who rode over for quick repartee and for gallops. Not once did Rocky Mountain Jim presume upon their Longs Peak intimacy nor violate the behavior of a gentleman. Jim had the qualities that Isabella saw in him, her occasional hyperbole only an indication of how deeply he appealed to her. If Jim had been shallow, or a flirt, or interested in her because he thought she had money, Isabella would have seen through him. About one such pursuer, a former colonel in the Southern army who proposed to her ten times and a year later was jailed in Boulder on a charge of bigamy, she declared that "making love was the only phrase that could be used, delicate flattery...by which he supposed he could make himself agreeable. I never spoke but to snub him but a man bent on money is not easily snubbed." She looked to Jim to protect her from such unwelcome company.

Nor was Isabella one to suffer fools; she had control of a sharp tongue. But about Jim she wrote, "He has pathos, poetry, and humor, an intense love of nature, strong vanity in certain directions, an obvious desire to…sustain his reputation as a desperado, a considerable acquaintance with literature, a wonderful verbal memory, opinions on every person and subject, a chivalrous respect for women…a great power of fascination…his conversation is brilliant, and full of the light and fitfulness of genius."

A powerful magnetic current attracted Isabella Bird and Jim Nugent to each other. A more disparate combination, the clergyman's daughter and the outlaw, was unlikely. Jim appealed to that part of her nature that had found no expression, that had been systematically weeded out, punished, starved, but that found an outlet at last in the wild horseback riding, in the freedom of the wilderness far from the corridors and salons of polite society, and in Jim's speech, and manner. No one ever knew his true background—a former schoolteacher? A defrocked priest? Speculation was rife. One thing was certain: Jim Nugent was a gentleman. From his treatment of "good women," one can surmise that Jim found in this gentle, soft-spoken English lady, who always treated him with respect, his idealized "pure" woman. In his reckless life, in his heart, Jim had cut the traces and was a rebel. Under Isabella's sober black silk beat a rebel's heart.

Isabella lost her heart to Jim, but she had not lost her mind. She interrupted her tribute to him by remarking that time might stale the pleasure of his discourse, and she concluded that "he is a most painful spectacle. His magnificent head shows so plainly the better possibilities which might have been his life, in spite of a certain dazzle which belongs to it, is a ruined and wasted one, and one asks what of good can the future have in store for one who has for so long chosen evil?"

The "certain dazzle" and the enjoyment of such "splendid company" continued, until, finally, Isabella did tear herself away. "I really think (though for the fifteenth time) that I shall leave tomorrow." The allure of the unknown beckoned her as it would all her life. That she was running away from Jim, that the space Jim usurped in her heart alarmed her, was undoubtedly true. Isabella had avoided commitment to anyone other than to Hennie. She had chosen, at the risk of loneliness and derision, to be single although she had had several offers of marriage. Despite the echoing, reverberating resonance that Jim awoke within her, she would resist.

The cold abated. A hunter reported that the snowdrifts were passable. On October 20, she and her Indian pony, Winchester, left with her "indispensables," including the black silk, reduced to a twelve-pound pack, on a trek that took her away from Estes Park for almost a month. Her reflections about Jim remained as reasoned as they had been. But passion, as we know, is unruly, and is not governed by reason's cool dictates. Images, memories, fantasies about seeing him again, the embrace of his warm hand accompanied her wherever she went.

Her journey was truly astonishing. Five hundred miles, on horseback, alone, without compass or guide, trusting that she would find a homesteader to shelter her at night, through country that could not be traversed, at a time of year when the peril of sudden storm or paralyzing cold was extreme. Isabella thought nothing of it, writing to Hennie about the weather, the scenery, the trail, the infant cities of Denver and Colorado Springs, the people she met, unaware of how singular a trip it was. She had no intention of publishing these letters, as they were purely personal and not ballasted with textbook information.

The musical French Canadian accompanied her out of the mountains on the morning she finally tore herself away from Estes Park on the way to Longmont. No smoke was rising from Jim's cabin, and with a lurch of her heart, Isabella realized how much she had been hoping to see him once again. Then she saw a "fearful object in the distance" who turned out to be Jim, whose "appearance was frightful." But "as soon as he spoke he was fascinating."

He is a most extraordinary man, Isabella thought.

Jim leaned on Isabella's horse and said, "I'm so happy to have met you. So very happy," and "his poor disfigured face literally beamed."

Her musical companion remarked what a thorough gentleman Jim was and "how very much he likes you."

Isabella confided, "I do like a gentleman who always knows the right thing to say and do." She thought that Jim was locked in the keepsake of her memory and safely imprisoned there.

"Steer south and keep to the best beaten path," the directions Isabella was given for the thirty prairie miles to Denver, were "like embarking on the ocean without a compass." She saw lone horsemen, rifles slung across their saddles, herds of cattle, groups of wild horses. She saw a drove of Texas cattle driven by three men bristling with firearms. She saw bleached carcasses, and two prairie wolves that she followed to get a closer look. They resembled "jackals, with gray fur, that bounded away in long leaps." She had a hard time finding the trail again. She did not see cabins or settlers. She learned to call a wagon with a white tilt a "prairie schooner," and she lunched with a disheartened man and woman with their children who had been three months on the thousand-mile weary journey from Illinois, burying a child and losing several oxen en route. They invited her to come along with them, but their gaunt oxen pulled too slowly.

A cold wind arose, and storm clouds lowered, which she raced to get to shelter. She expected to see Denver at the top of every prairie roll, but it wasn't until late afternoon that the "great braggart city" of sixteen thousand people lay spread out "upon a brown and treeless plain."

To preserve Victorian proprieties, she dismounted, put on her black silk skirt, and mounted sidesaddle as best she could on the standard cattleman's saddle to enter Denver. "To ride sidewise now seems to me as if having the use of two feet one was compelled always to hop on one."

The storm began, blotting out the city, but Winchester carried her over rough ground and trenches to Evans's shanty, where Winchester had been once before. The night was intensely cold; six inches of snow fell, and Isabella thought of the family on the prairie huddled together against the drifted snow and the wind that "doubled one up."

The Evanses' cabin was comprised of a kitchen with a bed in it, and two bed closets, in one of which Isabella slept with his niece, but they welcomed Isabella and were eager for her news. Next morning everyone was too cold to get up to start the fire, so breakfast wasn't until eleven. Isabella called on the heavily bearded ex-governor Hunt, to whom she had been given a letter of introduction.

"I was told you were an invalid," said Hunt, "but I could not believe such a horsewoman could be."

Riding sidesaddle, the short distance was as difficult for her, she thought, as a few hours of the restraints of civilization were for the frontiersmen.

In Denver she enjoyed sharing her Longs Peak experiences with William Byers, the peripatetic editor of the *Rocky Mountain News*, who, in an unsuccessful attempt to climb Longs Peak in 1864, had stayed with Joel Estes, who had given the park its name. In 1868 Byers was the first white man to reach the summit. His articles in the *News* extolled the beauties of Estes Park. In his personal column Byers wrote, "Miss I. Bird...a noted traveler in new and strange countries is in Denver...She travels almost altogether on horseback and has laid out a pretty good winter's work for herself."

Hunt and Byers encouraged her to ride horseback to Colorado Springs; Hunt gave her a map and a letter of introduction to ranchers and wrote down where she was to stop on her way. As there were no hotels or inns, it was the custom for travelers to be put up by the settlers and to be charged what they would have had to pay at a hotel.

The bank panic was over, and Isabella cashed two checks. She bought a bear jacket, she ate three mutton chops in an English-style restaurant, but the "harlequin" town exhausted her. The streets were thronged with men:

> Hunters and trappers in buckskin clothing; men of the Plains with belts and revolvers, in great blue cloaks, relics of the war; teamsters in leathern suits; horsemen in fur coats and caps and buffalo-hide boots with the hair outside, and camping blankets behind their huge Mexican saddles; Broadway dandies in light kid gloves; rich English sporting tourists, clean, comely, and supercilious looking; and hundreds of Indians on their small ponies, the men wearing buckskin suits sewn with beads, and red blankets, with faces painted vermilion and hair hanging lank and straight, and squaws much bundled up, riding astride with furs over their saddles.

All day she saw only five white women.

Denver was the hub of an enormous area. The Kansas Pacific Railroad served it, there were connections to Cheyenne and the Union Pacific, and the Denver and Rio Grande had built two hundred miles of its projected track to Mexico. There were an impressive number of saloons, and it was to Denver that men—ranchers, homesteaders, frontiersmen, prospectors, miners, hunters, men such as Jim—gravitated, to go on sprees and dissipate their hard-won money. There were enough asthmatics to warrant holding an "asthmatic convention," and scores of invalids who had come to be cured. There were outfitting stores where one could get a wagon, driver, horses, tent, bedding, and stove and start for the mountains.

The mountains were where Isabella longed to be. At five thousand feet, Denver had a magnificent view of the entire range, Longs Peak to the north, Mount Evans to the west, and Pikes Peak a purple blur to the south. Isabella spent one day and two nights in Denver and said that if she had had to stay a week, "the sight of those glories so near and yet out of reach would make me nearly crazy."

In describing these "glories," she used the same words that she used to describe Rocky Mountain Jim: "Perhaps this scenery is not lovable, but, like a strong stormy character, it has an intense fascination." Later, she amended this to acknowledge that she did find the austere beauties of the mountains "lovable."

After two days in Denver, she already yearned to be back in Estes Park. Both Jim and Isabella loved the mountains. She wrote about Jim, "Like all true children of the mountains, he pined even when temporarily absent from them." She was pining for the mountains and for him.

The next morning she was grateful to escape Denver and to head south through the rolling country at the base of the Rockies. The warm sun made the snow look a contradiction. She passed wagons on the trail and every half mile or so a settler's house. She found a muff containing $500 and later found its owner. That night revealed the hazards of depending upon settlers for lodging. A couple, with a house "papered and carpeted" at the mouth of Plum Creek, and with two hired girls, were not pleased to take in Isabella and offered her only a bed on the sofa. Isabella commented that the "hired men" and the "hired girls" ate with the family, a remark in keeping with her upper-class background, but that seems a curious observation now. At Griff Evans's ranch, workhands and guests ate in relays, as the dining space was too small to accommodate everyone at once.

Isabella had no tolerance for pretension; she enjoyed camaraderie, but she was not entirely successful in eradicating her English awareness of class. Her insistence again and again that Jim was a "gentleman" refers not only to his manners and sensibilities but also to his background. Jim looked the ruffian, but beneath the costume was the genuine article.

Despite signs of an impending storm, Isabella started forth early in the morning on her route that hugged the foothills. When she saw the toy cars of the Denver and Rio Grande whirl past—trains averaged twenty miles an hour on that section—she rather wished she were all "cushioned and warm" instead of on the bleak hillside.

The impending storm developed, and Isabella sought refuge in a cabin with other "wretched" travelers. She made herself so "agreeable" peeling potatoes and making scones that she was charged nothing for her stay. A break in the storm, and she was on her way. While crossing a frozen creek, the ice broke, and Winchester crashed into the water. On the trail by herself, a surefooted horse under her, challenged by keeping to the path, Isabella should have been buoyant.

In Tahoe, the evening ride through the dark forest from Donner Lake had exhilarated her. Not now. "I cannot describe my feelings on this ride, produced by the utter loneliness, the silence and dumbness of all things, the snow falling quietly without wind, the obliterated mountains, the darkness, the intense cold, and the unusual and appalling aspect of nature." All life was in a shroud. The landscape reflected her own heart. Why was she going south with every step of Winchester's short gait, when Jim and hours of perfect companionship were north? Why did they meet now, when there was no hope for a future together? Isabella could enjoy what might dismay another woman: living in isolation in the mountains, doing physical work. She could be a pioneer woman, but she could never accept a man in thrall to whiskey, a man subject to rages and violence as Jim had been.

As the dark deepened, Isabella found a small cabin, presided over by an old woman with a bullfrog's voice and a clay pipe who railed at the English and their manners, considering that "please," "thank you," and the like were "all bosh." Isabella did not talk in the nostril-pinching fashion of many of the English. She did not give herself airs. As she was often mistaken for a Swede or an Australian, she heard comments about the English that might not have been said if she had identified herself earlier.

The night was so cold that the churn was put on the stove, so cold that the stock came round appealing for shelter, so cold that even with the rag rug pulled over her, Isabella was icy, the coldest night that she had ever experienced. The cold penetrated her, and the hopelessness of her situation with Jim penetrated her.

The cold and the realization stayed with her. Another fearfully lonely day the track untrodden, seeing neither man nor beast. Balls of snow collected in Winchester's feet, and without a hoof-pick to remove them, Isabella was compelled to walk. The weather became too ominous to continue. She was glad to approach a ranch, the home of a millionaire who was making his fortune with cattle. The accommodations were luxurious. Five servants attended; the table boasted delicacies, and the bedroom hot water.

The comforts did not tempt her to prolong her stay. With eight inches of glittering snow on the ground the next morning, she broke her own way for two miles, until she could follow the track of a single wagon. Another lonely day passed in crossing the Arkansas Divide: The babble of the streams was bound by fetters of ice. No branches creaked in the still air. No birds sang. No one passed or met her. There were no cabins near or far. The only sound was the crunch of the snow under Winchester's feet. Winchester refused to cross an improvised bridge (Isabella was later told that the bridge was treacherous), but broke through the ice in water up to her belly. Winchester was "the queen of ponies."

When she reached the cabin on Evans's list, it was too full of other snowbound travelers. Almost frostbitten, she stumbled on another half a mile. The women in this clean, sweet cabin massaged her feet, and the renewed circulation "almost deserved the name of torture." She climbed a ladder to her loft bed.

The next day she again saw no travelers for miles and lost her way in a savage canyon. She stopped for feed for Winchester and milk for herself at a large house with eight boarders, "each one looking nearer the grave than the other." She passed through the "wild and romantic" Glen Eyrie, through a decayed-looking cluster of houses known pretentiously as Colorado City, and at last from a ridge saw Colorado Springs, the "Little London of the West." Once again, mindful of the amenities, Isabella put on her long skirt and rode sidesaddle, "though the settlement scarcely looked like a place where any deference to prejudices was necessary."

Isabella had ridden 150 miles on horseback through intense cold, had twice lost her way, had twice plunged into icy water, but her cheerful spirits returned. To her sister she wrote, "There are no real difficulties. It is a splendid life for health and enjoyment. All my luggage being in a pack, and my conveyance being a horse, we can go anywhere where we can get food and shelter."

The five-day journey from Denver had cost her ten shillings a day, the total less than the fare on the cozy toy car of the Denver and Rio Grande.

CHAPTER 26
ISABELLA LEAVES JIM

Isabella's horse, Winchester, was loping along, which suited Isabella after their invigorating gallop. She enjoyed the delicate scent of pine, the feel of the strong animal under her, and the patterns of shadow the late-afternoon sun cast on the scrub pine and sage. She was in no hurry to unsaddle and go to Evans's place for the evening meal. Jim's horse, Diamond, had galloped far past her, until Jim turned him around and trotted back to Isabella.

"Want another gallop?" Jim asked with practiced nonchalance.

"No," Isabella lied. "If I don't show up for dinner, Mrs. Evans is bound to worry."

"I'll come by for you later."

Isabella nodded. Everyone on the ranch considered that she and Jim were partners, so whose reputation was she trying to protect by refusing? Besides she hadn't yet told Jim that she was planning to leave tomorrow. She had postponed her departure as long as she dared. If she were to board the *Atlanta*, she had to get to New York within three weeks. And that required close connections. Thinking about it caused Isabella's spirits to droop; the parsonage in England without this elastic air would feel little better than a prison. How could she live without the gallops she so enjoyed? Or, honesty compelled, without Jim's daily presence?

In Jim's familiar cabin, he said, "Isabella, I have a request. Will you call me by my baptismal name? Robert. Robert Chavaliar."

"Of course. It's a privilege, Robert. In front of others?"

"No. We best wait for that."

Isabella's heart fluttered at his speaking of them as a pair that might have a future together. She couldn't tell him now that she was leaving and destroy a tender moment.

"Here, our tea's cold," he said. "I'll make a new pot. I'll use orange pekoe to celebrate."

"Robert." As he looked up from his tea making, she hesitated, then said, "I just like the sound of it. 'Jim' doesn't suit you at all. Robert."

To herself Isabella lectured, *This is ridiculous. Just tell him. It's not such a big event. It's not as if I were going to marry him. Marry him, is that what I've been thinking? Oh sure, marry a whiskey-drinking desperado with no definite income who hasn't even asked me to marry him. On the mark, Isabella.*

"Robert, I must tell you. I have booked passage on the *Atlanta* to go to Liverpool, and I must leave tomorrow if I'm to make it."

"Don't go. It would be devastating without you. No, you mustn't go."

"You forget, Robert, that England is my home. That my sister is waiting for me."

"Tell her to come here."

"She wouldn't like this life at all."

"You don't know until she tries it."

"Believe me, Robert, my gentle little sister doesn't fit into this vast landscape."

"But you do. That's not a question; it's a statement."

"Yes, I think I do. I've always been something of a tumbleweed. And I definitely love this limitless sky."

"Isabella, you don't know how thankful I am that you've blown in my direction."

"Thank you, Robert. I shall treasure that compliment the rest of my life."

"It is not a compliment. It's a statement. Because of you, I've given up whiskey. I've given up waylaying people and charging them for crossing my property. I've given up whoring around. Excuse me, ma'am. I don't know how else to say it. I don't want any other woman to clutter up my life."

"I'm sure, Robert, that these are things you've long yearned to do. I just happen to be here at the right time. The catalyst. But I'm happy to hear these changes. And," she added archly, "I'm a piece of clutter. That's something to cheer me when I'm feeling blue."

"Isabella, you know how I feel about you. If I were a decent sort, I could ask you to be my partner for life."

"You are a decent sort. I can't stand your talking about yourself like that. The irony is that I am treated in this so-called wilderness better than I have ever been treated in England. And now you've made these improvements. I'm glad for you, Robert."

"It sounds so good to hear you say my name."

"We could have a little burial service and tamp all those bad, destructive habits in the ground."

"Yes, but they'll all come back if you leave."

"That's not true. You feel virtuous about yourself, and that's worth fighting for. Robert, you've made giant steps that you know are in keeping with your true character. And you're not going to discard them. They don't depend upon me. They have much stronger support. They depend upon you. And you have a true friend in our Lord Jesus Christ. You have only to ask him, and he will be a steadfast partner." As Isabella spoke, her eyelashes became dense with tears.

Jim felt a familiar tide of cynicism rise, with its customary taste of bile. He was losing the one grown-up, mature woman in his life. "Will you consider staying here as my partner? That is, my wife?"

Isabella wanted this moment to last forever, but at the same time, she felt faint and had to exert control to remain upright. There was no way she could marry Jim, or Robert. He was not a man of the church. She pictured her father in heaven, next to God, behind a low balustrade, looking down at her, aghast! His right arm was raised, and he stood, sputtered a few words to God, and left the small box seat where he could sit and watch his loved ones struggling below.

"No, Robert," she stammered. "We are perfect as friends. Let's keep it this way and avoid the expectations marriage would bring. I cherish you beyond expression." Isabella's thoughts turned to the baby marriage would bring, with its dirty diapers, midnight wake-up calls, and the myriad other dreadful aspects of motherhood.

"Very well. Isabella, perhaps you know that my father was a surgeon. I know that here he would advise a clean cut. But remember"—Robert's voice became hollow—"I'll be at your side when you need me."